KV-042-197

Case Studies
in Industrial
Relations

Case Studies in Industrial Relations

Kevin Hawkins

Kogan Page

First published in 1982 by
Kogan Page Ltd, 120 Pentonville Road,
London N1 9JN

Copyright © Kevin Hawkins 1982

British Library Cataloguing in Publication Data

Hawkins, Kevin
  Case studies in industrial relations.
  1. Industrial relations – Case studies
  I. Title
  331'.0722   HD6961

  ISBN 0-85038-418-4

Printed in Great Britain by the Anchor Press
Ltd and bound by William Brendon & Son,
both of Tiptree, Essex

Contents

5. Unfair Dismissal 138

6. Race and Sex Discrimination 173

7. Notes for Tutors: Analysis of Cases 182

Introduction

The purpose of this book is to provide an aid to the teaching of industrial relations. Despite the proliferation of textbooks in this field over the past few years, there is still a surprising dearth of published collections of case studies. Yet most teachers of industrial relations would agree that case studies can play an invaluable role in the learning process by conveying something of the real flavour of problem-solving in this important area of management activity. The case studies used in this book fall into two categories: those intended for individual analysis followed by class or group discussion and those designed to test and develop individual negotiating skills. The former end with questions for discussion and analysis. The latter present a situation and describe the positions of the interested parties. As well as discussing the implications of the problem and assessing the negotiating position of each party, roles representing each should be assigned to group members and the course of the negotiations acted out.

No attempt has been made to cover every aspect of industrial relations; the substantive content of the cases merely constitutes a reasonable cross-section of problems, themes and 'situations'. The book should be read and used in conjunction with both the present writer's *Handbook of Industrial Relations Practice* (Kogan Page, 1979) and Michael Armstrong's *Case Studies in Personnel Management* (Kogan Page, 1979).

The cases have been written from an explicitly managerial perspective. This perspective recognizes the existence of 'problems' in industrial relations and attaches considerable importance to the task of improving the analytical skills of those who have (or may in the future have) some managerial responsibility in this field. A sensible approach to the analysis and resolution of industrial relations problems requires the following basic steps:

1. Establish what has gone wrong and what is likely to go wrong if no action is taken.
2. Decide what you want to achieve, both immediately and in the longer term.

7

3. Ensure that you have all relevant information and check the accuracy of the evidence.
4. Analyse the evidence and establish what has caused the problem. If there are several causes, put them in some order of priority.
5. Consider and evaluate alternative courses of action by listing costs and benefits. Consult other interested parties, such as trade union representatives and other colleagues, and ask for their views.
6. Decide what to do and communicate your decision to the interested parties. Start negotiations if appropriate. Otherwise ensure that your decision is implemented.

Within the limitations imposed by the analysis of case studies in the classroom the simple approach outlined above should be followed. In real life, of course, problems involving people, whether as individuals or in groups, are seldom simple. Feats of tactical and strategic brilliance achieved in the classroom may prove to be impossible when the same problem occurs on the shop floor and the people involved are not role-playing. Nevertheless, provided that case studies are accepted for what they are — a stimulus to thought and an opportunity to gain insights into practical problems and into opposing views of those problems — their obvious limitations need not diminish their value.

To some extent the protagonists in an industrial relations dispute are always role-playing. The behaviour of an individual, whether employer or employee, is determined partly by his own personality and individual needs and partly by the role in which he has been cast by the position he holds. The rules and conventions of the bargaining process impose a considerable degree of artificiality on the behaviour of the parties to the process. A negotiation simulation exercise in which the participants are relatively skilled, experienced practitioners of their art can in this sense be almost as realistic as it would be if it were taking place on the shop floor. The use of such exercises with groups of students who have had little or no contact with industrial relations in the workplace and, equally important, find difficulty in making the appropriate mental leap is obviously likely to be less rewarding. Within the confines of the training or seminar room, however, it is certainly possible for someone who is accustomed to taking a relatively narrow managerial view of industrial relations problems to gain some appreciation of how a trade union representative would view the same problems simply by playing the appropriate role.

All the cases used in this book are based on industrial disputes and 'situations' which have actually occurred over the past few years. All have been disguised and most have been amended or altered in some way to underline the appropriate teaching/learning points. Each chapter is prefaced by a brief introduction to the themes which the cases are designed to illustrate and the final section of the book (Chapter 7) contains an analysis of the cases and information for the assistance of tutors and trainers.

I would like to thank Mr Brian McAndrew, city personnel officer of Bradford Metropolitan District Council, for assisting me with some of the case studies and Mrs Lucy Suddaby for typing the manuscript.

1. Establishing Collective Bargaining

The sharp fall in aggregate union membership which has occurred in the UK since 1979 signals the end of the period of sustained expansion which began in the late 1960s. If unemployment remains at its current level or, more likely, increases over the next few years, it is reasonable to suppose that many unions will be devoting most of their efforts towards maintaining their existing membership. Another problem for the unions will almost certainly arise from those provisions in the Employment Bill currently before Parliament (April 1982) which cover the review of all closed shops. If closed shops are subject to periodic review through the mechanism of a secret ballot, it is likely that many will not pass the support level of 80 per cent specified in the Bill and will thus become unenforceable. In workplaces where this happens there will be a significant decline in union membership. As a result, unions such as ASTMS and the TGWU which are industrially and/or occupationally open to new members will be seeking to replace losses either by recruiting non-members or merging with smaller unions.

A trade union which is locked into static or declining industries and occupations can only maintain its membership base by merging with other unions. Those unions, however, which have established strong footholds in expanding industries and services and are 'open' in occupational terms are still likely to pursue a strategy of 'natural' growth. The most outstanding example of such a union is ASTMS, which has recruited white collar workers in virtually every job territory. This aggressive policy has yielded immense gains in terms of membership but often at the price of disputes with other unions on whose territory ASTMS has encroached. The 'Redwood Garden Tools' case below furnishes a typical example of how this union's recruitment policy has aroused opposition from other unions. Other white collar unions, notably APEX and BIFU, have also pursued relatively open recruitment strategies, though with less aggression and less success than ASTMS. It would seem that ASTMS has been particularly effective in tapping the feelings of resentment, alienation and frustration which many white collar workers, including those of managerial status, have expressed over the past decade or so.

10

It follows that while there will almost certainly be more emphasis on growth through merger activity during the present decade, it is unlikely that the more aggressive unions will overlook the scope for natural growth which still exists in some industries and services. In the private service sector there are still many organizations in which union membership is either low or non-existent and, since this is the only sector of the economy in which employment opportunities are likely to expand over the next few years, the trade union movement as a whole cannot afford to ignore any opportunity to establish a stronger bridgehead here. Two obstacles are likely to stand in the way of an effective campaign for membership and bargaining rights. First, the private service sector contains many employers who are strongly opposed to trade unionism. Second, the same prejudice seems to be shared by a large proportion of the workforce in this sector who, to the extent that they are interested in collective representation, are more favourably disposed towards a staff association than a trade union.

Two of the cases which follow illustrate how the combination of employer hostility and employee indifference can frustrate a union recruitment campaign. All three cases, however, underline the significance of the employer's attitude and behaviour. Delay, as the saying goes, is the deadliest form of denial. It is often open to an employer who is facing a recognition claim to play for time in the hope that the level of employee interest in union membership will soon begin to decline. Most employees are not interested in joining an organization which is unable to represent their interests and negotiate with management. If, therefore, the employer can gain a breathing space and take counter-measures, which might include encouraging the formation of a staff association, he may well succeed in taking the steam out of the union's campaign. Time won through delay, however, must be put to good use. If a strategy of playing for time merely reflects indecision on the part of the employer, or a wishful belief that if ignored the problem will resolve itself, it is unlikely to succeed. There is often a danger that during the period in which no decisions are taken by management, a second, possibly rival union may begin recruiting members. As a result, the problems of defining bargaining rights and devising appropriate bargaining structures will be more complex than they would otherwise have been.

While several tactical points emerge from the following cases, however, the underlying strategic significance of trade union recognition must also be emphasized. The decision to concede full bargaining rights to a trade union is likely to have a major effect on the structure of authority within the organization. Management has to come to terms with the fact that issues of substance which have hitherto been determined unilaterally must henceforth be subject to joint regulation. Managers must also learn to accept that union representatives will have to be consulted on a wide range of day-to-day problems before action is taken. More fundamentally, senior managers and directors are well advised to accept a pluralist view of the organization, which recognizes both the legitimacy of conflict and the importance of resolving it through collective rule-making. In some cases, and certainly in two of those which follow, it is this ideological trauma which has proved to be the most fertile source of strife and disorder in union recognition disputes.

CASE 1: Great Northern Stores Ltd

Background

1. Great Northern Stores Ltd is a major departmental retail organization with 120 stores situated in various towns and cities in the UK. The stores sell a range of foods, textiles, fancy goods and toiletries. The company was founded by the Muller family in the 1890s and members of this family currently occupy seven of the 12 seats on the board. The present chairman, Lord Muller of Sidcup, has been running the company since the late 1950s and is 62 years old. Of the other 11 directors, eight are over 55.

2. Ever since the foundation of the business, the Muller family has prided itself on its sense of responsibility for the welfare of its employees. At the 1980 annual meeting of the company, for example, Lord Muller said: 'We have always been great believers in the principle that the success of any business depends on real teamwork. We totally reject the conventional wisdom that a third party can look after the interests of employees more effectively than those who own and run the business. Our staff have always recognized that the success of the business is essential to their own well-being. We, in turn, believe that merit and loyalty should be rewarded.'

3. The company established itself as a leading national retailing organization during the post-war period. Its commercial success was based on a range of own-branded textile goods and foods which achieved an unrivalled reputation for quality. In 1945 the company owned 60 stores, mainly in Yorkshire, Lancashire and the West Midlands; by 1970 it had built a further 40 stores in Scotland, the East Midlands and the South. Between 1970 and 1980 a further 20 stores were added, mainly in the Home Counties, East Anglia and South Wales. Simultaneously, the board embarked on a major programme of rebuilding and refurbishing its older stores, although this programme is still far from complete and some of these properties are in need of considerable modernization.

4. This programme of expansion and rebuilding was partly a response to the changing and increasingly competitive environment in which the company found itself during the 1970s. The growth of supermarkets

and of other multiple retailers began to erode the company's market position. The company found itself forced to reduce profit margins and trim back its quality standards in order to compete. It was also obliged to move into areas such as footwear, wines and spirits, toiletries, books and home furnishings in which it had not previously been involved and in which its own brand name carried relatively little weight. As a result of all these factors the increase in sales volume fell from an average of 15 per cent per year in 1967-73 to 7 per cent in 1974-79. In 1980-81 sales volume grew by only 3 per cent, which was a decline in real terms.

5. Since 1974 the board has been pursuing a policy of 'good house-keeping' to hold down operating costs. This has mainly taken the form of trimming back on staff costs at store level. Between 1974 and 1981 some 600 (full-time equivalent) jobs were lost through natural wastage, despite the store expansion programme. Although most of these savings have been made in full-time and part-time sales staff, economies have also been made in managerial overheads. Many medium-sized stores which once had assistant managers and assistant staff manageresses no longer have them, while in the larger outlets significant reductions have been made in the number of departmental managers, clerical support staff and management trainees. As a result the administrative workload which store management has to carry has greatly increased in recent years. By contrast, few manpower reductions have been made in warehouse staff or at head office.

6. The company currently employs 15,000 staff, of whom 7000 are part-timers. More than half the part-timers are Saturday-only staff. The total includes over 3000 managerial and clerical staff who are employed in the company's head office and computer centre in Manchester and in the stores. It also includes over 1500 warehouse staff at store level. Almost all the sales staff are female, while the warehouse staff are male. Every store is run by a manager (male) assisted by a staff manageress whose primary task is to control staffing levels in the store and administer the company's welfare policy.

7. Labour turnover averaged 20 per cent a year up to 1979-80, since when it has dropped to 10 per cent. Turnover varies, however, with size of store and the state of the local labour market. It tends to be highest, regardless of size or location, among the Saturday-only staff and is currently running at nearly 20 per cent in this grade. Turnover among full-time sales staff and warehouse staff, by contrast, is currently less than 5 per cent.

8. The management structure of the company is highly centralized. All merchandising is done by specialist staff in head office and stores receive centrally determined allocations of stock. Until 1978 store managers were allowed discretion in food merchandising, but this

function is now performed by a department in head office. Store managers are responsible both to an area superintendent (the stores are grouped into seven areas) and to various functional executives in head office. The staff management structure, however, runs directly from store level to the personnel department at head office. The area superintendent has no responsibility for staff relations or welfare.

Employee relations policy

9. The company's staff relations policy has traditionally been based on the need to attract and retain good-quality staff by providing them with above average terms and conditions of employment. Full-time sales assistants are currently (October 1981) paid £64 for a 40 hour week and part-timers on a *pro rata* basis. After 15 years' service full-time staff receive an increase of £1 per week, after 20 years' service a further £1 and after 25 years a further £1.50 with *pro rata* increases for part-timers. Full-time warehouse staff are currently paid £82 per week, with a *pro rata* scale for part-timers and the same long-service payments as sales staff. There is a contributory pension scheme and subsidized canteen facilities for all staff. Until 1979 staff also received free medical and dental inspections, but these services were discontinued on grounds of economy.

10. A formal staff appraisal system is in operation. At annual intervals, an assessment of every employee is made by his or her immediate superior and the staff manageress. The appraisal is discussed with the employee and is then forwarded to head office. Merit payments are given for exceptional performance, but this is a rare occurrence. There is little scope for overtime and no sales commission is paid. Staff who wish to purchase the company's goods must do so at the full retail price, except in the case of 'out-of-life' foods which can be bought, if available, at half price.

11. The company has always placed great emphasis on the importance of character and personality in its managerial and supervisory staff. Although most of the younger store managers and a few staff manageresses are graduates, the company attaches no particular importance to academic qualifications. Managers are occasionally requested to attend courses at head office, run by the personnel department, on specific topics such as interviewing techniques. Attendance is, however, entirely voluntary. The company's philosophy is that practical experience is the best tutor.

12. The company's employee relations policy is based on a belief in the importance of good communication. If employees have a personal problem or grievance they are expected and encouraged to see the staff manageress and discuss it with her. In the unlikely event that the matter

cannot be resolved at store level, employees have access to the personnel department at head office. In addition, since 1977 every store has been required to hold periodic meetings of 'communication groups'. These groups comprise representatives of sales staff, supervision, warehouse staff and office staff, chaired by the manager or staff manageress. Minutes of all meetings are sent to head office. Initially there was considerable interest in these groups on the part of the staff, but more recently they have come to be regarded as powerless talking shops and most are, in fact, concerned with relatively trivial, day-to-day issues.

13. The company does not belong to an employers' federation but takes into account the improvements in terms and conditions which are periodically announced by the wages council covering the retail drapery, outfitting and footwear trades. The board reviews pay and other conditions every April. In recent years it has become customary for store managers to take soundings through the communication groups during the two months leading up to the annual review and to report the views of staff on what the size of the annual pay increase should be. Usually, however, the actual award has been significantly lower than staff have expected or wanted. This was particularly the case in 1981, when store managers reported to the area superintendents in March that most staff expected increases of 13-15 per cent. In the event, however, the increase announced was only 8.5 per cent, at a time when the general rate of inflation was running at about 13 per cent. The board sought to justify this award by pointing out that the economic recession had affected profits and that costs must be held down in order to avoid redundancies. Nevertheless, many staff, including store management, were very disappointed with their increase.

The Liverpool store dispute

14. The board has always made it clear that it does not regard trade unionism and collective bargaining as 'appropriate for a long established family business with a tradition of high-quality service to the customer'. In recent years Lord Muller has been an outspoken critic of 'disruptive and selfish' behaviour on the part of trade union leaders and shop stewards. In 1975 the Union of Shop, Distributive and Allied Workers (USDAW) attempted to recruit Great Northern sales staff in Manchester, Liverpool and certain other large stores in the North. Initially, the union had some success in Liverpool, where they recruited about one-third of the sales staff. As a result, it formally requested recognition and bargaining rights in respect of its members in the Liverpool store. The company refused the request on the grounds that since it had a centralized management structure, collective bargaining would also have to be organized on a centralized national basis rather than store-by-store. Since USDAW had only succeeded in recruiting a very small proportion of the total staff of the company, no recognition could be conceded.

15. Following this refusal, union membership within the company declined and USDAW called off its campaign. Nevertheless, a hard core of staff at Liverpool remained within the union and the store enhanced its reputation as the most 'difficult' in the company. The USDAW episode also helped stimulate interest in union membership among clerical and, to a lesser extent, managerial staff. It was rumoured that several staff in the central computer department at head office had joined APEX and that a few store managers had joined ASTMS. The board was made aware of these developments but decided to take no action, believing that the growth in union membership was a passing phenomenon which, if ignored, would soon be over.

16. This belief seemed to be justified until 15 July 1981, when a major dispute broke out in the Liverpool store. At the normal monthly meeting of the store's communication group in early July, the leading sales staff representative submitted a handwritten 'statement of grievances' to the staff manageress (the store manager who normally chaired the meetings being on holiday at the time). The statement drew attention to:

(a) The falling standard of living of the company's staff as inflation exceeded their last pay increase.

(b) The size of the pay differential between sales assistants (£64 per week) and warehouse staff (£82 per week), a differential which could not be justified by reference to the duties and responsibilities of the jobs involved.

(c) The fact that Great Northern Stores Ltd was no longer a leader in pay and conditions in the retail sector. Basic pay rates were no higher than those of other national retailing organizations, while certain fringe benefits (eg staff discounts) were less generous than those offered elsewhere.

(d) The lack of an effective means of communicating grievances to senior management in head office.

The staff manageress reacted angrily to these claims, describing them as 'deliberately provocative', and refused either to discuss them or to refer them to head office. A member of the communication group who sought to argue these points out with the staff manageress was threatened with dismissal. Thereupon a large proportion of the store staff at Liverpool, including the warehousemen, walked out and effectively closed the store.

17. On 17 July the personnel director wrote to all the Liverpool staff indicating that in the company's view they had broken their contracts of employment by walking out and would be dismissed if they did not return to work on 20 July. While a few staff turned up for work on 20 July, a greater number appeared outside the store and established a picket line. Simultaneously, an official of USDAW appeared on the

scene and signed up all those pickets who were not already members of the union. The regional secretary of USDAW promptly wrote to the personnel director stating that an official dispute now existed between the union and the company. On 22 July the company replied, denying the existence of such a dispute on the grounds that USDAW was not recognized by Great Northern Stores Ltd. In the meantime the company, having formally dismissed all the strikers, attempted to re-open the Liverpool store by transferring staff from neighbouring stores (Manchester, Warrington, Birkenhead, Wallasey and Southport) and there were some ugly scenes on the picket lines.

18. On 27 July the Liverpool store was re-opened with a skeleton staff of transferred employees, but the continuing presence of pickets and police outside the store discouraged many customers from entering the premises. On 28 July USDAW launched a major recruiting drive in other Great Northern stores in Lancashire, Cheshire and Yorkshire and, finding a sympathetic response from sales staff, signed up over 1000 members within a two-week period. The company took no further action beyond keeping the Liverpool store open until, on 10 August, the transferred staff refused to continue to man the store and demanded the reinstatement of the strikers. The company made no response to this demand beyond withdrawing instructions that any staff be transferred. The Liverpool store was then closed.

19. On 13 August the personnel director received a letter from the regional secretary of USDAW requesting a meeting to discuss the recognition of USDAW as the sole representative for bargaining purposes of all sales staff employed by Great Northern Stores Ltd. The letter stated that USDAW had now recruited 'a sufficient number' of employees to justify recognition and full bargaining rights. On 15 August the personnel director replied that the company intended to test the validity of the union's claim by conducting a secret ballot of all its sales staff. He added: 'If the result of the ballot indicates that there is substantial and widespread support among the sales staff for representation by USDAW the company will feel obliged to discuss with you the establishment of procedural relations. In the meantime the company hopes that, as a gesture of goodwill, you will use your best endeavours to secure a return to normal working at our Liverpool branch.'

20. The regional secretary of USDAW responded by asking his members to return to work at Liverpool pending a final settlement of the dispute. The store re-opened for business with its normal complement of staff on 22 August. The regional secretary also requested that he be consulted on the wording of the ballot papers. This request, however, was not acknowledged. Voting took place in every store on 29 August, and employees were presented with the following options:

(a) Are you broadly satisfied with the traditional arrangements within the company whereby you can voice your grievances as an individual direct to a member of management?
Yes ☐   No ☐   (please tick)

(b) Would you prefer to be represented in discussions with manage-. ment by an organization such as a staff association which would be run exclusively by and for Great Northern sales staff?
Yes ☐   No ☐   (please tick)

(c) Would you prefer to be presented by a trade union?
Yes ☐   No ☐   (please tick)

(d) If you have voted 'yes' to question (c), would you regard the Union of Shop, Distributive and Allied Workers as the appro- priate union to represent your interests?
Yes ☐   No ☐   (please tick)

21. Just over 85 per cent of the sales staff, supervisors and warehouse staff voted, with the following results:

(a) Twenty-five per cent voted 'yes'.
(b) Forty-eight per cent voted 'yes'.
(c) Twenty-seven per cent voted 'yes'.
(d) Of those voting 'yes' to (c), approximately one-third expressed a preference for USDAW. A significant number of staff had written in their preference for the TGWU. Management assumed that in all probability support for the TGWU came from ware- house staff in certain locations.

22. On 2 September the personnel director wrote to USDAW stating that the ballot made it clear that the union did not have sufficient support to justify recognition by the company. He added that, since a large proportion of the staff had expressed support for a staff association, management was taking steps to assist employees in establishing such an association. In his reply the regional secretary of USDAW made the following points:

(a) That the ballot paper was heavily loaded against USDAW and virtually invited staff to express other preferences.
(b) That under no circumstances would USDAW members in the company accept the formation of a staff association.
(c) That unless the company proceeded to recognize USDAW immediately, there would be a resumption of industrial action.

The personnel director made no reply to this letter.

23. On 6 September all staff received application forms for member- ship of the Great Northern Staff Association, the 'acting chairman' of which was a senior executive in the store operations department at head office. On the same day there was a spontaneous walk-out by sales staff in the Liverpool store. Warehousemen at the Sheffield store also

staged an hour-long stoppage in support of the claim for union recognition, although in their case the union concerned was thought to be the TGWU. Simultaneously, staff in the head office computer department sent a petition to the personnel director rejecting the proposed staff association and stating that, as members of ASTMS, they wanted full recognition and bargaining rights for their union.

24. On 7 September an emergency meeting of the board was convened to discuss what Lord Muller described as the 'gravest crisis in the company's history'.

Questions for discussion

1. What has caused the various industrial relations problems which have recently arisen?
2. What are the strategic and tactical alternatives which are now open to the board?
3. What course of action would you now advise the board to take?

CASE 2: The Huddersfield Abstinence Building Society

Background

1. The Huddersfield Abstinence Building Society has assets valued at over £500 million. The society's head office is in Huddersfield and it has 100 branch and sub-branch offices in various towns and cities throughout the UK. Of these branches 40 are in West Yorkshire, and eight are in the Huddersfield area. The society's business has grown rapidly in recent years and since 1972 20 new branches (all outside the West Riding) have been opened. The society at present employs 600 staff consisting of 450 full-time and 150 part-time staff. Of this total approximately 100 are employed at head office. The proportion of female staff employed by the society is about 75 per cent, including part-time staff.

2. The management structure at head office is as follows:

19

Below this level there are 14 departmental managers and below them 30 head office supervisors. There are 80 branch managers who administer the society's branches and sub-branches and report to the five regional managers.

The majority of the society's employees are female clerical staff and there is also a small number of ancillary staff including office cleaners and catering staff.

3. The society's personnel policy is determined by the board in conjunction with the general manager. Until recently all terms and conditions of employment were determined unilaterally by the society after 'consultation' with members of staff 'as appropriate'. The society maintains that it does not operate a salary structure but assesses the remuneration of each member of staff over the age of 21 on the basis of 'personal merit'. Personal assessments are made by the appropriate departmental manager (in head office) and by the branch managers. Staff under 21 are paid according to an age-related scale coupled with a merit award based on the assessment of their departmental head of branch manager.

4. In March 1976 a personnel adviser was appointed. He is now involved in the recruitment of staff at head office and branch level.

5. All cases of dismissal are referred to the general manager or to his deputy for decision.

The recognition dispute

6. Until the mid-1970s few members of the society's staff belonged to a trade union. In February 1978 the West Yorkshire area organizer of BIFU wrote to all the full-time staff employed at head office and in the West Yorkshire branches informing them of their legal right to join a trade union and indicating the advantages which they would gain from 'membership of a large and powerful organization representing over 100,000 employees in the financial sector'. The letter contained the address of the regional office of BIFU in Bradford and indicated that all staff who wished to join the union should contact this office directly.

7. On 21 March the West Yorkshire area organizer wrote to the general manager stating that BIFU had recruited a 'substantial' proportion of the society's staff and requesting a meeting to discuss the possibility of negotiating a recognition and procedure agreement with the society. The general manager replied to this letter on 6 April, informing the area organizer that the board of directors did not see that 'any useful purpose' would be served by a meeting 'at this stage'. On 23 April the area organizer again wrote to the general manager, stating that in the month of April alone 'a further 30 members of staff' had joined BIFU and that, unless the society adopted 'a more positive attitude' towards

this request for a meeting, it would be necessary for the union to refer the matter to the Advisory, Conciliation and Arbitration Service under the Employment Protection Act 1975.

8. On 27 April the general manager replied that 'an informal meeting to discuss the question in general terms might be possible' but that at present he was 'too busy'. Eventually, a meeting was arranged for 17 May. On 7 May the society gave all its staff a salary increase which amounted to the maximum permissible under the current phase of the government's incomes policy. In a general letter to all staff the general manager explained that the board had departed from its normal policy of considering salary awards on an individual basis because of 'the extraordinarily rapid rise in the cost of living during the past year'. He also stated that the board hoped that members of staff would 'continue to value the established methods of personal communication' which the society had developed over the years. He concluded by thanking all staff, on behalf of the board, for their 'loyalty and enthusiasm' during what had been 'a very busy and taxing phase of the society's progress'. He hoped that if any member of staff felt that he or she had a problem, they should always feel free to consult him personally about it. 'The maintenance of good human relations', he said, 'is something to which the society attaches the greatest importance.'

9. The meeting between the general manager and the area organizer of BIFU took place on 17 May. Apparently no progress was made and the general manager terminated the discussion after half an hour. On 24 May the general secretary of BIFU wrote to all members of the society's staff in all the branches and in head office in which he reiterated the benefits of joining BIFU and stated: 'A meeting has already taken place between the West Yorkshire area organizer and the society's general manager with a view to establishing a procedure and regular negotiating arrangements.' All these letters were sent to the home addresses of members of staff.

10. On 28 May the general manager wrote to all members of his staff, informing them that he 'deplored' the recent letter from BIFU and 'emphatically denied' that any negotiations were in progress with this or any other trade union. He continued: 'My board feels that the majority of the staff of the society do not believe that their interests would be materially served by the establishment of formal collective bargaining relationships with an external organization. Such a relationship would probably bring with it an element of compulsion and we believe that all members of our staff should have a right to choose whether or not they wish to belong to such an organization.' The letter went on to say that the board 'would be pleased to hear that all staff have joined in forming a staff association in the interests of improving communications throughout the society.'

The staff association

11. In June a working party was set up by the general manager in order to study the various methods by which a staff association might be established. The working party was chaired by the deputy general manager and comprised several departmental managers, the personnel adviser and the management services manager. On 15 June the general manager received a letter from the assistant general secretary of APEX, claiming that 'a significant number' of the society's staff had joined the union and requesting a meeting to discuss the possibilities of establishing 'procedures for consultation and representation' between the union and the society. On 18 June the general manager replied, stating that the whole question was 'under review' at the moment and that a secret ballot would be conducted 'to ascertain the wishes of the staff'. Until the results of the ballot were known there was 'little point' in meeting to discuss the matter of representation.

12. On 20 June a memorandum and a covering explanatory letter were sent out to staff with a ballot form. The form offered the staff the following alternative forms of representation:

(a) A staff association.
(b) BIFU.
(c) APEX.

The ballot was held on 22 June. On 24 June the general manager wrote to all members of staff informing them that the ballot had revealed an 'overwhelming preference' for a staff association and that one would be set up 'as soon as possible'.

13. On 25 June the working party produced a draft constitution for the proposed staff association. The general manager accepted this constitution after making one or two minor alterations. On 29 June all employees were invited to join the staff association and were notified of an open meeting to be held at head office on 9 July. It was also stated that any member of staff employed in any branch who wished to attend the meeting was free to do so and that the society would defray any travelling expenses incurred.

14. During the course of June a number of BIFU members at head office formed an action committee and on 18 June distributed membership application forms to a large number of head office staff. Some of these forms were later discovered to have been stuffed down one of the ladies' toilets. On 21 June the deputy general manager sent a note out to all branches forbidding any member of staff to be involved in trade union activities during working hours without the permission of management.

15. The staff association held its open meeting on 9 July and some 80 members of staff attended. An executive committee of 10 members was

elected, together with a chairman, secretary and treasurer. The draft constitution and rules were then submitted to the meeting and approved. Apparently, however, a number of provocative questions were put to the committee members and officers by a small group of employees who attended the meeting. They alleged that the staff association had been set up by the general manager and could not possibly provide an independent system of representation for members of staff. A good deal of recrimination ensued and threats of physical violence towards association officials were made. The meeting ended in some confusion.

16. On 11 July the general manager wrote to all members of staff informing them that henceforth the society would recognize the staff association as the 'sole representative' of all employees. The elected officials of the association would be able to discuss any matter of mutual importance, including salary scaler, with the general manager and/or his deputy. The association would also be able to represent an individual member of staff in grievance and disciplinary matters with senior management. In its first newsletter to its members, issued in mid-August, the association announced its intention of seeking certification as an independent trade union under the Trade Union and Labour Relations Act 1974.

17. On 31 July the assistant general secretary of BIFU informed the society that he was referring the union's claim for recognition to ACAS under the Employment Protection Act 1975. An exploratory meeting between a senior conciliation officer from ACAS, the area organizer of BIFU and the deputy general manager on 6 September failed to produce any agreement. BIFU stated that it would accept nothing less than sole bargaining rights for all the society's staff up to and including the level of head office departmental management. APEX also wrote to the society and ACAS, claiming that a significant proportion of the staff had joined the union and declaring an interest in any conciliation proceedings.

18. The claim was then formally referred to ACAS by BIFU. At a meeting in London between the general manager of the society, the general secretary of BIFU, the chairman of the staff association and the assistant general secretary of APEX, the senior conciliator suggested that another secret ballot should be held, but that this time it should be conducted by the Electoral Reform Society and the results made available to all members of staff and other interested parties. After a lengthy discussion this suggestion was agreed. The ballot was held on 13 November. The following questions were put to the staff on the ballot form:

(a) Are you a member of BIFU?
(b) If you are not, would you become a member if BIFU was recognized by your employer and was able to negotiate on your behalf?

(c) Are you a member of APEX?

(d) If you are not, would you become a member if APEX was recognized by your employer and was able to negotiate on your behalf?

(e) Are you a member of the staff association?

(f) Are you satisfied that the staff association continues to enjoy exclusive negotiating rights on your behalf with the society?

(g) Do you belong to an employee organization of any kind?

19. The results of the ballot were declared on 15 November. Of the 410 staff who voted (a participation rate of 70 per cent), the responses given to each question were as follows:

	Yes	Percentage answering yes	No
(a)	70	17.0	340
(b)	40	9.7	300
(c)	25	6.0	385
(d)	60	14.6	325
(e)	185	45.1	225
(f)	195	47.5	215
(g)	280	68.2	130

All staff up to but not including head office departmental managers were eligible to vote.

20. A meeting has now been convened by ACAS for November 22nd to discuss the results of the ballot. Present are:

For ACAS: Mr Graham, senior conciliator, ACAS (chairman)
For the society: Mr Clough, general manager, HABS; Mr Ackroyd, deputy general manager, HABS
For the staff association: Mr Waddington, staff association chairman
For BIFU: Mr Harris, assistant general secretary, BIFU
For APEX: Mr Bondfield, divisional organizer, APEX.

Points for the society's case

1. The society has already granted exclusive bargaining rights to the staff association, and the ballot clearly shows that the staff association has twice the membership of the two trade unions added together. In these circumstances, recognition of either one or both of the trade unions for bargaining purposes alongside the staff association would needlessly fragment the structure of employee relations in the society.

2. The society believes, as do nearly half the staff, that the staff association is best able to represent the interests of the society's employees. Although it is conceded that the initiative for establishing the association came from the society, the association is now run

exclusively by the staff and anyone at the level of head office departmental manager or above is excluded from membership.

3. The disorderly behaviour which occurred at the open meeting on 9 July suggests that there is a very small group of politically motivated staff who are trying to undermine the credibility of the association. The chairman of the society's board of directors is very concerned about this meeting and is anxious that the society should not be seen to be giving way to 'militants'. There is also evidence, admittedly hearsay, that a few of those present at the meeting on 9 July were not employees of the society, but were 'planted' by an unnamed political organization.

4. It is believed that membership of the association is still increasing and that the association would be more likely than either BIFU or APEX to attract the support of the 30 per cent of the staff who did not choose to vote in the secret ballot. Consequently, it is only a matter of time before the association has a clear majority of the staff in membership.

5. The results of the society's own secret ballot conducted in June, compared with the ACAS ballot, suggest that support for BIFU is tending to fall while support for APEX is static. The longer the society can stave off the demands of BIFU and APEX and generally 'play for time', the more likely is the strength of both unions to decline.

Points for BIFU's case

1. At the time of its initial request for recognition in April, the union had 140 of the society's staff in membership. The society must have had a strong indication of the level of support for BIFU in their June ballot and their subsequent strategy has clearly been to play for time so that a staff association could be firmly established. This in itself underlines the weakness of the association's claim to be independent of the society. The association was initiated by senior management as a 'soft' alternative to a genuine trade union. It has neither the resources nor the expertise to be an effective bargaining agent.

2. The union has been placed at a considerable disadvantage by the society in competing for membership against the association. Since July the chairman of the staff association has had access to all new recruits and to the society's notice boards and internal mailing system. The senior management of the society has made it clear that they would prefer to see employees joining the association and this is likely to have influenced many hitherto uncommitted employees.

3. It is imperative that some form of recognition is won from the society as soon as possible. Since June membership of BIFU has fallen from 125 to 70. Some members have been lost to APEX but most have

gone to the staff association, presumably in the belief that BIFU was unlikely to obtain recognition for bargaining purposes from the society. The longer the present discussions go on, the weaker the union's position will become.

4. It must also be emphasized that the HABS is a key middle-ranking society. For several years the union has been campaigning for membership and bargaining rights in the building society movement. It has had some success with small societies but has achieved little progress among the large and middle-sized societies. The achievement of even joint bargaining rights at the HABS would be an important psychological breakthrough which could have a positive spin-off in other societies. A defeat would have the reverse effect.

Points for APEX's case

1. Although the actual level of membership in the society is low, the actual plus the potential membership as revealed by the ACAS ballot adds up to just over 20 per cent of those who voted. This level of support is all the more remarkable in view of the fact that, unlike either BIFU or the staff association, APEX has as yet made no serious attempt to increase its membership in the HABS. On the assumption that more BIFU members could be induced to join APEX and that some of the 30 per cent of the staff who did not vote in the ACAS ballot might also be persuaded to join, it is quite possible that within the next few months the union could build its membership up to 100.

2. This objective would be greatly facilitated if the society could be induced to concede joint bargaining rights with the staff association (but *not* BIFU). APEX has already established a foothold in several middle-sized building societies and is determined to establish itself as a major force in this sector.

CASE 3: Redwood Garden Tools Ltd

Background

1. The Bilston factory of Redwood Garden Tools Ltd manufactures lawn-mowers and other garden equipment and employs about 1000 people. Although a long-established firm in the West Midlands, the capacity of the Bilston plant has been rapidly increased over the past three years as part of a programme of rationalization involving the closure of three smaller factories elsewhere. As a result the number of employees at Bilston has doubled since 1977.

2. The company's relations with its employees, who are organized by the AUEW and ASTMS, have traditionally been regarded as 'good', ie there have been very few strikes or other forms of industrial action.

Over the past 18 months, however, there has been a deterioration in relations at Bilston and 10 stoppages have occurred, together with several other 'incidents'. Although none of these stoppages has lasted more than a day, nine have occurred in one department of the factory known as C section. None of these disputes was taken through the agreed disputes procedure and none was officially supported by a trade union.

3. There are at the present time 130 people employed in C section, including 20 inspectors, 20 setters, six chargehands and one section manager. The section consists of four assembly lines on which electric lawn-mowers are assembled. Nearly half the operatives are semi-skilled and work a three-shift system. The six chargehands are all long-serving employees and have at various times been promoted from the skilled production grades. Most of their duties are supervisory. They are responsible for maintaining output and for liaison with other sections in the plant; they coordinate the work of inspectors and setters and, together with the section manager, attend meetings with higher management and shop stewards. They are also required, however, to carry out any 'practical' work which is necessary to keep the assembly lines going. One such duty is to ensure that there is a constant supply of oil to the machines in the section.

4. Two years ago the company decided in principle to upgrade the status of the chargehands, both at Bilston and in its other factories, and to call them assistant section managers. The new grade has the same responsibilities as the old but carries with it full staff status, which means the payment of a monthly salary and inclusion in the Redwood pension scheme. Progress, however, has been slower than anticipated and at the time of the current dispute the chargehands at Bilston were only halfway towards staff status, ie they were on monthly salaries but had not yet been included in the company pension scheme.

Union membership and collective bargaining

5. The AUEW has traditionally organized all employees below managerial level, but no written recognition agreement exists and the union's bargaining unit has never been formally defined. In the Bilston plant several chargehands are members of the AUEW but, until recently, the majority were not members of any union. In many cases they had once been members of the AUEW but, on becoming chargehands, had allowed their membership to lapse. In September 1981, however, a majority of the 40 chargehands at Bilston decided to join ASTMS. Of the six chargehands in C section only one is now a member of the AUEW, the other five being members of ASTMS.

6. The company is a member of the Engineering Employers' Federation and, as such, observes all national agreements in the engineering industry.

When, as a result of the recruiting drive which ASTMS mounted at the Bilston plant in 1981, a majority of chargehands (along with section managers and many other members of middle management) joined the union, the company felt obliged to recognize that ASTMS had the right to negotiate on behalf of its members in those grades where it had recruited a majority of the employees. The company also considered, however, that it could not refuse to negotiate with the AUEW in respect of its members, even if these were in a grade where ASTMS had majority membership.

7. Early in October 1981 the AUEW convenor at Bilston informed the company that AUEW members would no longer accept instructions from chargehands who were ASTMS members. Most setters and inspectors still belong to the AUEW. On 24 October the personnel manager at Bilston wrote to the divisional organizer of the AUEW asking him to instruct his members to call off sanctions against ASTMS chargehands and to allow the dispute to be resolved by the full-time officials of the two unions concerned.

8. On 10 November an informal meeting was held at the Bilston plant between senior management, the AUEW convenor and the AUEW divisional organizer. It was agreed at this meeting that the area officer of ASTMS should be invited to discuss with the AUEW divisional organizer a formula for resolving the dispute based on 'freezing' the pattern of union membership in the Bilston plant. A meeting was arranged for 15 November, but did not take place because of the dispute which broke out in C section on 14 November.

The oil tap incident

9. For several weeks prior to this dispute, relations in C section between the chargehands and the rest of the workforce had been deteriorating. Several minor acts of vandalism and sabotage were reported by the section manager to the production director, while one chargehand's car was sprayed with an aerosol in the car park. The section manager had strong suspicions as to who the culprits were but in the absence of concrete evidence no action was taken. By 14 November the atmosphere in C section was very bad.

10. The incident which precipitated the dispute occurred at 8.30 am on 14 November, when it became evident that one of the assembly lines was not working because of a deficiency of oil. The operation of turning the appropriate tap to supply oil is normally performed by a chargehand, but if one is not immediately available a setter will do the job. On this occasion a chargehand, Mr Burr, asked one of the setters, Mr Smith, to turn the tap, a task which Mr Smith and other setters had often performed. Mr Smith was about to turn the tap when he was approached by a fellow setter, Mr Riley, and after a brief conversation

he returned to Mr Burr and said he would not do the job.

11. Mr Burr then approached the section manager and told him what had happened. The section manager then told Mr Burr to arrange the oil supply himself. Mr Burr then operated the tap, allowing the oil to flow. The senior AUEW steward in C section then informed the section manager that the line was 'blacked'. Shortly afterwards a similar incident occurred on another assembly line in C section, which the setters similarly declared 'black'. The section manager formally warned all the setters in the section that they would be suspended unless they undertook to work normally. When they refused to give such an undertaking, they were all sent home. The setters on the other two shifts walked out in sympathy with their colleagues. As a result the entire workforce in C section was sent home by management.

12. On 17 November the divisional organizer of the AUEW met the area officer of ASTMS and agreed that work should be resumed on the basis of a temporary standstill on the recruitment of chargehands by ASTMS. The company accepted this formula and communicated it to the setters who had been sent home or were on strike. The setters, however, rejected it and their rejection was endorsed by the AUEW district committee.

13. A meeting at the local office of the EEF was convened on 23 November when the AUEW divisional organizer, having consulted the district committee, put forward the following formula for a resumption of work:

(a) The six chargehands in C section should be moved to another department in the factory where they would not be required to supervise AUEW members.
(b) The setters in C section would, in turn, be prepared to accept any additional duties arising from the removal of the chargehands.
(c) Discussions with the company should immediately follow with special reference to the bargaining unit covered by the AUEW.

14. The company replied that they would be willing to place the six chargehands on 'paid holiday leave' provided that ASTMS would accept this arrangement. The area officer of ASTMS, however, rejected this proposal and deadlock ensued. The dispute was then referred by mutual agreement to ACAS.

15. The first meeting between a conciliation officer from ACAS and representatives of all three parties is now convened (3 December). Present are:

For ACAS: Mr Glover, senior conciliation officer (chairman)
For the company: Mr Sterling, production director; Mr Elliot, personnel manager
For the AUEW: Mr Harrison, divisional organizer; Mr Friar, factory convenor, Bilston
For ASTMS: Mr Woodley, area officer.

The submissions of the parties

THE AUEW

1. It is argued on behalf of the AUEW that the resolution of any difficulties between themselves and ASTMS will not resolve the fundamental causes of the deteriorating industrial relations at the Bilston plant. Relations have deteriorated to a point where the AUEW shop stewards have no confidence in the management and the AUEW district committee believes that only an impartial inquiry into labour relations in the plant will provide the basis for a genuine settlement of grievances.

2. Two years ago the majority of chargehands in the factory were members of the AUEW. Early in 1980 management expressed dissatisfaction with a situation in which AUEW shop stewards working as setters were representing chargehands and proposed that the latter should have shop stewards of their own. This was agreed and as part of these discussions management further agreed that the AUEW should have exclusive negotiating rights for all chargehands who were supervising AUEW members. Although this agreement was never put in writing, verbal confirmation that the AUEW had sole negotiating rights for chargehands was given by the personnel manager at an informal meeting with AUEW stewards on 27 October 1981. It is argued that these exclusive negotiating rights automatically preclude chargehands from joining ASTMS.

3. In recent weeks, however, there has been a recruitment drive among chargehands by ASTMS. Chargehands have been 'poached' by ASTMS and this matter must now be resolved by the TUC under the 'Bridlington' procedure. Until this is resolved, ASTMS chargehands must carry out supervisory duties only and not attempt to do the work of AUEW setters. There must be a standstill on recruitment by ASTMS and the ASTMS chargehands in section C must be transferred to another department in the factory.

THE ASTMS

1. The ASTMS view is that this is not an inter-union dispute. No formal complaint of 'poaching' by ASTMS has yet been made by the AUEW. The real problem is one of inflamed industrial relations. There have been no difficulties with the AUEW in other plants where ASTMS chargehands or foremen are supervising AUEW members. ASTMS has not been involved in any of the previous 10 disputes at the Bilston plant. Any problem of union membership can be resolved by negotiation with the AUEW or, as a last resort, through the 'Bridlington' procedure.

2. Most of the Bilston chargehands were not members of any trade union when ASTMS recruited them. Moreover, they joined ASTMS without any special approach from the union, although there has

recently been a widely publicized national recruiting drive by ASTMS. Of the 40 chargehands at Bilston, 27 were members of ASTMS, four were members of the AUEW, seven had applied to join ASTMS and the remainder were not members of any trade union. Nevertheless, ASTMS does not claim exclusive negotiating rights for all the chargehands.

3. It is agreed that prior to 1981 none of the chargehands at Bilston was a member of ASTMS; it was in September 1981 that Bilston chargehands began to apply to ASTMS for membership. The present dispute has arisen for reasons peculiar to the Bilston plant, one of which must be the transition of the chargehands to assistant section manager status. To attempt to resolve this difficulty by transferring the ASTMS chargehands to another department would simply reinforce the unreasonable authority which was being built up in section C.

THE COMPANY

1. Management argues that this is an inter-union dispute. It also contends that it has the right to appoint workers to all supervisory posts in the factory. It is admitted, however, that there have been managerial weaknesses and that industrial relations have been allowed to deteriorate to a point where in October 1981 the atmosphere in the factory could only be described as hostile. This deterioration, however, stems from the attitude and activities of a small group of AUEW members who are largely responsible for the outbreak of unofficial and unconstitutional stoppages.

2. All the chargehands in section C are skilled men promoted from the shop floor and no one has claimed that they are not properly qualified to do their jobs. Nor did any of them at any time do work which was not part of their normal duties. It should be pointed out that for six weeks before the start of the present dispute, certain AUEW members refused to accept instructions from chargehands who had become members of ASTMS. Moreover, since May 1981 the same AUEW members have refused to work with four work study engineers who are members of ASTMS.

3. It is clear from the events leading up to the current dispute that inter-union rivalry has been reinforced in section C by personal bitterness between AUEW stewards and ASTMS chargehands. It is equally clear that the dispute was to some extent planned in advance. It is believed that the degree of personal bitterness in section C is now so great that the only solution is to remove the ASTMS chargehands from the department until alternative posts can be found for them. It is admitted, however, that they can only be replaced by chargehands from other departments who are also members of ASTMS. Consequently, it is up to the AUEW and ASTMS to resolve the problem of union membership and bargaining rights.

2. Negotiating and Implementing Change

The severe economic recession which began in 1979 and, at the time of writing, has barely begun to lift has had a major effect on the attitude of managements, union representatives and workers alike to the problem of efficiency. While some impressive increases in productivity have been achieved during the recession, it must be recognized that there was immense scope for improvement. From 1973 onwards British industry was, at least by the standards of the rest of the EEC, remarkably inefficient. Low productivity was not simply a matter of 'overmanning' or 'union restrictive practices', but also, and perhaps more importantly, a function of bad management. Managerial failings extended beyond technical areas such as product design and the organization of work to the field of human relations. The retention of out-dated class distinctions on the factory floor, the prevalence of autocratic, uncommunicative styles of management and the survival of near-Victorian working conditions and practices all helped to produce a pattern of behaviour on the shop floor which the media labelled 'bloody-mindedness'.

The recent recession has not in itself resolved any of these problems, but it has given employers, union representatives and employees alike an incentive and an opportunity to re-examine certain attitudes and practices. Faced with a stark choice between survival and liquidation, some managements have 'opened the books', spoken frankly to their workforce about the company's position and listened to suggestions and constructive comment which has come from the shop floor. Employees for their part have accepted pay settlements far below the prevailing level of inflation together with much tighter manning standards and more efficient working practices. Even in the public sector some progress has been made and both British Leyland and the British Steel Corporation have achieved remarkable increases in productivity. There is, moreover, some evidence to suggest that the gains may be permanent. When the level of economic activity recovers, many employers who have shed labour over the past two years and reorganized their operations on a much lower manpower base will be very reluctant to go back to the old standards. It is to be hoped that they will be equally reluctant to forget the lessons which have been learned in the field of 'man management'.

What are these lessons? First, the task of improving efficiency requires a *joint* commitment, and this is unlikely to be achieved without genuine, two-way *communication*. A conclusion which researchers drew from the experience of productivity bargaining during the 1960s has been heavily underlined during the recession, namely that if management wishes to elicit a constructive response from union representatives and their members, it must be prepared to 'come clean' about the state of the business. This means disclosing hitherto confidential information about profits, costs, prices, investment plans, cash flow, etc and being prepared to explain and justify policy decisions. The disclosure of such information presents several problems for both parties. In the past many well-intentioned efforts in this field have failed because union representatives and their members have been unable to understand the information which management has disclosed. This is partly the result of management's own failure to present the information in a comprehensible form and partly a reflection of the inadequate training and education which employee representatives have received from either their company or their trade union. A decision to disclose, unless supported by adequate preparation on the part of management and a willingness to learn on the part of union representatives, may therefore provoke *more* conflict and mutual mistrust than would have arisen if there had been no disclosure at all.

Second, if communication is effective, uncertainty will be reduced. One reason why employees and their representatives may react to the prospect of change in a way which management considers 'irrational' is that they are uncertain about the future. Distrust of management's intentions, apprehension that concessions made today will be used as a precedent in tomorrow's negotiations and lack of confidence in the ability of management to cope with the crisis may combine to produce a defensive, uncooperative response from the workforce. In some cases management may have to overcome the legacy of many years' neglect of employee relations in a relatively short time. There is no painless formula which can resolve such problems. The severity of the recent recession, however, and the reality of over three million people out of work has undoubtedly concentrated many minds on the business of survival. Workers who are facing the prospect of a long spell of unemployment may be less inclined to listen to those who urge obdurate resistance to management and more receptive to rational argument, provided, of course, that the argument is put across to them in terms which they can understand and that an opportunity is given for them to respond and, if necessary, make counter-proposals. Bad news may, in this sense, evoke a better response than continued uncertainty.

Third, the potential contribution of individual *employees* to a survival strategy can often be very positive. In any workplace there are likely to be several workers, some of whom are not union representatives, who as a result of experience and observation are in a position to offer management constructive suggestions on how to cut costs and improve efficiency. Some may be radical (eg the elimination of a tier of supervision), some may be marginal and some may be impracticable, but all may be worthy of consideration. If some are adopted, the spin-off in terms of higher morale and greater commitment to the organization may be significant. Although the role of union officials and shop stewards should not be undermined, it must be recognized that in a crisis *their* objectives and priorities may be significantly different from those of the 'silent majority' of the workforce. Whereas union representatives may be pursuing what they conceive to be the longer-term collective interests of their members, the employees themselves may be much more concerned with their own short-term individual interests (ie the preservation of their own jobs). In these circumstances it is hardly surprising that in some companies with a reputation for shop floor militancy, shop stewards have found themselves being virtually repudiated by their members when conflict has arisen with management over a major issue of substance such as a pay claim and the stewards have taken a 'militant' stand.

Finally, there is little doubt that the recent recession has shifted the balance of bargaining power in favour of management. This change may well outlive the current recession, particularly if the level of unemployment remains close to its current level. In these circumstances some employers may be tempted to adopt a hard-line, punitive strategy, involving the dismissal of militant shop stewards, the imposition of new working practices without consultation and, possibly, the exploitation of the new legal rights which both the 1980 Employment Act and the Employment Bill currently before Parliament confer on employers. A more sensible approach, however, would be based on the belief that fear is unlikely to produce an organization which enjoys high morale and a high degree of trust. The following cases illustrate some of the problems which the need to introduce change at the workplace can create. In each case there is a range of strategies which can be pursued by both management and union representatives. The challenge facing management is that of achieving short-term, pressing economic objectives while, simultaneously, winning the support and active cooperation of the workforce and thereby improving the climate of industrial relations in the longer term. The process of reconciling these two imperatives will not only tax the negotiating skills of both sides to the full but, more important, will test their commitment to the concept of management by agreement.

CASE 4: Bullman's Brewery Co Ltd

Background

1. Bullman's Brewery Co Ltd was founded in the 1880s by the Bullman family and is based in the Toxteth area of Liverpool. The company owns two breweries, one in Toxteth and one in St Helens, together with 400 public houses and off-licences situated in Liverpool, Merseyside and South Lancashire. The two breweries together produced 190,000 barrels of beer in 1980, although at their peak output in 1976 they turned out 240,000 barrels. Excluding the company's tenants, some 1500 people are employed at the breweries, in distribution, in the small soft drinks subsidiary, in administration and as public house managers.

2. From its foundation until 1978 the company was run by the Bullman family, who owned the majority of the shares. In 1978, however, the largest single shareholder, Sir Gervase Bullman, died and the remaining family directors decided to accept an offer to acquire the business from Grand Central Hotels Ltd, a large, London-based leisure and catering business. There were no significant changes in the management following the takeover. Sir Gervase Bullman's son, Edward, continued as chairman and managing director. Grand Central's finance director, B C Grizzard, joined the Bullman board but took no part in the day-to-day management of the business.

3. Against the national trend in beer output, the company's sales declined from 240,000 barrels in 1976 to 215,000 in 1979, before slumping to 190,000 barrels in 1980. At the company's annual meeting in January 1981, the chairman blamed the fall in sales on the 'catastrophic' level of unemployment on Merseyside. Nevertheless, the new managing director of Grand Central, Harry Bell, decided to take a personal interest in the management of the brewery and in February 1981 he visited Liverpool on a 'fact-finding' mission. Having talked to Edward Bullman and other members of senior management, he inspected the two breweries, the five depots and several public houses. He came to the conclusion that Bullman's needed a radical overhaul. As a result he commissioned a firm of chartered accountants, Rice Bogghouse & Co, to undertake a thorough appraisal of the business and report their findings to the Grand Central board.

4. Their report was completed by May 1981, and was accepted by the Grand Central board at their June meeting. With only a few amendments, the report was redrafted as a consultative document entitled *A Plan for the 1980s* and was sent out to the officials of the various trade unions recognized by the brewery: the TGWU, NALHM and the Bullman's Brewery Staff Association. At about the same time, Edward Bullman was asked to resign as chairman and managing director and became a non-executive director of the company. Three other family

directors were retired from the board. Their places were taken by senior management from Grand Central. A new managing director, G B Gilchrist, was appointed with effect from 1 August 1981. He had formerly been manager of Grand Central's casino business and came to Liverpool with a reputation for toughness.

5. One of his first actions was to convene meetings of Bullman's employees and explain to them the seriousness of the company's position and the need for drastic action. He did not conceal from them the likelihood of extensive redundancies but warned that any opposition to management's plans might well result in the closure and sale of the entire business. Officials of the TGWU and NALHM protested about the lack of consultation. As a result, in early September the management convened a meeting of all union and staff association officials in order to 'exchange views' about the company's future. The TGWU, however, refused to attend on the grounds that it would not sit down at the same negotiating table as NALHM or the staff association. Management agreed, therefore, to meet representatives of NALHM and the staff association on 15 September and to meet TGWU officials and shop stewards on 16 September. Present at the meeting on 15 September are:

For the company: Mr Gilchrist (managing director); Mr Maloney (personnel manager); Mr Smallwood (finance director).
For the trade unions: Mr Piper (regional secretary, NALHM); Mr Rhodes (chairman, Bullman's Staff Association); Mr Whiteley (secretary, Bullman's Staff Association).

Present at the meeting on 16 September are:

For the company: as above.
For the TGWU: Mr Watson (regional secretary); Mr Page (shop steward, Liverpool brewery); Mr Grimshaw (shop steward, St Helens brewery).

'A Plan for the 1980s'

Information document for consultation meeting with trade union representatives (August 1981)

Background

The main problem facing the brewing industry in 1981 is excess capacity, arising in turn from low demand and falling output. During 1980 total beer production fell by 3.8 per cent and this year it is expected to fall by a further 4.6 per cent. Forecasts for 1982 suggest a very modest recovery which will still leave the industry with a good deal of surplus capacity. Most of the large brewery companies have responded to the fall in demand by closing their small, high-cost production plants and depots. As a result, the number of jobs in the industry is declining at the rate of 5000 per year. There has also been a marked increase in competition for the free trade to a point where, in some cases, profit margins have been cut to vanishing point.

Despite this fall in consumption, lager has continued to increase its share of the total market. Bitter sales have also expanded slightly due to the introduction of new brands of cask-conditioned ale:

% of total consumption					
Draught beers	*1974*	*1976*	*1978*	*1979*	*1980*
Mild	13.8	12.6	11.9	11.4	11.3
Premium bitter and stout	16.8	15.2	13.8	13.2	12.3
Bitter	30.6	30.7	31.8	31.5	32.2
Lager	12.6	18.5	20.6	22.1	23.0
	73.8	77.0	78.1	78.2	78.8
Packaged beers	*1974*	*1976*	*1978*	*1979*	*1980*
Light, pale and export	11.7	9.9	8.5	8.1	7.5
Lager	3.7	5.1	6.3	7.0	7.7
Brown ale	3.5	2.4	1.9	1.8	1.6
Stout	5.9	4.3	3.7	3.5	3.2
Strong ale	0.6	0.6	0.6	0.5	0.5
Party cans	0.8	0.7	0.9	0.9	0.7
	26.2	23.0	21.9	21.8	21.2

Official forecasts suggest that by 1985 lager will account for 36 per cent of the total beer market, although much of this projected increase may well come from the continued growth of sales of canned lager through supermarkets.

Bullman's market position
The company is far too committed to static or declining sectors of the market:

% of Bullman's output					
Draught beers	1974	1976	1978	1979	1980
Mild	35.2	33.5	31.4	32.2	35.0
Premium bitter and stout	15.4	15.0	14.8	14.5	14.0
Bitter	25.5	24.0	25.0	27.2	26.5
Lager	5.0	6.5	6.0	6.2	6.8
	81.1	79.0	77.2	80.1	82.3

Packaged beers	1974	1976	1978	1979	1980
Light, pale and export	3.5	4.0	5.5	5.0	4.5
Lager	1.0	3.0	2.5	2.5	2.7
Brown ale	7.5	7.0	7.5	6.5	5.0
Stout	6.0	5.5	6.0	5.0	4.5
Strong ale	0.5	0.5	0.5	0.4	0.5
Party cans	0.4	1.0	1.8	0.5	0.5
	18.9	21.0	22.8	19.9	17.7

This obvious weakness stems from:

1. The company's failure to develop a good, popular draught lager. The present brand, 'Krumbach', was launched in 1973 and is brewed at St Helens. Despite the fact that it is now sold in 90 per cent of the company's tied houses, it has failed to compete with other, better known brands. It is thought that the wrong type of yeast is being used to brew this beer.
2. The failure to exploit the national trend towards cask-conditioned bitter ale. Although it is admitted that Liverpool is traditionally associated with dark mild beer, the company has allowed itself to become too heavily reliant on this sector of the market.

The company is also poorly represented in the free trade, both draught and packaged. Roughly 85 per cent of its total output is sold through its own tied outlets. The problem is that too many of these public houses are situated in declining areas of Liverpool and have no obvious potential for development. Some have, as a result, been neglected and are now in urgent need of structural repairs and internal improvements.

Of the company's total tied estate of 400 outlets, 380 are public houses. Of these, 220 are under direct management and the remainder are let to tenants. Many of the tenanted houses are let at peppercorn rents and are doing relatively little trade — three or four barrels a week being not uncommon. At the other end of the scale some 70 of the 220 managed houses are high-volume outlets, selling in excess of 15 barrels a week. Many of the remainder, however, are relatively small and could be transferred to tenancy. In the tenanted houses the tie for wines, spirits and soft drinks is not enforced and many tenants buy their supplies on a 'cash and carry' basis.

The present production situation

There are two breweries in operation. The Toxteth brewery dates from 1866 (refurbished and enlarged in 1897) and has a total production capacity of 100,000 barrels. At present, however, it is producing little more than 60,000 barrels. The plant and equipment are all virtually obsolete and there is a relatively high percentage of waste. All the company's output of dark mild ale is concentrated at this brewery. Since over 250 people are employed at this brewery, there must be a considerable degree of overmanning. Low productivity is, in turn, reflected in high unit costs. The company's head office is adjacent to the Toxteth brewery.

The St Helens brewery was acquired in 1936 as a result of a merger. It was partially modernized in 1968 when a kegging plant was added and further improvements were made in 1972 in preparation for the start of lager production. The present state of the plan is adequate but there is considerable scope for improvement. Total production capacity is 150,000 barrels a year, but only 120,000 barrels are currently being produced. At present the brewery employs approximately 370 people. Unless production can be increased, manpower costs must be reduced. Over the next few years it is estimated that the company will need to spend about £0.5m on technical improvements at this brewery, exclusive of normal repairs and maintenance.

There are four distribution depots, at Kirby, Warrington, Wigan and Garston, which in total employ 175 people, including draymen and their mates. With the exception of Kirby, which was built in 1966, the depots date back to the 1890s. Kirby and Warrington could both be extended if necessary but the other two are situated on very restricted sites which are not easily accessible to heavy vehicles.

The company has a small bottling and canning plant at Newton-le-Willows where its lager and pale and light ales are packaged for distribution to the retail trade. The plant employs 60 people. Its mild ales and stout, however, are bottled by a small agency in Liverpool. Adjacent to the Newton-le-Willows plant is the company's soft drinks subsidiary, Heywood & Co Ltd, acquired in 1948. The plant produces a range of mineral waters and squashes under the Heywood brand label, which are then delivered to the retail trade. It employs 75 people. The production plant itself, however, is now nearing the end of its useful life and if the business is retained it will need to be completely replaced within the next two years.

The present financial position
The profit and loss record can be summarized as follows:

Year	Net capital employed	Turnover (£m)	£m	% on net capital employed	% on turnover	Depreciation and retained profit (£m)
				Net profit before interest and tax		
1974	9.50	14.00	2.15	22.6	15.3	0.85
1975	9.79	14.80	2.20	22.4	14.8	0.92
1976	10.05	18.66	2.85	28.3	15.2	1.15
1977	10.15	19.20	2.65	26.1	13.8	1.05
1978	10.85	21.45	3.06	28.2	14.2	1.25
1979	11.45	22.15	2.90	25.3	13.0	0.85
1980	19.56*	21.80	2.65	13.4	12.1	0.75

The revaluation of assets in 1980 (asterisked in the table above) disclosed a rate of return on capital employed which is significantly less than that of other comparable firms. The assets are still conservatively valued and take full account of the current economic recession. The same can be said of net profits in relation to turnover. The growth of turnover up to 1980 is entirely attributable to price inflation since the volume of sales declined from 1976 onwards.

The company is short of working capital. The 1980 balance sheet reveals that current liabilities exceed current assets by £1.25 million. If the company was still an independent concern, it would undoubtedly be making a rights issue.

A plan for action
If the decline in the company's business is to be reversed, vigorous action is necessary. The following steps are considered essential:

Marketing
1. Develop and market a new lager which can compete with the market leaders.
2. Develop and market a new cask-conditioned bitter and/or light mild ale.
3. Penetrate the local take-home trade and develop the club trade using these new brands.
4. Rationalize the tied estate. Put the 50 lowest-barrelage houses up for sale and transfer all managed houses selling less than seven barrels a week (60 in number) to tenancy. Buy new outlets wherever possible outside Liverpool.
5. Devise an investment plan to improve the amenities and increase the profitability of the company's remaining public houses. Put tenanted house rents on a more realistic basis.

Production
1. Close the Toxteth brewery and concentrate all production at St Helens. This would enable St Helens to operate at full capacity and would thereby reduce unit costs.
2. Re-equip the St Helens brewery and extend the lager brewing capacity to 50,000 barrels a year. Transfer the company's head office from Toxteth to St Helens.
3. Rationalize the distribution arrangements so that one and if possible two depots can be closed.
4. Close the soft drinks subsidiary and 'buy in' proprietary brands on favourable terms.
5. Increase the efficiency of the bottling plant so that it can meet all the company's requirements for packaged beer.
6. These steps will reduce the labour force by anything from 300-400 and will in a full year produce savings in wages, salaries and other employee costs of nearly £1 million, excluding the cost of redundancy payments.

Finance
1. It is envisaged that the planned investment programme in new or improved production and distribution facilities will extend over a two-year period and will cost £1.2-1.5 million. The investment programme in the licensed estate will cost £2-3 million over a five-year period, although this will be partly offset by capital receipts from the sale of non-viable properties and by increasing the company's revenue from rents.
2. It would, however, be unrealistic to anticipate any short-term improvement in profit margins. Cost savings will have to be passed on to the company's tenants and free trade customers

in the form of greater discounts. The company's liquidity will, therefore, continue to be squeezed.

Industrial relations strategy

Until recently the company has not had an industrial relations strategy as such. The former management fought a long battle against trade unionism, although from the early 1970s onwards it was prepared to consult union representatives informally on a limited range of issues. One result of this tradition is that up to 1980 the average earnings of manual workers, public house managers and white collar staff were significantly below the average for the brewing industry. Most employees were, however, prepared to tolerate this adverse differential because they valued the security of employment offered by Bullman's. After the takeover by Grand Central, apprehension about their future security induced many employees to join the TGWU and take a more 'militant' attitude towards their pay and conditions.

The former management made extensive use of incentive schemes, all of which are now 'decayed'. Overtime also seems to be out of management control, particularly in distribution where it regularly accounts for 30 per cent of gross earnings. There are no method study or work measurement techniques in use. The personnel function has become more important since 1977 but is still regarded as a 'fire-fighting' service for line management.

The company must devise an industrial relations strategy which will help it to achieve its declared objectives in marketing, production and finance. This implies that management will have to take steps to:

1. Communicate its plans and proposals to the workforce and their representatives.
2. Reach a negotiated agreement with union officials covering redundancy, redeployment and other measures designed to reduce the labour force. No redundancy procedure has yet been discussed.
3. Take steps to improve productivity and reduce unit costs. This will involve changes in working practices and a fundamental reform of the wage system. The introduction of a job-evaluated pay structure would be necessary as a matter of priority.
4. Seek to avoid all stoppages of work and other disruptive action which will prejudice the company's attempts to increase its market share.
5. Secure the wholehearted commitment of the workforce to the objectives of the 'strategic development plan' and the long-term success of the company.

'A Plan for the 1980s'

Management document: industrial relations implications

Manning reductions

The closure of the Toxteth brewery would mean that most of its 250 employees would be made redundant. Although it would in theory be possible to phase production out gradually over a one-year period in the hope that some employees would leave voluntarily, this is not a realistic option. The brewery is situated in an area of very high unemployment with few or no job opportunities. Most of the brewery workforce live locally. They would have an obvious incentive to stay on and collect their redundancy payments. A few skilled personnel could be offered alternative employment at the St Helens brewery. This would, however, still mean redundancy for at least 230 workers at a total cost to the company in severance payments of roughly £140,000.

Of the four depots Garston is the most likely candidate for closure, being the oldest, least efficient and geographically least convenient. Again, unless the labour force could be reduced through natural wastage, about 40 employees would have to be made redundant. If the Wigan depot is also closed, this would entail about 35 additional redundancies. The estimated cost in redundancy payments would be £24,000 for Garston and £21,000 for Wigan.

The closure of the Heywood plant at Newton-le-Willows might be achieved without the same reliance on compulsory redundancy. Labour turnover has been running at 30 per cent over the last two or three years, although it has recently fallen to around 20 per cent. Nevertheless, the labour force is largely female and much use is made of part-time employees. Of the present labour force, it is reasonably safe to assume that only the longer-serving employees would need to be made redundant. This would involve about 30 employees, at a total cost of £18,000.

Early retirement

Although it is not envisaged that the introduction of an earlier retirement age (say 60 and 55 years for males and females respectively) would be much help in implementing the above programme of closures, it would be relevant to the general objective of reducing manpower costs.

Of the remaining workforce (ie those employed at St Helens, Warrington, Kirby and Newton-le-Willows, but excluding the public houses), there are approximately 80 manual employees

(70 males) who are either 60 years of age or above and could be encouraged to take early retirement. The only problem is that such a strategy would require the support of a good pension scheme or a mechanism for protecting the employees affected until their normal retirement date. As Bullman's do not have a pension scheme for manual workers, the cost of additional assistance would need to be investigated before this approach could be adopted.

The implications for the company's relationship with the trade unions

Clearly the TGWU has most to lose in terms of membership and, perhaps, credibility from the proposed closures and rationalization measures. Until the mid-1970s the TGWU represented less than half of the manual labour force, the majority being non-union. It was not until the acquisition of Bullman's by Grand Central that union membership began to increase and then it rose rapidly. At present it is estimated that 85 per cent of the manual labour force belongs to the TGWU. Under the former management there was no formal recognition of the TGWU for collective bargaining purposes, although the union was allowed to represent individual members in grievance or disciplinary proceedings, etc. In July 1979, however, the union was granted full recognition following a four-week strike at the Toxteth brewery which cost the company a great deal in lost sales.

The strike was organized and led by Fred Page, a prominent union activist at the Toxteth brewery. A former car assembly worker at Halewood, 'Fred the red' (as he is popularly known) enjoys a great deal of support among the Toxteth workforce, although he is distrusted as a 'commie' by many workers at the St Helens brewery. His declared intention in organizing the strike for union recognition was to 'drag Bullman's into the twentieth century' and to show Grand Central that the brewery workforce had industrial muscle and were prepared to use it in defence of their jobs. Since the strike he has negotiated a 20 per cent increase in wages in April 1980 and an 11 per cent increase in April 1981 on behalf of his members, together with improved fringe benefits.

The Bullman's Brewery Staff Association was formed in 1972, largely at the initiative of management, and currently has 90 members. Although in theory membership is open to all grades of employee in the company, most of the association members are clerks, typists, supervisors and middle-ranking executives. At its peak in 1975 the association had 160 members but since then it has gradually lost support. In 1976 it applied for a certificate as an independent trade union under the Trade Union and Labour Relations Act 1974, but its application was refused. The chairman of the association, Bill Rhodes, is the company's transport manager. The company 'consults' the staff association on salaries and other terms and conditions of employment. In 1980 the staff were awarded a 16 per cent salary increase and a 10 per cent increase in 1981.

The company's 220 public house managers are represented by NALHM, to which over 200 of them belong. This union was recognized by the company for 'consultative' purposes in 1973 and was formally given full bargaining rights in 1979. The Bullman managers belong to the Liverpool branch of NALHM, one of the union's strongest branches. The regional secretary, Harry Piper, has a reputation for effective negotiating and has successfully staved off threatened redundancies among public house managers in other Lancashire breweries. Relations between NALHM and the TGWU, both nationally and locally, are very strained. When Fred Page tried to launch a recruitment drive for ACTSS among the public house managers, Piper accused him of poaching and threatened to refer the matter to the TUC. The recruitment drive never got off the ground. Since formal recognition was granted in 1979 the TGWU has refused to sit down at the same negotiating table as NALHM and vice versa. Both unions, however, are strongly opposed to the loss of jobs among their members.

Implications for management style

Considerable pressure will be brought to bear by the TGWU in order to preserve the Toxteth brewery. Fred Page has already said that if the company tries to close it, the workforce will organize a 'brew-in' and keep the plant going by selling beer to labour and trade union clubs in Liverpool. There is no doubt that Page is hoping for a 'hard-line' response from management, which will enable him to play his favourite role of militant champion of the working class. How much support he would get from TGWU members elsewhere in the company, however, is debatable.

By contrast, both NALHM and the staff association will press for the fullest possible consultation and participation in the decision-making process. NALHM in particular may well put forward constructive alternatives to the company's proposals and if it does so it will expect its counter-proposals to be seriously considered. It would therefore be appropriate for the company to vary its management style depending on which union it is facing.

Strategic development plan: points for the TGWU's case

JOB SECURITY

1. The policy of the trade union is to maintain current levels of employment and preserve job opportunities as far as possible. The union is therefore obliged to resist anything in the strategic development plan which involves voluntary or compulsory redundancy. *This is a key union objective.* Management must be reminded that the success of the strategic development plan will depend very much on the active support and cooperation of TGWU members.

2. The union must, however, have a fall-back position. If, after hard bargaining, the union's objective of 'no loss of jobs' cannot be achieved it must seek a *quid pro quo.* This might, for example, take the form of redundancy payments well in advance of the statutory minima. It might also entail assurances on the part of management to create new jobs as soon as the plan begins to succeed, together with a pledge of no compulsory redundancy for those TGWU members not involved in the current redundancy proposals. There must, above all, be a categorical assurance by Grand Central's management that the St Helens brewery will not be closed.

WAGES

3. The union requires higher wage rates for operating new, more capital-intensive equipment and for its members' cooperation generally with those sections of the strategic development plan which are eventually agreed. Additionally, all incentive payments must be raised. The union will make inter-company comparisons within the brewing industry to ensure that all new rates and incentives are in line with the best currently operating.

4. The union cannot agree to the introduction of job evaluation, which it sees as a management 'con-trick'. Job evaluation is seen as a technique whereby management can set one workgroup against another in arguments over pay differentials.

5. The union has long been aggrieved by the way in which their members have been treated as 'poor relations' compared with the white collar staff. The aim of the strategic development plan is to make the company more profitable and this in turn will depend to a large extent on the efforts of the manual workforce. Their commitment to the plan would be greatly enhanced by the extension of the pension scheme currently enjoyed by white collar staff to cover the manual workforce.

6. The union cannot take much account of any argument by management to 'make haste slowly' with pay and pension improvements because of tight financial constraints while it strives to improve its profitability. Bullman's Brewery Ltd is now only a small part of the

Grand Central empire, which has been consistently profitable for many years. Grand Central is obviously financing the strategic development plan and can, by the same token, make sufficient funds available to improve wages and conditions.

7. The union will require management to provide appropriate facilities for a full-time convenor to carry out his duties at both the Toxteth brewery and the St Helens brewery, including an office, telephone etc. It will also require management to give serious consideration to negotiating a union membership agreement covering all manual grades in the company, subject to the terms of the Employment Act 1980.

Strategic development plan: points for NALHM's case

OVERALL STRATEGY

1. The association welcomes the development of a strategic development plan to ensure the future viability of the company. It realizes, however, that there will be problems in reaching agreement on details of the plan and therefore proposes that *all* trade unions involved should set aside those honest differences of opinion which have occurred in the past and present a common, united front in the forthcoming negotiations.

2. If a common approach cannot be agreed, NALHM will 'go it alone' and put the interests of its members first. The general principles of the association's viewpoint are set out below.

JOB SECURITY

3. The association is totally opposed to redundancy and loss of job opportunities. In the case of public house managers such a loss could arise either from the permanent closure of managed houses and the extinction of their licences or from the transfer of houses from direct management to tenancy. The strategic development plan envisages that at least 60 of the company's 220 managed houses should be transferred to tenancy. This proposal is totally unacceptable to NALHM *unless* the managers of those houses are given a prescriptive right to become tenants and appropriate financial assistance to enable them to do so.

4. The association would, however, be prepared to discuss with the company a scheme which would enable its members to retire at any time after they have attained the age of 55. This would be feasible under the company's existing pension arrangements for public house managers. Of the 60 managers whose jobs are threatened by the plan, 27 are over 55 years of age and could benefit from such a scheme.

SALARIES

5. The company has always adhered to the basic minimum salary scales

for managers agreed by NALHM and the Brewers' Society. An incentive scheme geared to the barrelage sold through each house was agreed in 1974 and has remained unchanged since then. The scheme is now so far out of line with those operated by other brewery companies, large and small, that a completely new bonus system must be introduced as a matter of priority. The agreement of NALHM to the strategic development plan is conditional on a formal recognition by the company of the need to effect a substantial improvement in the pay and conditions of its members.

Strategic development plan: points for the staff association's case

OVERALL STRATEGY
1. The staff association welcomes any initiative by the company which is likely to protect the employment of the members of the association and improve their salaries and conditions. It would welcome a joint response by all employees' organizations to the company's proposals and notes with great regret the apparent refusal of the TGWU to participate in such a response.

2. The association's main objective is to protect and enhance its own position as the only organization which is capable of representing the interests of the clerical, technical, administrative and managerial staff of Bullman's Brewery Co Ltd. To this end it must ensure that any loss of employment is strongly resisted and that, if such loss is ultimately agreed by all parties to be unavoidable, the members of the association suffer no loss which is proportionately greater than that suffered by any other group of employees.

JOB SECURITY
3. The association observes that there is no specific reference in the strategic development plan to redundancies among its members. The association can only assume from this omission that senior management do not regard the level of staffing in the clerical, technical administrative and managerial grades as excessive or inappropriate.

4. The association recognizes, however, that measures to hold down all manpower costs may be necessary in the short term. It is therefore prepared to discuss with the company the possibility of an early retirement scheme for members of staff on the understanding that when the company's financial position improves additional staff employment will be created.

SALARIES
5. The main reason why the association's membership has declined in recent years is that too many members of staff have perceived it as weak and ineffective. The fact that the salary increase negotiated in

1980 was 4 per cent less (at 16 per cent) than that achieved by the TGWU was particularly resented. The fact that in 1981 all groups received the same percentage increase (11 per cent) has done nothing to mollify the association's members.

6. The salary structure for staff employees has become hopelessly warped over the years, largely because of the *ad hoc* system of merit awards. This system has been much abused by personal favouritism and has given rise to a great deal of resentment. Repeated requests by the association for the abolition of this system have been refused. The association is pleased to note that the company apparently believes that the application of job evaluation techniques is now necessary. The association would, therefore, be prepared to cooperate in a job evaluation exercise on a joint basis with management.

7. In return for this cooperation, the association will require management to discuss methods whereby members of staff who currently do not belong to the association may be persuaded to join.

Personal profiles

G B GILCHRIST
Managing director of the company since August 1981. Formerly managing director of Grand Central Casinos Ltd, and before then chief accountant of Grand Central International Hotels Ltd. An accountant by training, he has a reputation for being able to 'turn round' failing or inefficient businesses. His previous business career has not, however, given him much exposure to collective bargaining and he has never dealt with a labour force and union representatives in the Merseyside area.

JOHN MALONEY
Personnel manager of the company since 1980. Formerly staff relations officer in Grand Central's leisure services division and before then a free trade salesman and area manager with one of the largest brewery groups in the UK. Since his appointment to Bullman's he has greatly modernized the personnel function, introducing new systems and procedures and seeking to improve communications with the workforce. His experience of negotiating with trade union representatives is, however, limited.

BRIAN SMALLWOOD
Finance director since May 1981. Previously senior consultant with Rice Bogghouse and Co and virtually wrote the latter's report on Bullman's himself. He has had many years' experience as a consultant involved in rescuing small firms from difficulties and has been very successful. A chartered accountant by training, he holds strong views

Case Studies in Industrial Relations

on trade union militancy and believes that many of Britain's problems are attributable to wreckers and subversives on the shop floor. He believes instead in the need to talk directly with 'real' workers on the shop floor.

TOM WATSON
Regional secretary of the TGWU. He has occupied this post since 1965 and is due to retire in 1983. He is a tough and experienced professional negotiator who has been bloodied by many battles with recalcitrant employers on Merseyside. His main concern now, however, is to reach retirement without too many problems and upsets. Two years ago he suffered a heart attack and has tended to take things easier ever since.

FRED PAGE ('THE RED')
Senior TGWU shop steward at the Toxteth brewery. Shop steward at Ford's Halewood plant from 1971 until he was made redundant in 1974. Member of the Militant Tendency and of Liverpool City Council. An extremely effective organizer and negotiator with a very strong personal following both in the brewery and in the local community. He organized the four-week strike at the Toxteth brewery in July 1979 which resulted in full recognition for the TGWU at Bullman's after many years of fruitless pressure. The following year he negotiated a 20 per cent wage increase for the manual workforce. He is determined to survive any redundancy programme and to displace his longer-serving rival at St Helens, Bill Grimshaw, as the union's 'number one' steward at Bullman's. His aim is a full-time position with the TGWU or a parliamentary seat.

BILL GRIMSHAW
Senior TGWU shop steward at the St Helens' brewery and a Bullman's employee since 1965. A political moderate who believes in the 'softly-softly' approach to collective bargaining. Had he been dealing with a progressive, enlightened management during his career with the company, he might have achieved much more than he has. As it is, he feels resentful that the change towards a more go-ahead management style since the takeover by Grand Central has coincided with the rise of Fred Page. Grimshaw detests Page and would not lift a finger to save Page's job at Toxteth. Whatever happens, he is determined that none of 'his' members' jobs at St Helens will be axed under the plan.

HARRY PIPER
Regional secretary of NALHM since 1972. A thoroughly professional negotiator with a record of solid achievement in bargaining with other companies. A brewery man to the core, he suspects that the new management of Bullman's has little or no idea how 'the trade' operates and will seek to 'steamroller' their proposals through, regardless of

50

objections or counter-proposals. He is aware that one or two other brewery companies in the region are waiting to see the outcome of Bullman's attempt to switch 60 managed houses to tenancy. If Bullman's succeed they will follow suit. He is therefore determined to stave off this move as long as possible or, alternatively, extract a costly *quid pro quo* from management.

BILL RHODES
Chairman of the company staff association since late 1980. He took over at a low point in the association's fortunes after a 'palace revolution' by the membership at the 1980 AGM had displaced the former leadership. The association was formed in 1972, largely at the initiative of management, and currently has 90 members. Most of its members are clerks, supervisors, typists, technicians and middle managers. At its peak in 1975 the association had 160 members but began to lose support when it failed to achieve any tangible improvements in terms and conditions. Rhodes is committed to reviving its fortunes and to obtaining a certificate of independence as a trade union. He has, however, had very little experience of collective bargaining and is unsure how many of his members would support him if it came to a showdown with the company.

PAUL WHITELEY
General secretary of the staff association since 1980. He shares Rhodes's general objective of regenerating the staff association, but is more cynical about the prospects of achieving it. His present job is that of tenanted trade supervisor for Central and West Liverpool and, as such, he realizes that he could be made redundant if the strategic plan's objective of selling off all the less viable tenanted houses is realized. He sees the takeover by Grand Central as an opportunity to further his own career and get out of Bullman's Brewery.

CASE 5: Cleckleydale Metropolitan Council

Background

1. The Metropolitan Borough of Cleckleydale employs 18,000 employees in three main groups: administrative, professional, technical and clerical (APT & C staff), teachers and lecturers, and craft and manual workers. It provides the normal range of services allocated to metropolitan district authorities under the Local Government Act 1972, namely education, social services, housing, refuse collection and other technical services associated with highways, drainage, parks, cemeteries, etc. From its inception in 1974 until May 1980, Cleckleydale was Conservative-controlled. In May 1980 Labour won a narrow majority and the present political balance on the council is 35 Labour members,

28 Conservatives and 17 Liberal and SDP Alliance members.

2. Between 1974 and 1977 the controlling Conservative group operated a system of reasonably tight recruitment control, whereby certain vacancies were left unfilled and the employment of seasonal workers was curtailed. By this method the total number of employees on the council's payroll fell from 17,600 in 1975 to 16,700 in 1977. From 1977 onwards, however, pressure for improved council services induced the controlling group to relax the controls on recruitment and, as a result, the total number of employees on the payroll began to rise, reaching 17,900 in March 1979. This increase was brought about partly by filling vacancies within the existing establishment (ie the agreed manpower budget and organization structure) and partly by creating new posts.

3. While permitting day-to-day recruitment to increase, the leadership of the council was, at the urging of the chief management services officer, actively seeking methods of reducing the council's longer-term demand for labour. In 1978 the leadership decided to introduce word processing technology into its typing services. It was calculated that this new technology would enable the council to reduce the number of typists on its payroll by 50 per cent within three to four years without any adverse effect on the throughput of work. In April 1978 the branch officials of NALGO were informed that word processing equipment would be introduced throughout the organization, starting the directorate of technical services.

4. The reaction of NALGO was hostile. The Cleckleydale branch passed a resolution deploring the lack of prior consultation on the introduction of word processing equipment. It also demanded that the council give a guarantee of no compulsory redundancy to all those staff who were likely to be affected by the new technology and that an enhanced rate of pay be awarded to these staff in technical services who were being asked to operate the new equipment. The leadership of the council agreed to achieve the projected reduction in staff numbers by natural wastage and offered a marginal increase in pay to the typists who were to use the new equipment. When NALGO rejected this offer on the grounds that it was inadequate, the council went directly to the typists concerned and asked them if they were prepared to operate the new equipment on the terms offered. By an overwhelming majority, the staff accepted the management offer and NALGO were left with no alternative but to accept this as a *fait accompli.*

5. Between June 1978 and May 1980 the installation of word processing equipment enabled management to reduce the typing staff in technical services by nearly 50 per cent. But although a provisional timetable had been sketched out for the extension of the new technology to other departments of the council, no further progress had been made in this respect when the Conservatives lost their majority in May 1980.

The development of a manpower strategy

6. The change of government at Westminster in May 1979 was followed by the imposition of sizeable reductions in Cleckleydale Council's budget. In the course of the financial year 1979-80 the council was required to reduce its planned revenue expenditure of £95 million by £2 million. At a strategy meeting in June 1979, the senior members of the Conservative group decided that £0.75 million of the total reduction would be found from savings on the manpower budget, to be achieved by the reintroduction of strict recruitment control. Over the next few months the chairman of the personnel sub-committee personally scrutinized every vacancy and, by leaving a substantial proportion unfilled, achieved the target saving.

7. Initially NALGO and the other trade unions recognized by the council (the NUT, NAS/UWT, TGWU, NUPE, GMWU, AUEW and EEPTU) reluctantly acquiesced in the new controls on recruitment. As the operational effects of unfilled vacancies became increasingly apparent, however, so the union representatives came under greater pressure from some of their rank and file members to resist recruitment control. This pressure was particularly strong within NALGO where it was felt, with some justice, that the APT & C grades were shouldering more of the burden of recruitment control than any other group of staff. As a result, in December 1979, NALGO began to pursue a policy of 'non-cooperation', which meant that staff were instructed not to take on extra work as a result of unfilled vacancies.

8. This action led to a fundamental reappraisal of the council's approach to manpower and industrial relations. The leadership realized that day-to-day recruitment control, unsupported by a longer-term manpower strategy, would neither achieve the desired reduction in spending nor, because of its *ad hoc* and unpredictable effects, would it ensure that the controlling party's declared intention of protecting essential services was fulfilled. After several weeks of intensive discussions, at member and officer level, the leadership announced a five-point strategy which, it was said, would be pursued during the financial years 1980-81 and 1981-82:

(a) That further reductions in the council's budget would be achieved primarily by cuts in manpower costs.

(b) That these cuts would be effected by a combination of voluntary severance, early retirement and continued recruitment control. There would be no compulsory redundancy. The severance payments and 'golden handshakes' would be financed from the council's cash balances as a 'once-and-for-all' charge which would in time be more than fully recouped by the savings made on the manpower budget. No employee who accepted voluntary severance or early retirement would be replaced and his or her post would be eliminated from the establishment.

53

(c) That the APT & C grades would be required to absorb a greater percentage reduction in numbers than either the teaching force or the craft and manual workers on the grounds that the latter groups were more closely identified with essential or 'sharp-end' services to the public. The APT & C grades, by contrast, were regarded as the 'bureaucracy' and, as such, less important to the general public. The number of posts in the APT & C grades would therefore be reduced by 10 per cent and in all other grades by 5 per cent. For the APT & C grades this implied a loss of 400 posts, while the teachers' and lecturers' grades would lose 250 posts and the craft and manual workers 425 posts. A significant proportion of these posts (especially in the craft and manual grades) would be part-time.

(d) That a comprehensive review of the management structure of the authority, the results of which would mirror the reductions in APT & C numbers, would begin immediately and be ready for implementation on 1 April 1980.

(e) That new, labour-saving technology would be gradually introduced throughout the authority, with the agreement and cooperation of NALGO, and that the savings in manpower costs so derived would be applied partly to finance further cuts in spending and partly to improve the terms and conditions of the remaining APT & C staff.

9. Once this strategy had been agreed at member level, the leader of the council and the chairman of the personnel sub-committee met the local branch officials of NALGO in order to explain their intentions and invite comment. The official response of NALGO was that the union was opposed to any reductions in local government spending and would actively resist such reductions in Cleckleydale as elsewhere. However, the branch officials indicated informally that they would be prepared to consider any detailed proposals which the council put before them on the proviso that none of their members would be made compulsorily redundant. They also made it clear, however, that they were not prepared to accept any discrimination against NALGO. Any reductions in manpower must, they argued, be applied equally to all groups of employees. They further argued that *all* the financial savings from new technology should be applied to improving the terms and conditions of remaining NALGO members.

10. In the light of this response, the leadership of the council considered the problem of applying the same percentage reduction in manpower across the board. The council's rate support grant for 1980-81 implied a further reduction in spending of £4.5 million. A cut of 10 per cent in APT & C staff, combined with a 5 per cent cut in teachers/lecturers and craft/manual employees, would achieve this reduction target. It was calculated that to achieve the same numerical reduction in staff by

applying an across-the-board formula would imply a cut of roughly 6 per cent in the total number of employees on the payroll (see table below).

	Original formula (10% APT & C, 5% all others)			NALGO formula (6% across the board)		
	Reduction in numbers	FTE	Saving (£m)	Reduction in numbers	FTE	Saving (£m)
APT & C	400	320	2.8	245	200	1.6
T & L	250	180	1.4	310	225	1.57
C & M	425	200	0.6	520	275	0.82
	1075	700	4.8	1075	700	3.99

The NALGO formula would, however, not only have left the council £0.5 million short of its reduction target but would have entailed politically unacceptable cuts in 'sharp-end' service employees. For these reasons the council's leadership told NALGO that their counter-proposal was unacceptable.

11. NALGO responded by refusing to enter into further negotiations with the council and by declaring that they would 'vigorously oppose' any attempt by management to reduce staffing, whether by declaring redundancies or recruitment control. They further called upon all other unions recognized by the council to join them in resisting any further reductions in local government spending. The other unions formally declared that they were opposed to spending cuts and would resist any redundancies with industrial action. Privately, however, the biggest teachers' union, the NUT, and the largest manual union, NUPE, both indicated that they would be prepared to discuss with management ways and means of avoiding compulsory redundancy.

12. In the light of NALGO's refusal to continue discussions, the leadership of the council decided to communicate directly with the APT & C staff and 'test the market'. Early in March 1980 all 4000 APT & C staff were contacted in order to discover how many were interested in taking (a) early retirement and (b) voluntary severance. Some 300 staff said that they were 'definitely interested' in early retirement, while a further 150 said that they 'might be interested' depending on what kind of terms were offered. A further 200 staff said that they were or might be interested in voluntary severance, again depending on the terms offered.

13. Encouraged by this response management proceeded to work out the terms of an early retirement/voluntary severance offer and, simultaneously, to reorganize the authority on the basis of a 10 per cent cut in APT & C staff. By 15 March the terms of the offer had been agreed at member level and were circulated to all APT & C staff

55

(see Appendix I). A similar offer was put on the table for discussion with the NUT. By the end of April some 200 APT & C staff had formally accepted early retirement, 50 of whom had already gone. The balance were due to leave at various times between 1 May and 1 September. A further 220 were 'actively considering' the offer. Some 70 staff had accepted voluntary severance and had either left or were in the process of leaving.

14. On 5 May 1980, however, the annual municipal elections were held and the Conservatives lost control of Cleckleydale Council. A minority Labour administration assumed control and immediately suspended the early retirement/voluntary severance offer. The Labour group had long made it clear that they were strongly opposed to the policy of 'golden handshakes' and had given a pledge that there would be no further contraction in council employment. This pledge was reiterated during the election campaign. Indeed, they declared that they would expand council employment by increasing the direct works organization's labour force.

The post-election strategy

15. Shortly after assuming control of the council, the Labour leadership realized that since they were obliged to work within the Conservative group's budget for the financial year 1980-81, they would also be obliged to follow through their predecessors' manpower strategy. The Labour leader, councillor Ducket, sounded out the NALGO branch chairman, Tony King, about the prospects for a package deal and received a reasonably positive response. Ducket made it clear to King, however, that in his view the Conservatives' terms were too generous. The authority had insufficient cash balances to make an offer to all potential volunteers for early retirement or voluntary redundancy. As a result, either some volunteers would be disappointed or the terms on offer would have to be watered down somewhat. The only way in which this downward revision could be avoided was by the speedy extension of word processing equipment throughout the authority, which would achieve a rapid reduction in clerical and secretarial staff. King indicated that such a revision might be negotiable.

16. Shortly after this discussion, however, King was taken seriously ill and was effectively out of action for several months. He was replaced as acting branch chairman by Alan Blake, who took a more 'militant' view of the agreement. Blake quickly let it be known that there was no possibility of NALGO agreeing to any downward revision of the existing terms. The leader of the council reluctantly accepted that significant changes in the terms and conditions of the early retirement/voluntary severance package were not feasible. He was still anxious, however, to secure NALGO's commitment to a strategy aimed at reducing manpower

costs during 1980-81 and protecting employment within the council in the longer term.

17. In preparation for their meeting with NALGO, management submitted a draft agreement (Appendix II). This is on the agenda of the first formal meeting between the elected members, senior management and NALGO constituting, respectively, the management side and the staff side of the council's joint consultative committee. The meeting has been called for 7 June 1980. Present are:

For the council: Cllr Bowman (chairman of the JCC and chairman of personnel sub-committee); Cllr Ducket (leader of the council); Cllr Horton (leader of the Conservative group); Mr B Gregory (chief personnel officer); Mr C Clarkson (principal industrial relations officer).

For NALGO: Mr A Blake (acting chairman, Cleckleydale branch); Mr S Rye (vice-chairman); Mr G Floggett (branch secretary); Mr P Beasley (branch organizer); Mr R Franklin (regional officer).

Appendix I: Terms of the offer to APT & C staff

Early retirement terms

In the interests of achieving necessary economies and protecting essential services to the public, the council is prepared to consider applications for early retirement made by any member of its APT & C staff who meets the following criteria:

1. Is over 50 years of age.
2. Has five years' qualifying service for the council's superannuation scheme.

Employees whose applications are accepted will receive immediate payment of accrued superannuation benefits and will be credited with a notional period of service. This period will not exceed the shortest of:

1. Ten years.
2. A period equivalent in length to the employee's qualifying service.
3. A period which, when added to the employee's qualifying service, does not extend it beyond 40 years.
4. A period equivalent in length to the time from retirement date to the sixth-fifth birthday.

Voluntary severance

Any employee who volunteers for redundancy will, if his application is accepted, be offered a payment additional to any statutory redundancy pay and to the return of any superannuation contributions, frozen benefits or transfer of benefits, whichever is applicable. This payment will be made on the following scale, irrespective of the age of the employee, and is applicable to all full-time and part-time employees:

Length of service	Payment
Less than 1 year	2 weeks' pay
1 year but less than 2 years	7 weeks' pay
2 years but less than 3 years	8 weeks' pay
3 years but less than 4 years	10 weeks' pay
4 years but less than 5 years	11 weeks' pay
5 years but less than 6 years	12 weeks' pay
6 years but less than 7 years	14 weeks' pay
7 years but less than 8 years	15 weeks' pay
8 years but less than 9 years	17 weeks' pay
9 years but less than 10 years	18 weeks' pay
10 years but less than 11 years	20 weeks' pay
11 years but less than 12 years	22 weeks' pay
12 years but less than 13 years	23 weeks' pay
13 years but less than 14 years	24 weeks' pay
14 years and more	26 weeks' pay

Length of service is taken to be unbroken local authority service to date.

March 1980

Appendix II: Draft agreement dealing with the manpower implications of new technology and cutbacks in financial resources

Preamble

1. This agreement is made between Cleckleydale Metropolitan Council and the staff of the JCC for non-manual workers (excluding teachers).

2. The purpose of this agreement is to provide a means of dealing with the application of a reduction in the labour force brought about by either cutbacks in financial resources or the introduction of new technology.

3. The council will attempt to minimize harm to individuals by offering the terms and conditions contained in this agreement.

4. The staff side accepts that, in return for the terms and conditions offered in this agreement, its members will cooperate with all reasonable steps, including the introduction of more flexible working practices, taken to reduce manning levels, for the reasons detailed in (2) above.

5. The calculations of the benefits under this scheme are subject to an overriding maximum which is that the sum cost to the council of payments in the first year shall not exceed one year's salary plus on-costs.

6. The agreement should apply until one of the parties to the Agreement gives three months' notice to the other of its intention to terminate the agreement.

7. Section 'A' of this agreement deals with reductions in the labour force brought about by cuts in financial resources and section 'B' those reductions in the labour force related to new technology.

8. The terms and conditions of this agreement do not form any part of any employee's conditions of service or individual contract.

Section 'A'

In the event of reductions in manning levels being declared as a result of cuts in financial resources, Cleckleydale Metropolitan Council offers, and the staff side accepts, the following conditions being applied to affected employees:

1. No employee will be made compulsorily redundant. Those employees who are not found jobs in the section or department affected will be offered reasonable alternative employment if such is available.

2. The staff side agrees to cooperate in the redeployment of staff and the achievement of more flexible working practices.

3. Any employee who is displaced will be offered a payment additional to any statutory redundancy pay and to the return of any superannuation contributions, frozen benefits or transfer of benefits, which may be applicable. This payment will be made on the following scale, irrespective of age, and is applicable to all full-time and part-time employees:

Length of service	Payment
Less than 1 year	2 weeks' pay
1 year but less than 2 years	7 weeks' pay
2 years but less than 3 years	8 weeks' pay
3 years but less than 4 years	10 weeks' pay
4 years but less than 5 years	11 weeks' pay
5 years but less than 6 years	12 weeks' pay
6 years but less than 7 years	14 weeks' pay
7 years but less than 8 years	15 weeks' pay
8 years but less than 9 years	17 weeks' pay
9 years but less than 10 years	18 weeks' pay
10 years but less than 11 years	20 weeks' pay
11 years but less than 12 years	22 weeks' pay
12 years but less than 13 years	23 weeks' pay
13 years but less than 14 years	24 weeks' pay
14 years and more	26 weeks' pay

Notes:

(a) Length of service is taken to be unbroken local authority service to date and shall apply to both redundancy payment and additional payment calculations.

(b) A week's pay will be calculated with no upper earnings limit for both redundancy payment and additional payment.

(c) An employee is not entitled to a payment if he or she has reached age 65 on the Saturday of the week in which his or her contract terminates. For an employee who is nearing age 65 when he or she is displaced, the payment is reduced progressively as follows: for each complete month by which the employee's age exceeds 64 on the Saturday of the week in which his or her contract terminates, the payment to which he or she would otherwise have been entitled is reduced by one-twelfth.

(d) The payment made to an employee eligible for 'enhanced years' retirement benefits will be reduced by the cost to Cleckleydale Metropolitan Council, during the first year of retirement, of the additional lump sum and pension payments.

4. Any displaced employee who is over 50 years of age, and has five years' reckonable qualifying service for the superannuation scheme will be offered early retirement. Such employees will receive immediate payment of accrued superannuation benefits and will be credited with a notional period of service. This period will not exceed the shortest of:

(a) Ten years.

(b) A period equivalent in length to the employee's reckonable and qualifying service.

(c) A period which, when added to the employee's reckonable service, does not extend it beyond 40 years.

(d) A period equivalent in length to the time from retirement date to the sixty-fifth birthday.

(e) Dependent on his or her circumstances the offer of a notional period of service need not be taken up by an employee accepting early retirement.

5. Alternative posts may be filled on the basis of:

(a) Full-time employee filling a full-time post, or

(b) Two part-time employees filling one full-time post, subject to full-time staffing levels not being exceeded.

Section 'B'

1. The council and the staff side agree that the extended intro-duction of new technology is essential to the maintenance of an efficient and effective service to the public. The severance conditions laid down in Section 'A' will apply to those employees who are displaced by new technology.

2. It is agreed that the savings accruing to the council from any particular application of new technology will be identified and certified as savings by the director of finance. After account has been taken of any payments arising out of the general conditions offered in Section 'A' and out of any specific conditions, if applicable, savings then remaining will be applied to the protection of employment within the council.

3. In the light of (2) above the authority will immediately enter into negotiations with the staff side for the introduction of word processing equipment into the directorates of housing, social services and education. In addition to the general conditions offered in this agreement, the following terms and conditions shall also apply:

(a) Word processing operators will be paid on the word processing operators' grade.

(b) Existing MC 82 operators who are currently paid on a scale which extends to spinal column point 14, and who can already be regarded as word processing operators, will receive a one-off lump sum payment of £300 as a disturbance allowance.

(c) The authority will immediately enter into negotiations with the staff side to examine the savings and to allocate them in accordance with this agreement.

June 1980

Points for the management side

1. The budget for 1980-81 was put together by the previous controlling party on the basis that the reductions required by central government – £4.5 million – would be found by cuts in manpower. The present controlling group has no alternative but to pursue this strategy during 1980-81. If it was felt desirable to achieve a reduction of £4.5 million by cutting expenditure on non-manpower items then a great deal of detailed forward planning would be necessary to minimize the effect of such cuts on the public. No such planning, however, has been done; there is, therefore, no alternative but to reduce manpower costs.

2. It is essential that renewed progress is made in the application of word processing technology to the whole of the council's operations. If the union's agreement is forthcoming, it is estimated that this objective could be achieved by 1984, with considerable savings in staff costs. It is likely that most of these savings could be achieved by natural wastage, ie by non-replacement of secretarial and clerical staff who leave between now and the full and final introduction of word processing equipment in 1984.

3. There is little doubt that several departments within the council are overmanned in terms of APT & C staff and have been for some years. Prior to the introduction of strict recruitment control in May 1979, there were 500 more staff (mainly APT & C) on the council's payroll than in April 1974 when the council was first established, despite the opportunities to make economies of scale which local government reorganization was supposed to provide. If central government continues to reduce local government spending over the next few years, as seems likely, the council will sooner or later be unable to fulfil its current pledge of 'no compulsory redundancy'. While it is admitted that early retirement and voluntary severance will involve a loss of job opportunities, the terms on offer are generous and are considerably better than many redundant employees in the private sector have received.

4. While there may be some room for manoeuvre on the distribution of

the manpower reductions as between APT & C staff and other groups, something near to the formula adopted by the previous controlling group must be maintained. The average current cost of employing one APT & C employee (with on-costs) is nearly £8000 per year; the corresponding figure for teachers is £7000 and for craft and manual workers £3000. It is obvious, therefore, that if concessions are made in terms of APT & C reductions in line with NALGO's demand, redundancies among teachers and manual workers will have to be increased on more than a straight one-for-one basis. This, in turn, would involve significant changes in staff/pupil ratios in the authority's schools and cuts in basic services such as refuse collection which are politically unacceptable.

5. Nor is it practicable for management to rely exclusively on recruitment control to achieve cuts in manpower. The previous administration achieved its planned saving of £0.75 million through recruitment control, mainly at the expense of APT & C grades. If this policy was to be rigorously pursued without the support of a more general severance package deal, the organization would sooner or later end up with all kinds of staffing anomalies and imbalances. Recruitment control is a blunt instrument in so far as it operates against efficient as well as inefficient departments. It also depends on a factor which is outside management's control — namely the rate of turnover — which obviously varies from one department to another and, in a period of rising unemployment, is likely to fall. For these reasons, recruitment control can never be a substitute for a proper manpower strategy.

Points for the staff side

1. The union cannot accept any discrimination against APT & C staff. If cuts in manpower have to be made — and NALGO strongly opposes any such cuts — they should be done on either an across-the-board basis or in a way which reflects the service priorities of the controlling party. The present proposals, however, are based on a crude prejudice against 'bureaucrats' and on an equally simplistic belief that the council is over-staffed. If this is so the council itself must bear the responsibility and it is unfair to penalize APT & C staff for years of sloppy management.

2. APT & C staff have already made a disproportionately large contribution to the previous administration's £2 million cutback in 1979-80. Most of the £0.75 million savings on recruitment control were achieved by leaving APT & C vacancies unfilled. The union's membership will not tolerate continued discrimination of this kind. Indeed, the branch executive committee is already coming under pressure to instruct members not to 'cover' unfilled vacancies by accepting additional work or responsibility without suitable additional remuneration.

3. The draft agreement submitted by management for discussion is inadequate in several respects:

Section A:
(a) What is meant by 'more flexible working practices'? In what ways are current practices 'inflexible'?
(b) The additional payments offered in A3 are by no means generous. Anyone with less than one year's service should receive the equivalent of four weeks' pay, not two, and so on through to an employee with over 14 years' service who should receive 52 weeks' pay.
(c) No mention is made of assisting displaced staff to find alternative employment, either within or outside the council, by providing them with suitable training or retraining at the authority's expense. A provision to this effect must be included.

Section B:
(a) The union can only agree to the loss of job opportunities arising from the introduction of new technology if part of the cost savings which the Council receives are applied to the *creation of new employment* as well as to the protection of existing jobs. The council must also recognize that part of the savings may be applied to the improvement of terms and conditions for existing staff.
(b) If new technology is to be extended throughout the authority, it will require careful and sensitive management. Many secretarial and clerical staff are apprehensive about the new equipment. Management and union representatives will together have to spend a good deal of time explaining to staff what the new technology means for them as individuals. A repetition of the unfortunate experience of 1978 could easily destroy the chance of further progress. Consequently, NALGO branch officials *must* be formally involved in a joint consultative structure which will supervise the introduction of new technology and iron out the day-to-day operational problems.
(c) No mention is made of those staff who, having had the benefits of the new equipment explained to them, would still prefer to work on conventional typewriters.

4. The draft agreement makes no reference to the procedure by which employees who do *not* wish to accept early retirement or voluntary severance are to be assimilated into the new, reduced establishment of the authority. Every means must be used to find suitable employment within the council for such staff and, if no suitable job is available, they must be given 'supernumerary' status at *no* loss of salary. A suggested procedure appears below.

Suggested procedure for 'assimilation'

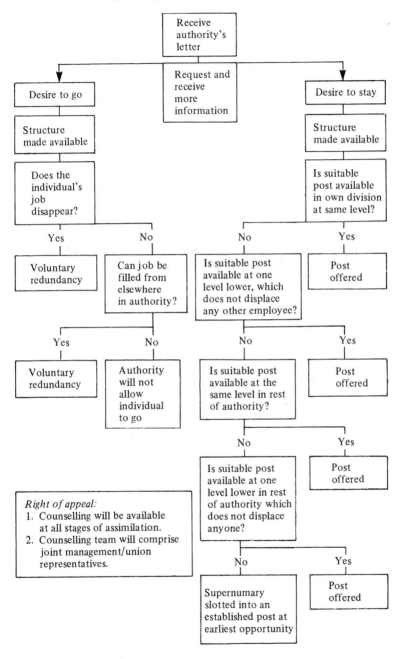

5. What is to be the role of recruitment control *after* the new establishment has been finalized and agreed? The union's position is that since the number of APT & C staff is being reduced, the revised establishment which emerges at the end of the day must be fully staffed. There can be no further justification for leaving vacancies unfilled, whether 'supernumerary' staff are available to fill such vacancies or not.

CASE 6: Burntisland Heating Co Ltd

Background

1. Burntisland Heating manufactures a wide range of domestic heating appliances. Until 1979 the company was owned and directed by members of the McCracken family who had established the firm in 1937. In 1979, however, the company was acquired by Wires Inc, a New York-based corporation with worldwide interests in domestic appliances and textiles. Since then there have been a number of sweeping changes in the senior management of BHC. Whereas before 1979 seven of the eight directors were McCrackens, by 1981 only one director (in charge of research and development) belonged to the family. The managing director, marketing director and finance director are all American. The production director was, prior to his appointment at BHC, employed by IBM and the personnel manager has been recruited from the Ford Motor Co Ltd. So far only one departmental head has been replaced, but there is a general feeling that middle management will soon be 'purged'.

The factory is situated in Fife, Scotland, a declining coalmining area with a high level of unemployment. The plant is located on the Glenrothes Industrial Estate and is one of the largest employers in the district. It has never had any difficulty recruiting labour. Some of the skilled workers have had previous experience in shipbuilding or engineering, but most of the semi-skilled and unskilled employees have been with the company all their lives. Labour turnover has averaged between 3 and 4 per cent over the past 10 years.

2. The company expanded steadily between 1950 and 1979. In 1950 it employed 100 people; by 1980 it employed 1000 hourly paid workers (40 per cent female) and 400 weekly and monthly paid staff. A new plant may be built on an adjoining site in 1983 but the board is said to be looking at alternative sites in Yorkshire and East Anglia.

Since 1966 the factory has operated on a double day shift system, ie 6.00 am to 2.00 pm and 2.00 pm to 10.00 pm. The efficiency agreement of 1980 introduced a third shift from 10.00 pm to 6.00 am, partly at least as an answer to the high levels of overtime which were being worked in the evenings.

Since 1979 production has been based on market analysis and sales forecasting. The company has no 'order book' as such and trade tends to fluctuate seasonally. This is a highly competitive field and rapid turnround and punctual delivery are essential.

Trade unions and collective bargaining

3. No trade unions were recognized until 1974, when the company experienced the first strike in its history. The strike was called by TGWU and SMWU members in support of their claims for recognition and negotiating rights. As a consequence of the strike, full recognition was conceded to these two unions in respect of production workers. The AUEW and the EEPTU subsequently organized all the craftsmen in the plant and quickly won full recognition and bargaining rights from the management. There are now 100 craftsmen in the plant.

4. Although no formal agreement was drawn up to this effect, the craft union shop stewards soon developed the practice of meeting and negotiating with management separately from the TGWU and SMWU stewards. The practice was justified by the craft stewards on the grounds that many of the skilled workers were paid on a different basis from the direct production workers (flat hourly rate as opposed to piece-work). Management expressed its dislike of this arrangement but acquiesced in order to avoid any further difficulty. Between 1974 and 1979 there was no further industrial action within the company. Over this period earnings rose by 100 per cent and the company maintained its traditional position as one of the 'best paying' employers in the area.

The efficiency agreement 1980

5. The first major initiative of the new management team in the post-merger period was to formulate an efficiency agreement. The managing director called a meeting of all employees in the factory during the lunch break one day and explained to those present (about 35 per cent of the total labour force) that a 'new approach' would be adopted in respect of the management of the company's resources. He disclosed that over the past year the company had made a loss (£150,000) for the first time in its history and that the parent company in New York expected a speedy return to profitability. He said that unless there was a substantial improvement in productivity the company would lose a great deal of business and that would mean redundancies. He asked for the cooperation of the workforce in ensuring the survival of the company and said that he would be discussing specific plans with union representatives over the next few days. Four TGWU and two SMWU shop stewards were present at this meeting. The craft stewards were attending a 'coordinating' meeting of their own to discuss routine problems.

6. Several days later the managing director called a meeting of all the shop stewards, including the craft stewards, and outlined the key features of the efficiency agreement to them:

(a) A single negotiating committee for all hourly paid employees.
(b) A high day rate system of payment.
(c) A job-evaluated wage structure.
(d) A three-shift system.
(e) A ban on all restrictive practices and the achievement of total flexibility.
(f) A clearly defined grievance procedure.
(g) A legally binding agreement of fixed duration.
(h) A statement of managerial functions.

In return, the company offered to accept a system of departmental closed shops and to operate a 'check-off' procedure for members' subscriptions. A guarantee of no compulsory redundancy was also offered.

7. The initial reaction from the shop stewards to these proposals was negative and negotiations only started when the managing director threatened to close down the entire plant and transfer its operations elsewhere. After six months of negotiation it was announced that agreement had in principle been reached on objectives (b), (c), (d), (f) and (h). The stewards intimated that they would accept a fixed term agreement which was *not* legally binding. They refused to accept objective (e) in any form. The craft stewards declared that objective (a) was totally unacceptable to them.

8. As a next step management invited a firm of consultants to examine the wage structure and devise a system of job-evaluated grades. This project was considerably delayed, however, by a breakdown in negotiations caused by the consultants' refusal to give the craft stewards an undertaking that the differential between Grades 5 and 6 would be widened. Management then instructed the consultants to press on with the exercise unilaterally. This they did and submitted their final report in April 1981. The report proposed that six job grades be established ranging from skilled work (Grade 6) to unskilled work (Grade 1). The wage rates proposed were as follows:

Grade	Wage rates (£)*
6	128.00
5	120.00
4	114.00
3	108.00
2	100.00
1	91.50

*Paid for a 40-hour week to employees aged 20 or over

9. The consultants also proposed, and management accepted, that an 'annual improvement factor' be introduced. Incentive payments of any kind were to be abolished and the old system of merit awards discontinued. The annual improvement factor would be based on the profitability and productivity of the company and management envisaged that increases in earnings should come only through the AIF. It was proposed that each AIF increase should be negotiated for the period January to December of each year. During the life of an AIF management would not discuss any increases in pay, beyond the possible regrading of individual workers under the job evaluation system. Arguments for increases based on criteria such as the cost of living or comparability would no longer be accepted by management.

10. By October 1981 the efficiency agreement had been drafted in its complete form and was submitted to all the shop stewards for negotiations. During these negotiations, which were conducted with the craft and non-craft unions separately, the managing director made it clear that in future all wage increases must be related to productivity, but he also intimated that the AIF might take account of 'movements in earnings in the local labour market' if these were having an adverse effect on recruitment. In November 1981 the TGWU and SMWU stewards agreed to a revised version of the draft originally put forward by management. The craft stewards agreed to 'go on talking' with management. Simultaneously an AIF of 10 per cent was agreed and paid to all the workforce.

11. Early in January 1982 the production director and personnel manager met the AUEW and EEPTU stewards for a general discussion on increasing flexibility between the various crafts in the maintenance section. Management proposed that:

(a) When a particular group is overloaded, the company has the right to draw men from other groups in order to assist the overload, accepting that the recognized trade group who normally do the work will still control, organize and be responsible for it.

(b) When required, small adjustments to machines can be made by any tradesman who is competent to do the job.

(c) Maintenance work on all plant and machinery may be carried out by any competent tradesman.

(d) When a 'mate' is needed but not available, a tradesman will perform the job on his own.

(e) Electricians will strip bearings from electric motors rather than pass this work on to fitters.

12. Management argued that these proposals were sanctioned by the 'rights and functions of management' section of the efficiency agreement. As such they did not necessitate any additional increase in pay.

It soon emerged, however, that the craft stewards would only agree to discuss these proposals in return for a 'substantial' wage increase for their members. After much protracted argument a compromise was reached whereby the flexibility provisions would be implemented on 1 February 1982 for a trial period of three months in return for an increase of £5.50 per week to the maintenance men involved. At the end of this trial period the savings achieved would be measured against the costs and the position reviewed to see if a larger increase was justified.

13. By the end of April management had formed the opinion that the savings achieved did not warrant any further increase. The shop stewards, on the other hand, felt that their members were working harder and had earned a further increase. They therefore claimed a further £3.50 per man per week. Management rejected the claim outright on 2 May. AUEW and EEPTU members in the maintenance section promptly replied by rejecting the principle of flexibility and announcing their withdrawal from further talks on the efficiency agreement. For the next four weeks the maintenance men worked to rule. Until then there had been a degree of informal, *ad hoc* flexibility between different crafts. Thus, for example, a fitter would often perform a minor electrical task without calling in the electrician. After 2 May, however, a rigid observance of demarcation lines was enforced. The same fitter would then call the electrician simply to turn off the power switch of his machine. In retaliation management withdrew the 'lead in' payment of £5.50.

14. Towards the end of May a mass meeting of all the craft union members was held outside working hours at which a vote of 'no confidence' in the AUEW and EEPTU stewards was passed. As a result they resigned and were replaced by more militant opponents of the efficiency agreement. On 3 June certain AUEW members objected that it was not appropriate for Grade 6 workers to undertake deburring with hand tools — a Grade 2 job — while there was no immediate work for them to do. Management maintained that this practice was sanctioned by the efficiency agreement. On 4 June three AUEW members were formally warned that they should follow management's instructions on this matter. They refused and were dismissed by the personnel manager. There was an immediate walk-out by all AUEW and EEPTU members. On 5 June management closed down the entire plant and sent the remainder of the workforce home.

15. The managing director simultaneously issued a statement to the effect that there had been an unconstitutional and unofficial withdrawal of labour and that the company would not 'negotiate under duress'. On 12 June, however, the AUEW made the strike official, followed on 15 June by the EEPTU. On 18 June the managing director wrote to the local full-time officials of the AUEW and the EEPTU requesting a

meeting. The AUEW divisional organizer replied that he would only agree to a meeting if the AUEW convenor at BHC was also present on an equal basis. Management eventually agreed and a meeting has now been arranged for 27 June. Present are:

For the company: Mr Nixon (managing director); Mr Agnew (production director); Mr Grindall (personnel manager).
For the trade unions: Mr McTavish (divisional organizer, AUEW); Mr Cameron (AUEW convenor); Mr Duff (EEPTU steward).

Efficiency agreement

Preamble

This agreement is made on 2 November 1981 between the Burntisland Heating Co (hereinafter referred to as the company) and the representatives of the Transport and General Workers' Union and the Sheet Metal Workers' Union.

The purpose of this agreement is:

1. To promote the efficient, economic and profitable operation of the company's business.
2. To promote the most effective use of the company's human resources.
3. To secure a prompt and orderly disposal of grievances arising between the company and its employees.

The company, the trade unions and all employees have a common interest in increasing productivity and efficiency. It is also a common desire that the wages structure and the general conditions of employment shall be appropriate to current circumstances.

To achieve these aims many obstacles will have to be overcome and many far-reaching changes will have to be implemented. Only by increasing our share of the market can we increase the wealth of the company, and thereby pay for the increased wages and better conditions of employment that we all desire. This additional business can only be obtained if we can make the right product, at the right time, at a competitive price. The customer has a vital interest in the efficiency of the company and considerable effort will be needed at all levels to provide our customers with a first class service.

Rights and functions of management

The company retains all the functions, rights and authority which have not been specifically abridged, delegated or modified by this agreement. Accordingly the rights and functions of management herein reserved shall include but not be limited to the rights to:

1. Hire new employees.
2. Retire employees prematurely, subject to mutual agreement.
3. Select, train, transfer, promote and demote employees.
4. Select supervisory personnel.
5. Manage the plant and direct the workforce.
6. Plan, direct, control, modify, extend, curtail or cease processes or operations.
7. Contract out any such processes or operations (without detriment to the existing workforce).

8. Discipline, suspend or discharge employees subject to the agreed disciplinary procedures set out in the factory handbook.
9. Introduce new or improved or change existing working methods and manufacturing facilities and change or discontinue jobs or job procedures, save that all such introductions, changes or discontinuances shall be subject to prior communication.
10. Establish and change work and production schedules.
11. Determine, designate, modify or discontinue occupational classifications.
12. Determine the number and types of employees required.
13. Transfer or suspend employees from duty because of lack of work or for other legitimate reasons.
14. Make such rules and regulations as the company considers advisable for the orderly and efficient conduct of its business and to require employees to observe such rules and regulations.

Disputes procedure

Stage 1
Any employee wishing to raise with the management any matter in which he is directly concerned will in the first instance discuss it with his foreman. The latter will (other than in exceptional circumstances) deal with the matter promptly. Both or either of the parties to the discussion may exercise the right to have the subject matter recorded in writing. This record should show:

(a) The facts and nature of the problem.
(b) The foreman's answer.
(c) If necessary, the anticipated period of time within which the problem is to be resolved at Stage 1.

Stage 2
If the employee is dissatisfied with the answer he may if he wishes bring the appropriate shop steward into the matter. The union branch chairman is not to be involved at this stage. Should the matter to be raised affect not one individual but a group the shop steward may approach the foreman at the outset together with a spokesman for such a group.

Stage 3
If a dispute still exists after the three parties have discussed the problem the manager (and/or supervisor) will be asked by the foreman to participate in the discussion. The union branch chairman may be requested by either party to be present to assist at any time during this stage.

Stage 4
If the issue is not settled after a reasonable length of time formal representations may be made to: (a) The union branch chairman and the personnel manager, and (b) by both sides in the dispute to the managing director.

Stage 5
The issue will, if not resolved at Stage 4, be submitted to final and binding arbitration. The arbitrator will be agreed by both parties.

Merit rating scheme
The parties agree that the new job evaluation scheme will provide a more equitable method of payment based on objectively assessed job values and levels of skill and responsibility. It is therefore agreed to discontinue the present merit rating scheme with effect from 1 October 1981, freezing all merit payments at their current levels.

Job evaluation scheme
1. It is agreed that the new job evaluation scheme will have effect from 1 January 1982. It is accepted that during the introductory period a number of anomalies could emerge as a result of regrading several jobs. It is agreed that these jobs are to be treated on an individual basis. In order to maintain an efficient scheme the company undertakes to update job values as and when necessary.
2. As an adjunct to the new structure it is agreed that in selected cases promotional opportunities will be given in the form of training for the next grade up the scale. Any employee so selected will be paid:

(a) From the commencement of training at a rate of half-way between the basic minimum rate for his job immediately prior to such commencement and the next grade up for which he is to be trained.
(b) At the full rate for the next grade up when:
(i) The training has been satisfactorily completed.
(ii) A vacancy exists in the next grade up.
(iii) Such employee has been confirmed as a full-time worker in it.
(c) At his former rate of pay if, on grounds of unsuitability or at the request of the individual or for any other valid reason, training is discontinued and the employee reverts to his former grade.

Shift rate

The company will increase the shift allowance by 10 pence an hour to 50 pence per hour effective 3 October 1981.

Flexibility

The criteria which will be used in order to determine whether a worker shall carry out a particular job will be whether:

1. He has been trained to the required standard.
2. He has the time and the opportunity.
3. He has the necessary tools and equipment.

The training department has been expanded to carry out all necessary training.

Time on the job

Time clocks will be installed at the entrance to each major department within the plant and clocking in will take place there when each employee reports for work. Clocking out will be at the same place. A period of five minutes will be added to the clocked time at the beginning and at the end of each day, making 10 minutes in all, as a contribution to washing, etc.

Activity sampling

The concept of activity sampling will be introduced. This will be done on a random basis. The purpose of activity sampling is to highlight shortcomings in the scheduling and organization of work which are retarding productivity.

Annual improvement factor

If the company's overall profitability will permit, an annual improvement factor may be negotiated with the trade union representatives in December of each year. Any increases agreed will operate from 1 January for the whole of the next calendar year. At no time in that year between 1 January and the renegotiation of the AIF will the company entertain any further claims for general wage increases. The AIF will be geared primarily to the profitability and efficiency of the company and will not be determined by the level of wage settlements elsewhere or by movements in the general price index.

Duration

This agreement will be effective until 31 October 1984. It may be terminated by either party at any time provided that six months' written notice is given.

Signed on behalf of the company: R Nixon (managing director); S Agnew (production director).

Signed on behalf of the trade unions: P L Wright (TGWU branch chairman); M Fergus (TGWU branch secretary); S Killin (Sheet Metal Workers' Union).

Points for the management case

1. The company cannot survive if its craftsmen continue to resist the principle of reasonable flexibility in their day-to-day work. It is estimated that labour productivity levels at the Glenrothes plant are 30 per cent below those of the least efficient American factory in the group. One major contributory factor is overmanning in the craft grades. The work study department estimates that the present volume of work could be done by 70 craftsmen, whereas the company employs 100. As a result the unions must accept both increased flexibility and lower manning levels if large-scale redundancy is to be avoided.

2. Management has made all reasonable efforts to persuade the craft unions to accept flexible working practices. The efficiency agreement has not been imposed on them, but since they accepted both the 10 per cent increase in the AIF and the three-month 'lead-in' payment of £5.50 they are morally obliged to continue to negotiate with management on the principle of flexibility. If they refuse, the plant will have to close since it could not be operated profitably. The efficiency agreement cannot be scrapped to suit the craftsman, even if management were prepared to do so, because it has been fully accepted by the TGWU and SMWU who are both committed to its principles.

3. During the three-month trial period, average productivity in the craft grades increased, although it is difficult to be precise about the size of the increase. Productivity throughout the factory as a whole, however, rose by 10 per cent. Since 2 May this productivity gain has largely disappeared. While the question of lead-in payments can certainly be discussed with the craft stewards, it must be made clear to them that:

(a) The TGWU and SMWU members received no lead-in payments at all, so that any concession to the craftsmen must not be large enough to provoke a counter-claim from them.

(b) Pay increases will in future be achieved only through the AIF which in turn depends on the company's profitability.

(c) No separate bargaining arrangements will be conceded in respect of craftsmen.

Points for the trade union case

1. The 'rights and functions of management' section of the efficiency agreement virtually gives management a blank cheque to change working methods unilaterally, without regard to custom and practice. This is unacceptable to the AUEW and EEPTU membership in the plant. They are not opposed in principle to greater flexibility, but expect to be consulted over the details of any proposed changes. No plan for improved efficiency, however necessary it might be, can be implemented without the active cooperation of the workforce. So far

management has given the impression that it is determined to impose flexibility on the craftsmen and this attitude will be resisted.

2. The role of 'lead-in' payments in persuading the membership to accept new working practices is crucial. Since management cannot, by its own admission, directly measure the craftsmen's productivity it must be prepared to take account of their own evaluation of the significance of productivity improvements. Since the cooperation of the craftsmen is generally seen to be vital to the success of the company, the 'lead-in' payments should be reintroduced at an enhanced level and the differential between Grades 5 and 6 should be increased. Nothing less will suffice to get the membership back to work. They are also demanding that management recognizes their status by conceding separate negotiating facilities.

3. It is unrealistic to base *all* pay movements on the AIF to the exclusion of criteria such as the cost of living and comparability. The AUEW does not accept that its members are primarily responsible for the declining profitability of the company and sees no reason why they should be penalized for managerial inefficiency. The defence of its members' earnings against inflation is one of the most important tasks of any trade union.

CASE 7: Aire Valley Yarns Ltd

Background

1. Aire Valley Yarns Ltd is a multi-plant company producing industrial and textile yarns. There are five company establishments in various locations throughout the North of England, but the Leeds factory is the largest and is adjacent to the company's administrative headquarters. For the past few years the company has been a wholly owned subsidiary of Yarns International, a large chemical and synthetic fibre corporation based in Pittsburgh, USA. The local origins of the firm in Leeds, however, go back nearly two centuries.

2. At the present time the Leeds factory employs 1635 manual workers (or 'weekly staff', as they are called within the company) and 454 monthly staff, subdivided as follows:

Weekly staff Production	As at 1 December 1981	As at 1 March 1982
Spinning	471	420
Drawtwist	590	500
Seaming	136	100
Inspection and packing	134	100
Warehouse	75	50
Staple	200	135
	1606	1305
Maintenance		
Skilled	170	170
Semi-skilled	70	70
Apprentice	15	15
	255	255
Others		
Personnel/canteen	65	65
Supplies, etc	10	10
	75	75
Total manual	1936	1635
Monthly staff	464	454
Total labour force	2400	2089

3. Roughly two-thirds of the weekly staff employees belong to a trade union, though membership is patchy in some of the production departments. The TGWU is the biggest union in the factory and organizes the production workers. The AUEW and the EEPTU represent the skilled men in the maintenance section.

Most grades of monthly staff are represented by ASTMS, which concluded a recognition agreement with the company in 1978. Relations between the two craft unions on the one hand and the TGWU on the other were once very good but have in recent years become strained due to disagreements over differentials. Traditionally, the stewards of all three unions have sat down together as the staff side of the company's joint negotiating committee but with increasing difficulty from the AUEW stewards who have expressed their preference for separate bargaining arrangements. The smaller EEPTU tends to follow the AUEW line.

4. The two craft unions have operated informal closed shop arrangements with management for many years. The TGWU has requested a formal union membership agreement on several occasions in the past, but management has consistently refused on the grounds that the overall level of union membership in the production departments is, at roughly 50 per cent, too low to justify a closed shop.

The staff status agreement

5. Until the early 1970s the company enjoyed a strong commercial position. The demand for the type of yarns made by the company was consistently high and there was relatively little domestic competition. In these circumstances the most important priority for management was to meet delivery dates. In industrial relations terms this policy was reflected in the piecemeal concessions made by management to union and workgroup demands and in the high level of earnings offered by the company. During this period a strong but largely informal shop steward organization developed inside the Leeds factory.

6. The takeover by Yarns International in 1975, however, was accompanied or followed by several changes at the Leeds factory. First, the market for yarns hardened and the company found that its profit margins were under increasing pressure. Second, employee morale began to decline and small-scale, unofficial stoppages of work began to occur. Third, there were several changes in senior management. In 1978 both the works manager and the production director at Leeds were replaced by younger men and in 1979 a new personnel manager was appointed.

7. In late 1979 a group of management consultants was called in to survey the company's industrial relations policies and practices. As a result of their findings, early in 1981 management launched its staff status agreement for manual workers. The declared aims of the SSA were:

(a) To achieve greater efficiency through a more effective use of plant, materials and people.

(b) To improve the rewards, status, security and job satisfaction of all employees.

The preamble to the SSA document stated that greater efficiency and job satisfaction would be achieved by employing each person to the fullest extent of his capabilities and by eliminating 'unnecessary and wasteful practices'.

8. The agreement distinguished between weekly staff (ie weekly paid manual workers) and monthly staff (ie monthly paid clerical, supervisory and managerial personnel), but all employees were to enjoy an agreed annual salary and stability of earnings. This would replace the existing incentive payments system which, management believed, had decayed to a point where it was out of control. Included in the terms of the SSA was a job evaluation scheme, based on the following steps:

(a) Each job in the factory was examined by a group of people, including the employee concerned, his shop steward, his foreman, the departmental manager and the work study officer. The job was examined with a view both to increasing the employee's effectiveness and to enlarging the job itself to achieve greater work satisfaction.

(b) A formal agreement was then produced by the group, embodying the 'best method' of doing the job, and a new job description drawn up.

(c) The job was then analysed by a management assessment team, with the participation of the appropriate shop steward. Jobs were assessed under four main requirements: mental, physical, personality and skill. Points were allotted under each of these headings.

(d) The total points value of each job was then used in order to place the job in the salary scale. There were 6 grades in the salary scale covering all workers from unskilled indirect employees (Grade 1) to skilled maintenance workers (Grade 6).

9. Management presented the SSA in draft form to a meeting of the Company's joint negotiating committee in March 1981 and, after several weeks of negotiating with the shop stewards on the JNC and their local union officials, the agreement was implemented in the form described above. The six salary grades were also agreed. It was further agreed that, while some employees might find themselves slightly worse off under the new salary structure than they had been under the previous incentive scheme, any anomalies would be resolved by the next annual pay review in December 1982.

By December 1981 the job evaluation exercise had been completed in the Leeds factory, except for the fitters in the maintenance section where management encountered a good deal of resistance. The stated reason for this resistance was the fear that traditional differentials, already compressed, would be eroded still further. The fitters' steward demanded a guarantee that a separate grade would be introduced for all skilled maintenance men which would reflect the *market* value of their work (ie the continuing shortage of time-served craftsmen in the local labour market). Management refused this demand on the grounds that it would upset the basis on which the entire job evaluation scheme had been built. In the course of the negotiations, however, the personnel manager gave a guarantee that there would be no compulsory redundancy in the maintenance sections. This guarantee is still 'live'.

10. On 5 December management announced that, owing to a sudden and sharp contraction in the company's order book, major redundancies would be necessary at the Leeds factory. As a result, 300 weekly staff in the production departments and 10 monthly staff were declared redundant in January and February 1982. Simultaneously, rumours began to spread on the shop floor that the entire company might be forced to close down if business did not pick up very soon.

11. Despite the redundancies, management proceeded with its attempts to induce the fitters to accept the job evaluation scheme. One problem which soon emerged was the significant imbalance which had arisen

between the number of fitters on shift-work and those on day-rota work. This imbalance required that 20 fitters be transferred from shift to day-rota work. Negotiations between the personnel manager and the AUEW shop stewards began on 1 March. Three days later the works manager reported that no more shift-work was available and notified the 20 fitters to transfer to day-rota work with effect from Monday 13 March. Management offered to maintain the agreed shift allowance for the next two months to enable further negotiations to take place. The AUEW stewards, however, consulted their union's district committee on the matter and subsequently instructed their members to report for normal shift working on 13 March.

12. The works manager held a meeting with the AUEW convenor and the other maintenance stewards on the morning of the 13 March, after which the following statement was issued:

Maintenance reorganization

A meeting of members of the AUEW and works management was held this morning to discuss the transfer of some shift-workers to day work.

The works manager referred to the official communication he had received from the shop stewards at this meeting to the effect that a branch resolution had instructed the shift-fitters to ignore the management's instruction and report at different hours from those the management had decided.

The works manager has made it quite clear that the company cannot allow the branch to run the factory. At the same time he is conscious of the difficult position the shop stewards have placed the men in by their action. For this reason he is not intending to take any action against any of the men today.

Nevertheless, to avoid any misunderstandings, he wishes to make it quite clear to the shop stewards, and will make it equally clear to the shift-fitters concerned that they are expected to work day-rota hours after today as laid down by the management.

If they refuse to do this they will be expected to stay at home without pay until such time as they decide to work the hours indicated to them. The choice is entirely with them and this is therefore not a question of suspension. If they come in at hours other than those indicated by the management they will be sent home until they are ready to make themselves available for work as instructed.

---

13. On Tuesday 14 March the fitters still reported to their normal shift and as a result three men were sent home. The immediate consequence was a walk-out by all AUEW craftsmen in the factory. On 23 March the strike was made official and over the next few days AUEW craftsmen employed in other factories within the company staged a number of short protest strikes. TGWU members at Leeds, however, continued to work normally and machines were serviced by management personnel. AUEW pickets then attempted to stop the delivery of raw materials to the factory and the despatch of finished goods. The police were called in and four pickets were arrested.

14. On Friday 17 March management decided to close the Leeds factory and send all staff home until the dispute with the AUEW was resolved. A subsequent letter to all employees signed by the managing director of the Leeds factory blamed the stoppage on the 'irresponsibility of a small minority of the workforce' and made it clear that, unless there was a full return to work by the AUEW before the end of

March, further redundancies would be necessary and the entire plant might be permanently closed.

15. Informal contacts between management and the local full-time official of the TGWU occurred over the next few days, with the result that a meeting of the JNC was convened for 24 March. The meeting did not, however, take place because of the refusal of the AUEW stewards to discuss their grievances in the presence of the TGWU. Eventually, following discussions between the AUEW divisional organizer and the district officer of the TGWU, the AUEW stewards reluctantly agreed to a JNC meeting which has now been arranged for 29 March. Present are:

> For the company: Mr Preston (managing director); Mr Garth (works manager); Mr Pullen (personnel manager)
> For the trade unions: Mr Walters (AUEW divisional organizer); Mr Brown (TGWU district officer); Mr Skelton (AUEW convenor).

Extracts from relevant agreements:
for the information of both sides

1. Staff status agreement
Instituted in 1981

Clause 8
'Where alterations to working or manning practices are necessary in order to improve efficiency, there should be joint discussion and agreement between management and union representatives. Work shall proceed in the meantime on the basis of existing practice.'

Clause 12
'Disputes arising between the parties to this agreement over the provisions of this agreement should be resolved as speedily as possible. In the event of a failure to agree being recorded, the matter shall be referred to conciliation or arbitration by an independent third party. In the meantime there shall be no stoppage or other disruption of work.'

2. Works rules agreement
Current version dating from 1974 and still, apparently, in force.

Clause 9
'Any employee may be transferred from one occupation to another, carrying either a lower or a higher rate of pay, without notice and at the discretion of management, who will have regard to custom and practice.'

Clause 11
'An employee may be put on day-work, night-work or shift-work at the discretion of management in accordance with the needs of the business. Every effort will be made by management to give reasonable notice of such changes.'

Points for the management case

1. Management's handling of the transfer of 20 fitters was as consistent with clause 8 of the SSA and clauses 9 and 11 of the WRA as the circumstances at the time permitted. A severe decline in the volume of business requires speedy and effective action in order to preserve the jobs of the majority of employees.

2. The resistance of the fitters to the job evaluation scheme is unreasonable in the circumstances. While recognizing that the maintenance men in general might be apprehensive at the prospect of losing the traditional linkage between their earnings and those of the highest paid incentive workers, it is believed that their position in Grade 6 accurately reflects the status and content of their jobs (see table below). It is accepted that the fitters transferred to day-rota work will lose their shift allowance of £20 per man per week, but this is being maintained for two months as a goodwill gesture to allow negotiations to proceed.

SSA salary grades	Weekly earnings (£)	Old PBR scheme (£)*
Grade 6	155	170 – 145
Grade 5	145	148 – 130
Grade 4	116	120 – 115
Grade 3	95	90
Grade 2	90	88
Grade 1	80	78

* Variations in weekly earnings due to overtime and shift premia
These rates are operative until 1 December 1982

3. A further point is that, following the redundancies in the production departments in December, the company is clearly overstaffed in its maintenance sections and the manning levels here will have to be reduced by natural wastage. If this proves insufficient, the guarantee of no compulsory redundancy will have to be withdrawn, although since there is a high proportion of long-service employees in maintenance (100 skilled men have between 12 and 35 years service) redundancy payments would be costly. This policy would also leave the company short of skilled labour when the next upturn in business arrives.

4. The real basis of the fitters' claim seems to be their demand for separate bargaining facilities for skilled maintenance men. This claim, however, is clearly not in the company's interest since it would obviously lead to an intensification of the rivalry between craft and non-craft unions in the plant, with predictable implications for labour relations in general and manpower costs in particular.

5. It is worth taking a calculated risk by standing firm, in the belief

that the AUEW full-time officer will put pressure on the fitters to modify their bargaining stance. If the plant was re-opened for production, it could probably be kept going at reasonable levels of output for several weeks with the help of management and semi-skilled volunteers. It seems clear that there is no support from TGWU or ASTMS members for the strike. As the prospect of a permanent closure draws nearer, so we may anticipate that there will be increasing pressure on the AUEW stewards to call off their action.

Points for the trade union case

1. Management has clearly violated the spirit of clause 8 of the SSA and, more to the point, clauses 9 and 11 of the WRA. It did not negotiate in good faith on the fitters' transfers. When the personnel manager began negotiations on 1 March he must have known that no shift work was likely to be available and the period of three days allowed for negotiations was totally inadequate.

2. Management's action was particularly provocative in so far as both the works manager and the personnel manager knew that feelings were running high among the fitters about the job evaluation scheme. It must be remembered that under this scheme fitters' average earnings, although guaranteed stability, will be significantly reduced, at least until the next annual pay review (see table below). In the fitters' view the differential between Grades 6 and 5 takes no account of the continuing shortage of craftsmen and thus undervalues their work. The very least they expect is that, as the price for their acceptance of SSA, the average pre-SSA earnings of all craftsmen should be maintained until the next annual pay review, when the job evaluation scheme would be renegotiated.

SSA salary grades	Weekly earnings (£)	Old PBR scheme (£)*
Grade 6	155	170 – 145†
Grade 5	145	148 – 130
Grade 4	116	120 – 115
Grade 3	95	90
Grade 2	90	88
Grade 1	80	78

* Variations in weekly earnings due to overtime and shift premia
† Average fitters' earnings are £165 per week
These rates are operative until 1 December 1982
The fitters believe that a fair Grade 7 salary would be £175 per week

3. A more effective, long-term solution to the problem, however, would be the designation of a special salary grade for skilled maintenance men which would have an agreed comparative relationship to Grade 6 and would maintain an appropriate differential over that grade. This would

recognise the contribution which the craftsmen have made to the success of the company in the past (bearing in mind that 100 of them have between 12 and 35 years' service) as well as ensuring that management would be in a position to recruit the best possible craftsmen when the next upswing comes. Once the principle of a separate grade has been agreed, there is no logical reason why management should continue to resist the claim of AUEW/EEPTU members for a separate negotiating committee.

4. Whilst it is admitted that there is little support for the AUEW case from the TGWU members in the Leeds factory, there are encouraging signs of solidarity from AUEW members in other plants within the group (Bradford, Dewsbury and Huddersfield) who realize that there is an issue of principle which has to be settled. Consequently, while management at Leeds might be able to maintain some kind of output (if they re-opened the factory) for a short time, sooner or later operations will come to a standstill.

3. Industrial Action and the Law

The Employment Act of 1980 and the Employment Bill of 1982 together constitute a radical departure from the legal traditions of British industrial relations. In 1906 the long argument between 'interventionists' and 'abstentionists' seemed to have been resolved in the latter's favour. The Trade Disputes Act of 1906 gave trade unionists protection against the two torts of conspiracy to injure and inducing a breach of employment contracts, provided, of course, that such torts were committed 'in contemplation or furtherance of a trade dispute' (the so-called golden formula). But since 'trade dispute' was defined in terms which covered virtually every type of industrial action, the authors of the 1906 Act doubtless anticipated that in practice trade unionists would be free to engage in collective bargaining with employers, uninhibited by legal liabilities. If employers, in the course of an industrial dispute, were legally free to lock out their workers, the workers must, in turn, be free to withdraw their labour.

Those who opposed the philosophy of 'abstentionism' argued that, far from standing aside from the conduct of industrial relations, Parliament and the courts should define what was permissible behaviour in an industrial dispute so that innocent third parties could be protected against coercion and interference. Between 1871 and 1906 the judges had sought to impose limits on the freedom to strike by developing new civil liabilities, even to the extent (in the Taff Vale judgment) of holding that trade unions were legally liable for the actions of their officials and members. The 1906 Act, however, reversed Taff Vale and made it impossible for trade unions as corporate bodies to be sued for damages arising from the actions of their officials and members 'in contemplation for furtherance of a trade dispute'. The assumptions which underpinned the abstentionist approach were, first, that judges and lawyers were ill-equipped to deal with industrial relations problems and, second, that the best guarantee of order and predictability in industry was a firm framework of voluntary, agreed procedures.

After 1906 there were only two arguments which could be used to outflank these immunities. One argument was that strike organizers were not acting within the golden formula, and the other was that, even if the golden formula did apply, wrongs had been committed for which no immunity had been given in the 1906 Act. The first of these arguments was successfully asserted in a handful of cases where the judges took the view that action against an employer had been motivated by a personal grudge or something else outside the golden formula. Once the judges had begun to develop an objective test in respect of action taken 'in contemplation or furtherance of a trade dispute', it was also possible for them to hold that the action was too remote from the dispute in question to be capable of furthering it. The second argument emerged in a series of cases during the 1960s in which it was held that the 1906 Act gave no immunity against the torts of intimidation, inducing a breach of a commercial contract and interfering with the performance of such contracts. The development of liabilities in respect of commercial contracts was a particularly significant threat to strike organizers. In many industrial disputes the only way in which strikers can bring sanctions to bear against an employer is by seeking to disrupt the supply of goods into and out of his establishments. If there is no immunity from the tort of inducing breaches of such contractual arrangements, many strike organizers are liable to be sued for damages.

These loopholes were closed up by the Trade Union and Labour Relations Act of 1974, amended in 1976. This legislation extended the immunities granted in 1906 to cover the 'new' torts of intimidation, inducing a breach of a commercial contract and interfering with the performance of such contracts. In so doing, however, TULRA simply inflamed the old controversy between interventionists and abstentionists. The development of new tort liabilities during the 1960s reflected the growth of public concern about the alleged abuse of trade union power. Immunities conferred upon relatively weak, struggling organizations in the early 1900s should, it was argued, be removed or severely limited in an era when those same organizations enjoyed enormous power both to inflict damage on the economy and disrupt vital public services. The Industrial Relations Act of 1971 sought to reduce the coercive power of trade unions by abolishing the traditional immunities. In accordance with interventionist beliefs, the Act defined what was permissible behaviour in industrial disputes ('fair and unfair industrial practices') and made trade unions legally liable for the actions of their officials and agents. The unworkability of the Act, however, proved to be only a temporary setback for the interventionists.

Public concern about the 'excessive' power of the trade unions received a sharp stimulus during the 'winter of discontent' of 1978-79. The widespread disruption which occurred during the 1978-79 pay round, particularly in the public sector, gave a new impetus to those who argued that, by extending immunities from tort liabilities, TULRA had aggravated the imbalance of power between trade unions and employers.

Particularly sharp criticism was directed towards industrial action taken against employers not involved in a primary dispute (secondary action) and against the associated form of secondary picketing. Concern has been expressed about the use of secondary picketing ever since the coalminers' strike in 1972 when the NUM inflicted severe disruption on electricity supplies by picketing power stations and coke depots in addition to the coalmines themselves. The winter of discontent saw the widespread use of secondary picketing, which, in turn, greatly increased the effectiveness of the action being taken.

The avowed intention of the 1980 Employment Act and the Employment Bill currently before Parliament is to redress the balance of power. Leaving aside the provisions in the 1980 Act which relate to individual employment rights and the closed shop, it is clear that the main purpose of the Act is to limit the scope of lawful industrial action and thereby give 'neutral' employers the right to sue strike organizers for damages. The Act does not remove immunity from *all* forms of secondary action. Instead, it limits immunity to secondary action which is taken 'in contemplation or furtherance of a trade dispute' against someone who is a supplier or customer of the employer and has direct contractual relations with him. Union organizers will not be liable for damages provided they can show that the purpose of their action is to prevent or disrupt the supply of goods and services to the employer and that the action is 'likely' to achieve that purpose. In other words, the Act permits the judges to develop their own objective test of whether secondary action is being pursued for purposes which fall within the golden formula. It further seeks to outlaw secondary picketing by protecting only such action which is confined to the workers' own place of work. Only trade union officials are allowed to picket a workplace in which they are not employed.

The current Employment Bill further restricts the golden formula by removing protection from disputes between 'workers and workers' (ie inter-union disputes), from strikes which are called as part of some national campaign rather than to further a dispute with an employer, and from strikes which are designed to force a contractor to use 'union-only' labour. More significantly, the Bill reintroduces the Taff Vale principle that trade unions are liable for any acts committed by their 'officials' (including shop stewards) which are unlawful under the terms of the 1980 Act. A scale of maximum damages which unions may have to pay is specified in clause 13 of the Bill. Furthermore, the Bill proposes to restrict a lawful trade dispute to disputes between an employer and his own employees, so that disputes between an employer and a trade union where the employer has no dispute with his own employees will be unlawful. This will, in effect, put all secondary action outside the golden formula.

The practical effects of this legislation have yet to be seen. The volume of case law will, of course, depend on the extent to which employers are prepared to enforce their new rights in the ordinary courts. If the experience of 1971-74, when the Industrial Relations Act was in force, is a reliable indicator of employers' attitudes to the law, it may be doubted that the new legislation will be invoked very often. The number of strikes has fallen very sharply since 1979 as unemployment has doubled to stand at over three million. It seems probable that in a period of severe recession, when many employees are more concerned to preserve their jobs than to take strike action in pursuit of pay claims, the impact of the new restrictions is likely to be marginal. The vast majority of employers will no doubt continue to regard a recourse to the law as a last step, to be taken when all else has failed and there is no voluntary settlement in prospect. Nevertheless, as in the past there will be a few employers who, for whatever reason, will seek to test their rights in court. The following two cases illustrate how the new legislation may, in practice, limit industrial action and also raise certain questions about its wider effects on workplace relations.

CASE 8: CCS Construction Ltd: dispute at the Duckhaven power station construction site

Background

1. The dispute arose on the site of a power station being built by CCS at Duckhaven on the coast of South Wales. A local firm, Blocket & Son Ltd, was employed by CCS as reinforcement sub-contractors. At the beginning of May 1981 it became apparent that there was a growing degree of unrest among Blocket's operatives on the site and allegations were made by the site stewards that the men were not being paid as much bonus as their hours worked entitled them to receive. Blocket's were accused of 'not keeping their books properly'. To emphasize their claim, Blocket's operatives began an unofficial work to rule on 6 May.

2. Several meetings were held between Blocket's representatives and the site stewards, with a CCS contracts manager in the chair. Blocket's accounts were audited by CCS and the allegations were declared to be without foundation. The site stewards were informed of this and were given the appropriate information in writing. The stewards replied with a demand for a guaranteed bonus of £2.50 per hour. Blocket's refused this demand and maintained that bonus payments must continue to be related to production, as was the firm's customary practice.

3. At the start of the Duckhaven contract in 1979 only a minority of Blocket's labour force were trade union members, mainly of UCATT and the TGWU. By May 1981, however, all the steel-fixers and a few joiners had enrolled in the Society of Joiners, Steel-Fixers and Pipe-

Twisters (SJSFPT) which was conducting a recruitment drive on many large construction sites throughout the UK at the time. Blocket's indicated that they would recognize and negotiate with SJSFPT representatives on the same basis as they did with UCATT and the TGWU.

The dispute

4. On 11 May three steel-fixers (all members of the SJSFPT) refused to obey legitimate instructions given to them by their foreman and were dismissed by Blocket's site manager. The rest of the steel-fixers on the site promptly went on strike and were supported by other members of the SJSFPT. The other members of the union returned to work the following day but the steel-fixers declared their intention of staying out until the dismissed men were reinstated. Management, however, in conformity with the rules of the Federation of Civil Engineering Contractors, refused to enter into negotiations while the men were on unofficial strike. A compromise was reached by putting the three men on suspension pending an investigation by a joint union/management tribunal. The men returned to work on 20 May and on that date an investigation into the dismissals was conducted by CCS management and the regional organizer of the SJSFPT. As a result it was agreed that the three steel-fixers should be reinstated.

5. The steel-fixers' site stewards accepted this decision but additionally demanded that:

(a) There should be no redundancies amongst SJSFPT members employed on the site as a result of the recent strike action.
(b) A formal closed shop should be operated for all steel-fixers, joiners and pipe-twisters on the site.
(c) An assurance should be given by Blocket's that there would be no attempt to violate the closed shop by the employment either of non-union labour or of members of other trade unions.

6. CCS and Blocket's replied jointly to these demands as follows:

(a) Decisions concerning the redundancy of any employees were exclusively the concern of CCS management, which would have regard to the needs of the business and the requirements of the law.
(b) Management would not recognize a closed shop for the SJSFPT in respect of any group of operatives. It would continue to recognize three unions (the TGWU, UCATT and the SJSFPT) as representing all the operatives. Furthermore, should a steel-fixer, joiner or pipe-twister who was not a member of any of these unions apply for a job, he would, if suitable, be engaged and no pressure would be placed on him to join any union. To do so,

management added, would be contrary to the provisions of the Employment Act 1980. This reply did not satisfy the steel-fixers and from 20 May onwards their output declined considerably, with adverse effects on the productivity of the whole site.

7. On 1 June, in response to an advertisement for steel-fixers which management had placed in the local papers, four new steel-fixers arrived on the site and requested employment. One of them was in possession of a note from the secretary of the Cardiff branch of the SJSFPT, asking that he be allowed to commence work, and the other three expressed their willingness to join any one of the three unions recognized by management. The steel-fixers' stewards refused their permission for these three men to start work and threatened a stoppage of work if they were employed. Management then telephoned Mr Morgan, SJSFPT regional organizer in Cardiff, who advised that the three men should be employed and instructed the steel-fixers' stewards to permit them to start work. The stewards, however, refused to accept this instruction. In the meantime the three men concerned decided to apply to join the SJSFPT and completed the appropriate application forms.

8. On 3 June the district secretary of the TGWU arrived on the site and interviewed all the applicants for jobs as steel-fixers, whose number had now increased to 20. A few of these already had TGWU cards; the remainder (including the three applicants for SJSFPT membership) were enrolled there and then as TGWU members. The SJSFPT stewards disputed the validity of the membership cards issued by the TGWU (these were subsequently accepted as valid by the SJSFPT organizer in Cardiff) and when the new steel-fixers started work at 8.30 am on 6 June the rest of the steel-fixers walked off the site. They were quickly followed by the other SJSFPT members, who established a picket line at the site entrance and effectively prevented all other employees from coming on to the site.

9. On 7 June Blocket's sent notices of dismissal to all SJSFPT members in their employment on the site. The picketing, however, continued and no employees or delivery vehicles could gain access to the site. The SJSFPT stewards then organized flying pickets to visit four other major construction sites in South Wales operated by other firms and sub-contractors and attempts were made to persuade SJSFPT members on these sites not to work. On three sites the flying pickets were successful and were replaced by pickets from the sites themselves. Work was, as a result, either seriously disrupted or brought to a halt. The SJSFPT organizer in Cardiff held several meetings with CCS management and the strike organizers over the next few days in an attempt to find a formula for resolving the dispute. No progress had been made, however, when on 15 June the national executive committee of the SJSFPT declared the strike official.

10. On 17 June CCS management received a letter from the general secretary of the SJSFPT, which stated that the dispute would continue until:

(a) Management agreed to reinstate all those SJSFPT members who had been dismissed.
(b) Management agreed to ballot SJSFPT joiners, steel-fixers and pipe-twisters in accordance with the Employment Act 1980 on the desirability of a closed shop for the union in respect of these groups.
(c) Management signified its willingness to negotiate a guaranteed bonus system for all operatives at the Duckhaven site.

11. CCS management categorically rejected these demands and on 21 June instituted legal proceedings against named members of the SJSFPT by applying for an interlocutory injunction.

Questions for discussion

1. What is the liability of the strike organizers under the terms of the 1980 Employment Act?
2. How would the provisions of the 1982 Bill (when it becomes law) affect this liability?
3. What is the effect of a successful court action by CCS likely to be on union/management relations at its various construction sites?

CASE 9: Grebworth Metropolitan Council

Background

1. Grebworth Metropolitan Council employs some 24,000 employees, of whom roughly 80 per cent belong to a recognized trade union. The Council also has a direct labour organization (DLO), which undertakes a wide range of building, maintenance, repair, cleansing and drainage work on behalf of the various departments of the authority. The DLO employs approximately 800 staff and, under the terms of the Local Government Act 1980, is required to achieve a return of 5 per cent by 1983. A union membership agreement has been operated by the council in respect of the DLO since early in 1980. The signatory unions are NUPE (which has over 60 per cent of the membership), the TGWU, the AUEW and EEPTU.

2. At the same time as the UMA was introduced the council also resolved that, while it would continue to invite tenders from private sector companies for a defined range of council contracts, no contract would be awarded to any firm which did not recognize a trade union

for bargaining purposes. The council soon encountered certain practical problems with this policy, however, particularly in the field of housing maintenance. The authority's housing stock of 50,000 council-owned dwellings was far too large to receive an adequate repairs and maintenance service from the DLO. Prior to 1980, the council had put something approaching 80 per cent of its repairs and maintenance contracts in housing out to competitive tender. With effect from 1 April 1980 non-union firms were automatically disbarred from submitting a tender. Since, however, over half the firms who normally tendered for this business were non-union, this caused great difficulty. As a result, the council's director of housing, Mr Brandon, persuaded the housing committee to relax its policy. From 1 August 1980 any firm could submit a tender, as long as they provided 'fair and reasonable' terms and conditions for their employees and were willing to 'open their books' for inspection by council officials if they were required to do so. The council also gave a guarantee to the DLO shop stewards that there would be no compulsory redundancy in the DLO as a result of the new policy.

The dispute

3. No difficulties were encountered with the new policy until May 1981. On 12 May the council invited tenders for a contract to construct 150 aged persons' flats on a site at Sandybanks, which was situated about three miles from the centre of Grebworth. The firm which successfully tendered for the job was Muttley Brothers Ltd, a local concern employing over 100 men, which had done work for the council on several occasions prior to 1 April 1980, when the company was disbarred because they had not recognized a trade union for bargaining purposes. Muttley Brothers also tended to use non-union sub-contractors on their various projects.

4. In 1976 the firm had been involved in a dispute with the TGWU over recognition. The TGWU succeeded in recruiting about 20 of Muttley's workforce and on this basis claimed full recognition and bargaining rights. The company, however, refused to consider any such claim and shortly afterwards, when redundancies became necessary, management made most of the union members redundant. Since then Muttley had encountered no further recognition claims and the level of union membership in May 1981 was negligible. A few attempts were made by the TGWU between 1978 and 1980 to 'black' Muttley's supplies and, although these were ineffective, the TGWU district secretary, Mr Ross, let it be known that he would 'get' the firm one day.

5. Anticipating that there might be trouble with the trade unions over the Sandybanks project, on 19 May Fred Muttley (managing director of Muttley Brothers) had informal talks with the regional officer of NUPE,

Mr Kelly, and assured him that Muttley Brothers paid wages and provided other conditions which were 'broadly in line' with those available in unionized construction firms in the district. Mr Kelly said that if this was so, there was no reason why Muttley's tender should not be considered on its merits. On 6 June the council awarded the contract to Muttley's.

6. Site works commenced on the Sandybanks project on 1 July. On 17 July it came to the attention of Mr McKinnon, a TGWU shop steward in the DLO, that Muttley Brothers were the main contractors on the project. On 18 July, pretending to be an unemployed construction worker in search of a job, he went on to the site and asked the site foreman what the going rate for labouring was. The foreman told him, but added that there were no jobs available. Mr McKinnon then compared Muttley's rate with the current rate paid by the council's DLO and found that the former was 10 per cent less than the latter. He promptly telephoned his district secretary, Mr Ross, who in turn sought a meeting with the council's chief personnel officer, Mr Lilleywhite. The details of their conversation were not disclosed, but Mr Lilleywhite promised that there would be a full investigation of Muttley's employment practices.

7. On 22 July Fred Muttley received a letter from Mr Lilleywhite stating that it had come to the attention of the council that the company was not complying with their contractual obligation to offer terms and conditions no less favourable than those available in unionized concerns. If Muttley's wished to continue with the work, he added, they would have to submit their records to an investigation by the council's audit department. Mr Muttley was angry at what he considered to be 'snooping' but said that he would accept any investigation. He then telephoned Mr Kelly of NUPE, who said that as far as he knew the action did not originate from his union but from the TGWU. Kelly later telephoned Muttley and told him that someone in the TGWU was 'out for his blood'.

8. Between 26 July and 30 July the audit department investigated Muttley's employment records. In the report to the council's director of finance the auditors indicated that there was insufficient evidence to suggest that Muttley's terms and conditions were 'significantly' less favourable than those on offer anywhere else in the local building industry. The director of finance then reported to the chief personnel officer that no breach of contract had occurred. Mr Lilleywhite so informed Muttley's, and work on the site was resumed on 4 August. On 6 August, however, a meeting of DLO shop stewards representing all four unions was held, which unanimously carried a resolution calling for the replacement of Muttley's as main contractor by the DLO. The meeting further resolved that, in the event of the council refusing to

change its policy, it should still accept the principle of consultation with DLO shop stewards on the choice of private contractors for council work. These resolutions were endorsed by Ross, representing the TGWU, but by no other full-time union officer. They were forwarded to the director of housing and the chief personnel officer, both of whom rejected them as contrary to council policy.

9. On 10 August about 25 DLO employees, led by Mr McKinnon, established pickets round the Sandybanks site and succeeded in turning back several vehicles carrying supplies for the site works. One vehicle, however, drove straight through the picket line, seriously injuring a TGWU picket. On 11 August the number of pickets increased to 55 and there were some ugly scenes, resulting in several arrests by the police. On the same day Ross wrote to the chief personnel officer declaring an official dispute with the council and demanding a return to the policy of April-August 1980, namely that non-union firms should not receive council contracts. Simultaneously, Muttley's sought an injunction against McKinnon and other named union members, restraining them from further action.

The legal evidence

10. *The Employment Act 1980:* Under S17 of this Act secondary action arises when a person:

(a) Induces another to break a contract of employment or interferes or induces another to interfere with its performance.
(b) Threatens that a contract under which he or another is employed will be broken or its performance interfered with, or that he will induce another to break a contract of employment or to interfere with its performance, if the employer under the contract of employment is not a party to the trade dispute.

If, however, the employer affected by the secondary action can show that he is in fact involved in a trade dispute and that a commercial contract between himself and the employer against whom the primary action being taken is, as a result, being broken, he is able to sue the organizers of the action for damages. Under S17 there is no immunity from liability for breach of a commercial contract unless:

(a) The secondary action is taken by employees of a supplier or customer of the employers in dispute and its principal purpose and likely effect is to prevent or disrupt supplies during the dispute going to or from the employer in dispute.
(b) The secondary action is taken by employees of an employer associated with an employer in dispute (or a supplier or customer to such an associated employer) to whom the employer in dispute has, because of the dispute, transferred

work; and the principal purpose and likely effect of the secondary action is to disrupt the supply of goods or services which, but for the dispute, would have been supplied to or by the employer in dispute.

11. *The definition of a trade dispute.* S29 (1) of TULRA defines a trade dispute as:

'A dispute between employers and workers, or between workers and workers, which is connected with one or more of the following:

(a) terms and conditions of employment, or the physical conditions in which any workers are required to work;
(b) engagement or non-engagement, or termination or suspension of employment or the duties of employment, of one or more workers;
(c) allocation of work or the duties of employment as between workers or groups of workers;
(d) matters of discipline;
(e) the membership or non-membership of a trade union on the part of a worker;
(f) facilities for officials of trade unions, and
(g) machinery for negotiation or consultation, and other procedures, relating to any of the foregoing matters, including the recognition by employers or employers'associations of the right of a trade union to represent workers in any such negotiations or consultation or in the carrying out of such procedures.'

12. Court of Appeal Decision in *McShane and Ashton* v *Express Newspapers Ltd (1979)*:

'There must be some limitation upon the words "in furtherance of a trade dispute". The correct construction of "in furtherance of a trade dispute" is narrower than "in connection with" or "in consequence of" a trade dispute. There is an objective element in whether an act is taken "in furtherance" of a trade dispute within the meaning of S13 (of the Trade Union and Labour Relations Act). It is not merely a subjective concept. For an act to be held to be in furtherance of a trade dispute, the party taking the act must establish both that he had a genuine intention to achieve the objective of a trade dispute and that the acts he did pursuant to that intention were reasonably capable of achieving the objective. "In furtherance of a trade dispute" is not synonymous with "in the belief that a trade dispute is being furthered". Thus a genuine belief that the action will further a trade dispute is not of itself sufficient to bring the act within the protection of S13.'

13. Court of Appeal Decision in *BBC* v *Hearn and Others (1977)*:

'Whilst the phrase "terms and conditions of employment" in the definition of a trade dispute in S29 (1) of TULRA is not restricted to contractual terms and conditions and includes those terms which are understood and applied by the parties in practice, or habitually, or by common consent, on the facts of the present case the dispute had not reached the stage of being a trade dispute connected with terms and conditions of employment. The dispute in contemplation was not a trade dispute. Rather, the present case was one of coercive action or the threat of coercion. To become a trade dispute, there would have had to have been a claim by the union for a clause to be inserted into contracts of employment or a condition to be understood that the union's membership would not be bound to take part in broadcasts to South Africa. If that request had been made, and not acceded to, there might be a trade dispute as to whether there should be a condition of employment . . . .'

The case for Muttley Brothers Ltd

1. In all probability the picketing of the Sandybanks site is secondary picketing and as such is unlawful under the terms of S16 of the Employment Act 1980. The pickets from the DLO can hardly claim that they are picketing their own place of work. Only McKinnon, as a trade union 'official', has any right to picket the site. The number of pickets present on both days was also well in excess of the limit prescribed in the government's code of practice on picketing.

2. The argument advanced by the TGWU that private contractors should not be employed at all, or at least only after 'consultation' with DLO shop stewards, does not fall within the orbit of a 'trade dispute' as defined by S29 of TULRA. The council has already made it clear that it will not change its existing policy on the use of private contractors. The action at Sandybanks cannot therefore be regarded as 'reasonably capable' of achieving the objective of a trade dispute. Nor, on the basis of Ross's declared intention to damage Muttley Brothers, can it be argued that he had a 'genuine intention' to achieve the objective of a trade dispute. His action was plainly motivated by a desire for some kind of revenge on Muttley's and not by a genuine concern to further a lawful trade dispute.

3. The disruption caused at the Sandybanks site has induced workers employed by both the council and by Muttley Brothers and their suppliers to break their contracts of employment. The pickets have thereby committed the tort of interfering with Muttley's business by unlawful means. S13 (3) of TULRA, which provided a statutory immunity for interference by trade union officials with commercial contracts by declaring that an act, which itself was not actionable or

was a breach of contract in contemplation or furtherance of a trade dispute, would not be regarded as unlawful for the purpose of establishing liability in tort. But this was repealed by S17 (8) of the 1980 Act, and there is no longer immunity in respect of interfering with the trade or business of a third party by unlawful means.

4. Since it is extremely unlikely that the defendants would be able to establish at a full trial that they were entitled to immunity under S13 of TULRA, an injunction should be granted.

The case for McKinnon *et al*

1. A lawful trade dispute existed between the union members and the council. The DLO stewards were legitimately concerned that, despite the council's declared policy of 'no compulsory redundancy', the decision to employ private contractors could pose a longer-term threat to job security in the DLO. At the very least it would discourage the expansion of employment opportunities within the DLO. The stewards were also legitimately concerned that Muttley Brothers and other non-union contractors were deliberately undercutting the DLO by paying lower wages and offering other less favourable conditions. These were clearly 'employment' matters and as such fell within the definition of a 'trade dispute' under S29 (c) and (g) of TULRA.

2. Furthermore, in terms of the Court of Appeal's decision in *BBC* v *Hearn*, McKinnon *et al*, by seeking to persuade the council to change its policy, were in effect also seeking to have their own contracts of employment amended so as to preclude the possibility of any DLO employee being required to work with non-union labour. As a result, the secondary action against Muttley Brothers is, in reality, primary action against the council.

3. The repeal of S13 (3) of TULRA by S17 (8) of the Employment Act 1980 does not create a new tort of interference with the business of a third party by unlawful means. The meaning of S13 is plain. S13 (1) states clearly that an act done by a person in contemplation or furtherance of a trade dispute shall *not* be actionable in tort only on the ground that it consists in threatening that a contract will be broken or its performance interfered with. The repeal of S13 (3) has in no way weakened or neutralized the effect of S13 (1).

4. Since it is likely that the defendants will be able to establish at a full trial that a trade dispute exists, the request for an injunction should be denied.

Questions for discussion

1. Are McKinnon *et al* liable for damages as alleged by Muttley Brothers?

2. Do the provisions of the Employment Act 1980 assist or hinder the resolution of this type of dispute?
3. What would be the effect on the defendants' liability of the provisions of the Employment Bill 1982?

4. Grievances and Discipline

The trends in case law arising from unfair dismissal claims are discussed and illustrated in Chapter 5. An important objective of the statutory protection against unfair dismissal, however, is to encourage employers to devise or improve *voluntary* procedures in this field. Managements should ideally be seeking to ensure that their own voluntary arrangements are so effective that none of their decisions is challenged before an industrial tribunal. The fact that many firms have never been faced with formal tribunal proceedings is partly the result of the effective working of their own procedures and partly a reflection of the strength of collective organization in their establishments. Since tribunals were given jurisdiction over unfair dismissal claims, employees in areas such as retailing, private services and construction have been disproportionately involved in tribunal proceedings. This, in turn, reflects both the preponderance of small firms and the limited penetration of collective bargaining in these sectors. By contrast, in those industries and sectors where trade unionism and collective bargaining are relatively well-established, an employee who believes himself to have been unfairly disciplined or dismissed is more likely to invoke the support of his shop steward or union official than complain to a tribunal.

Employers, employees and union representatives all share a direct interest in maintaining the authority of disciplinary rules. Management's fundamental right to discipline employees whose performance or conduct is unsatisfactory is hardly ever questioned, but the *way* in which this prerogative is exercised has become increasingly subject to social as well as legal constraints in recent years. The 'corrective' approach to discipline, as distinct from the older, 'punitive' approach, has been seen as a method of integrating the legal and the social norms of discipline. The corrective approach emphasizes the importance of:

1. Formalizing disciplinary rules and expressing them in clear, unambiguous language.
2. Ensuring that the rules and standards of behaviour are well known by those to whom they apply.
3. Following the principles of 'natural justice', which embrace the

employee's right to state his case, the right to be represented and the right of appeal.

4. Grading disciplinary penalties, so that warnings and opportunities to improve should precede dismissal in all but clear-cut cases of gross misconduct or 'irredeemable' incapability.

5. Agreeing on both equitable standards of behaviour and on the rules to be followed in the event of a breach of those standards with trade union representatives.

6. Formally involving union representatives in the operation of disciplinary procedures.

The corrective approach assumes that employees are willing to abide by standards of behaviour which employers and union representatives regard as 'fair' and 'equitable'. This assumption, however, like the corrective approach as a whole, oversimplifies the relationship between the legal and social norms of discipline.

Several cogent criticisms have been made of the corrective approach. First, it is said that it concentrates on the *procedural* aspects of discipline almost to the exclusion of the substantive norms which a procedure is supposed to enforce. In so far as this criticism is valid, it implies that substantive norms are primarily a matter for management's discretion. In other words, it is up to management to decide what, in a given set of circumstances, is 'satisfactory' performance and what is 'gross' misconduct. Second, it is argued that the corrective approach assumes that formalized rules are always superior to the informal variety. It would certainly be inappropriate for managers to regard a formal procedure as a means of avoiding both the need to consider every disciplinary case on its merits and the task of weighing evidence and exercising judgment. Excessive formality can lead to injustice. Third, it is argued that the corrective approach reflects predominantly managerial norms of fairness, and that this reflects only one dimension of industrial discipline. It is possible that in some situations the employee's trade union, or the workgroup to which he belongs, will have more disciplinary influence over him than will the employer, and the norms they enforce may not be the same as the employer's. This, in turn, means that the employer may only be able to make *his* norms effective with the assistance or through the mediation of union representatives. Finally, it is argued that the corrective approach sees discipline as an exclusively *individual* matter and ignores the fact that some disciplinary issues become negotiable. This again is a valid criticism and examples of 'bargainable' disciplinary disputes are included below.

A distinction should be drawn between the way in which management handles everyday disciplinary offences, particularly those involving some form of *misconduct*, and the less frequent cases in which the employee's problem is that of inadequate *performance*. The corrective approach rightly stresses the importance of a diagnostic as opposed to a punitive response on the part of management in cases where performance is unsatisfactory. After a proper investigation of the circumstances, it may be that the employee is not performing well because he has not been properly trained, or the targets set for him are unrealistic, or for some other reason which may entail a responsibility on the part of management.

A further problem may arise when performance standards are changed. In current circumstances, when senior management is under pressure to improve profitability and cut costs, performance standards which were once deemed adequate are no longer seen to be so. What, then, is the position of the employee who has achieved past standards but fails to achieve the more demanding targets of today? How much effort should management devote to the task of assisting him to bring his performance up to the new level? At what point is management entitled to say 'enough is enough'? If, by the same token, a customary rule or working practice which management has observed or tolerated in the past becomes too costly to maintain, how should management go about changing it? These and other issues are raised in the cases presented below.

CASE 10: Sally Brown

1. Sally Brown, who is 52 years of age, has worked for Great Northern Stores Ltd, a large retailing firm, for 35 years. She is unmarried and joined the company in 1955 as a sales assistant straight from school. She has never been regarded as an outstanding employee, but her work has always been considered satisfactory. Throughout her career with the company she has worked in its Sheffield store. Despite her long service in one location, she has few, if any, friends at work and since 1977 has spent most of her spare time looking after her bed-ridden mother.

2. In June 1979 the area manager, Mr Morrison, decided, despite opposition from the manager of the Sheffield store, that Miss Brown should be promoted to sales supervisor. She did not seem too pleased at the prospect of promotion, but felt that to refuse the new post would show ingratitude to the company.

3. Towards the end of 1979, after six months as supervisor, her colleagues began to notice a marked change in her behaviour at work. Her moods became much more volatile and unpredictable; she seemed unable to concentrate on a task for any length of time, and on more than one occasion was found weeping in the staff rest room. The staff she supervised became concerned when customers began to notice her odd behaviour and tried to ensure that she was never left alone with a customer. The staff manageress at Sheffield, Miss Crawley, spoke to

her and attempted to discover the cause of her behaviour. Miss Brown said that she was going through a difficult time with her mother and was finding it difficult to cope.

4. As a result, Miss Crawley discussed the matter with the manager, Mr Blaine, who, in turn, consulted Mr Morrison. Between them they decided that Miss Brown should see her doctor as soon as possible. In January 1980 she consulted her doctor, who immediately referred her to Dr Hargreaves, a consultant psychiatrist at the largest hospital in Sheffield. As a result of her consultation with Dr Hargreaves, she was admitted to hospital and spent two months as an in-patient. After her discharge in March, she spent a further four weeks on sick leave as an out-patient at the hospital.

5. Towards the end of April Miss Brown wrote to Miss Crawley saying that she was now entirely fit for work and would be returning to the store on Monday 2 May. Miss Crawley discussed this with Mr Blaine, who told Mr Morrison that in his view Miss Brown should not return to work until written confirmation of her fitness for work had been received from Dr Hargreaves.

6. Mr Morrison received a letter from Dr Hargreaves on 30 April, with a copy to Mr Blaine, which briefly stated that Miss Brown had suffered from a serious depressive illness from which she was now completely recovered. Dr Hargreaves further wrote: 'I am sure that, given appropriate sensitivity on the part of Miss Brown's superiors and subordinates, there will be no recurrence of her former symptoms.' Miss Brown returned to work on 9 May, as instructed by the store manager, and resumed her supervisory duties.

7. Two weeks later Miss Brown was the subject of a prolonged and heated discussion at the fortnightly meeting of the store's management team. Miss Brown's departmental manager, Mrs McArthur, said that the sales staff had begun to complain again about Miss Brown's behaviour. She made the staff nervous and anxious and special arrangements had to be made in order to ensure that she was never left alone with customers. Mrs McArthur said that the staff were getting 'fed up' with Miss Brown and one or two were threatening to write to head office if nothing was done about her in the near future.

8. Miss Crawley, however, argued that they had not given Miss Brown sufficient time in which to re-establish a normal pattern of behaviour. She further argued that dismissal was out of the question since the consultant psychiatrist had pronounced Miss Brown fit for work and, in addition, the area manager would not authorize the dismissal of such a loyal, long-serving employee. Mr Blaine, however, resolved that Miss Brown must be transferred to another store and wrote to Mr Morrison to this effect. He also told Miss Crawley that she should not discuss the matter with Miss Brown until area office had decided what

should be done.

9. Nevertheless, shortly afterwards Miss Brown heard 'on the grapevine' that the staff had made complaints about her and that the store manager wanted her out of the store. She became very distressed and went to see her union representative. He advised her to register a formal grievance, which she did in accordance with the company's individual grievance procedure. As a result, the local full-time officer of USDAW, Mr Ford, had an informal discussion with Mr Morrison, who conceded that the complaints against Miss Brown should have been put to her in writing. She should also have been given an opportunity to put her side of the case and be represented by USDAW in accordance with the agreed procedure. Mr Morrison promised Mr Ford that these procedural failures would be corrected and that Miss Brown would have a full and fair hearing before any decision about her future was taken.

10. Mr Morrison spoke to Mr Blaine and advised him to hold a full discussion of the matter at the next ordinary meeting of the store's management team and to invite both Miss Brown and her union representative to the meeting so that they could respond to anything that was said. Miss Crawley communicated this invitation to Miss Brown in writing and also had what she later described as 'informal and confidential chat' with Miss Brown. In the course of this conversation, Miss Crawley put it to Miss Brown that too many people in the Sheffield store were now 'against' her and that it would be better for all concerned if she were to request area office for a transfer to another store. Miss Brown rejected this suggestion and accused the store management of 'victimization'. The discussion ended with a declaration by Miss Brown that if necessary she would appeal to the chairman of the company if she continued to be treated unfairly.

11. The next ordinary meeting of the store's management team was held on 4 June. Miss Brown and her union representative sat outside the meeting room, waiting to be called in for the discussion. After two hours, however, the meeting ended without Miss Brown or her union representative being called in. Mr Blaine later explained that the members of the management team had already decided that Miss Brown should be transferred to another store and that no useful purpose would have been served by a potentially unpleasant personal confrontation. Miss Crawley added that Miss Brown should now take the 'good advice' she had been given about applying for a transfer.

12. When Miss Brown told Mr Ford what had happened, he was extremely angry. He immediately wrote to Mr Morrison, with a copy to the personnel director at head office, accusing him of breaking his word in failing to ensure that Miss Brown had a fair hearing. He described the way in which the company had handled the matter as 'abominable' and accused the store manager of trying to 'hound Miss Brown out of

the company'. He further argued that the prolonged acrimony and uncertainty which Miss Brown had experienced had directly affected her health and caused her a great deal of anxiety. He concluded by demanding that Miss Brown be given more time in which to re-establish her self-confidence and that Mr Blaine be replaced by a more 'sensitive' and 'sympathetic' manager.

13. Simultaneously, Mr Morrison received a memo from Mr Blaine requesting that Miss Brown be transferred as 'a matter of urgency' to another store. He argued that her continued presence in the Sheffield store was adversely affecting staff morale and efficiency and that she would cause further trouble in the future unless speedy and effective action was taken. He ended by saying: 'No manager should have to put up with a supervisor whose behaviour is so odd and unpredictable that staff and customers are, or are likely to be, alienated. In Miss Brown's case, things have now gone so far that nothing less than her permanent removal from the store is likely to remedy the situation.'

Questions for discussion

1. Comment on the way in which management has handled this problem.
2. What steps should the area manager now take?

Great Northern Stores Ltd: procedure on discipline and dismissal

General

1. The company and the trade union prefer that discipline should be voluntary and self-imposed. However, it is recognized that from time to time it will be necessary to take action against members of staff whose performance is below standard or whose behaviour is unacceptable. The purpose of this agreement is to ensure that, in the event of disciplinary action being taken, all members of staff, whether full- or part-time, shall be treated fairly and in accordance with the provisions of current legislation.

Conduct or performance unsatisfactory but not gross misconduct

2. This includes bad timekeeping and attendance, inattention to work, poor standards of work, foul or abusive language.

   (a) The employee shall be advised verbally by his or her supervisor or departmental manager that his or her conduct or performance is unsatisfactory or unacceptable. However, every assistance will be given by the company to the employee to improve his or her conduct or performance.

   (b) If the employee's conduct or performance fails to improve within a reasonable period of time, the supervisor or departmental manager concerned shall notify the store manager or staff manageress who will consider the matter and interview the employee. If in his or her judgment the offence or shortcoming is of sufficient gravity, he or she will send a letter to the employee which sets out the matter in detail and specifies a period, which shall be at least two months, in which the matter shall be rectified. This letter will specify the action which the company proposes to take in the event of a failure to improve within the time specified, and will make clear to the employee his or her right to be represented by an officer of the trade union at all subsequent stages of this procedure. In the event of an employee not being a paid up member of the trade union the officer of the trade union shall exercise his discretion on the matter of representation.

   (c) A copy of the letter shall be sent by the store manager or staff manageress concerned to the branch secretary of the trade union.

(d) At the end of the time limit, the employee must be interviewed by the store manager or staff manageress who will take one of the following courses of action:

(i) If the required improvement has taken place, the matter will be closed unless the same offence or shortcoming recurs within six months.

(ii) If some improvement has taken place but not to the standard required, the time limit shall be extended by a period from one to three months as appropriate to the particular circumstances.

(iii) If no progress has been made, the employee shall be advised of this and the matter will be immediately referred to the area manager or (in head office) functional manager, who will first consider whether the employee can fill another position satisfactorily and if so arrange for a transfer.

(iv) If a transfer is not possible the dismissal procedure will be employed.

Whichever course of action is taken, the employee and the branch secretary of the trade union shall be informed in writing.

Gross misconduct

3. An employee who is guilty of gross misconduct may be dismissed summarily, ie without the period of notice to which he or she is legally entitled. Under this agreement, gross misconduct is defined as:

(a) Dishonesty, including theft, fraud, breach of till procedures, misappropriation of funds and falsification of records.

(b) Deliberate refusal to follow the legitimate instructions of a superior.

(c) Drunkenness or drug abuse.

(d) Deliberate destruction of property belonging either to the company or to other employees.

(e) Physical violence.

(f) Deliberate disclosure of confidential information which is prejudicial to the interests of the company.

(g) Deliberate and serious neglect of duties.

4. In the event of any employee being charged with gross misconduct, the branch secretary of the trade union shall be immediately informed.

5. The employee shall be immediately suspended on full pay pending an investigation of the facts and circumstances by the area or functional manager. The suspension shall immediately be confirmed in writing by the store manager who will also advise in writing:

   (a) Details of charges.
   (b) That the employee may wish to send a statement to the area manager.
   (c) That the employee has the right to be represented by the trade union at any interview.

6. No employee shall be dismissed for gross misconduct, with or without notice, until a full investigation of the facts and circumstances has taken place. If the case is not proved the employee shall resume work with no loss of salary or status.

Dismissal

7. When the matter has been fully investigated, the penalty to be imposed shall be discussed at a meeting between the area or functional manager and the employee. An employee who is a member of the trade union is entitled to be represented by the appropriate officers of the union at this meeting.

8. Whatever decision is arrived at will be communicated in writing to the employee by the store manager within five working days. This communication will also advise the employee of his or her right to appeal against the decision, whether it involves dismissal or some lesser penalty, within 10 working days of the date of the meeting at which the decision was taken.

9. Any employee can appeal against dismissal, whether summary or otherwise, to the personnel director and any such appeal shall be heard as soon as possible. At the appeal, the employee shall have the right to state his case and to be represented by an officer of the trade union.

Great Northern Stores Ltd: procedure on grievances

General

1. If an individual employee has a grievance relating to his or her employment, he or she has a right to express it. Such grievances may arise from any term or condition of employment except a disciplinary matter, which should be dealt with under the procedure on discipline and dismissal. The company recognizes the right of trade union members to consult with and seek the assistance of the union in expressing and resolving grievances. It is the intention of the company and the trade union, however, that all individual grievances should be resolved as near as possible to their point of origin.

Stage I

2. The employee should arrange to discuss the matter with his or her store manager or staff manageress. Prior to this course of action, the staff member may wish to talk the matter over with the appropriate supervisor or departmental manager. He or she also has a right to consult the appropriate trade union representative who may, if the employee wishes, be present when the store manager or staff manageress discusses the matter with the employee.

Stage II

3. (a) If the employee is not satisfied with the result of this discussion he should ask his store manager or staff manageress to arrange a meeting with the area manager or (in head office) functional manager. This meeting should be arranged within three working days.

   (b) If the employee wishes to be represented at this meeting by the trade union, he or she is entitled to be so represented. Such representation may be made by a lay representative or by an officer of the union.

   (c) If the grievance is not resolved at this level, the employee or his union representative will notify the area or functional manager of this fact and the reasons why the grievance is still outstanding in writing and send copies to the personnel director and the branch secretary of the trade union.

   (d) The area or functional manager will furnish the personnel director with his view, in writing, of the grievance.

Stage III
4. The grievance will then be referred to the next ordinary meeting of the company's joint consultative and negotiating committee, or to a special meeting of the JCNC if the parties agree that the circumstances necessitate such a meeting, and will then be dealt with in accordance with the agreed negotiating procedure. The employee shall be present at all Stage III meetings and the decision of the JCNC shall be communicated to the employee in writing within three working days.

CASE 11: George Harney

1. George Harney has worked for Grubthorpe Metropolitan District Council since 1973. Initially he was employed as a swimming baths supervisor, but in 1976 he was promoted to the position of assistant manager at the Boreham Road Sports Centre. He was regarded as a wholly satisfactory employee until March 1981, when he was summarily dismissed for gross misconduct. The offence he was alleged to have committed was theft which, under the council's disciplinary procedure, is punishable by instant dismissal. With the support of his trade union, however, Harney exercised his right of appeal to a panel of three councillors, whose decision is final.

2. The evidence presented to the panel by Mr Wickham, the chief recreation officer (representing the management) was that a routine inspection of the accounts at the Boreham Wood Sports Centre by the council's audit division in February 1981 had revealed certain discrepancies. Specifically it was discovered that for the week ending 27 February the cash box showed a deficiency of £11.20. For the week ending 20 February, the deficiency was £9.50, and for the previous week it was £7.30. No further discrepancies were detected.

3. After examining the managerial rotas for the weeks in question and discussing the matter with the manager of the sports centre, Mr Summers, the audit officers decided that the balance of probabilities indicated the theft of money from the cash box. Every member of staff was interviewed, including Mr Harney, and all denied any knowledge of the missing money. Further investigation, however, narrowed the list of 'suspects' to two people: a temporary cashier, Mrs Smith, and Mr Harney. Both employees were interviewed again and both were warned that the police would have to be called in. Mr Harney then admitted that he had taken money from the cash box, but denied that he had stolen it. He was immediately suspended from duty on full pay, pending further investigations, in accordance with the council's disciplinary procedure.

4. His explanation was that during the three-week period in question (ie 6-27 February) the sports centre was very short of administrative staff. In a normal week, he said, he and the manager would expect to have two receptionist/cashiers and two clerical assistants in the office covering the standard daily hours when the centre was open to the public (ie 9.00 am − 9.30 pm). During February, however, there had been an unusually high level of sickness and absenteeism among the staff, with the result that on several occasions the office would have been completely unmanned if Mr Harney had not covered for absent staff. When, however, Mr Summers was on day-off or was otherwise absent from the centre Mr Harney had to act as manager. At such times he could not cover the reception office, but had to be mobile round the centre. The problem was particularly difficult in the early evening period when public usage of the centre was at its peak.

5. Mr Harney said that he had asked the area recreation officer, Mr Tudor, for temporary staff to cover the office side at peak times but that this request was refused. According to Mr Harney, Mr Tudor said that his staffing budget was already overspent and that there would be 'hell to pay' if he sanctioned any additional staff at Boreham Road. Mr Tudor told him, he said, to 'manage the best way he could'. In evidence to the appeals panel, however, Mr Wickham said he had interviewed Mr Tudor, who said that he had also advised Mr Harney to 'go higher' if he wanted to employ extra staff.

6. In the event Mr Harney decided, without consulting Mr Summers, Mr Tudor or anyone else, to bring his own wife into the office as a relief receptionist/cashier to cover the peak times. He simply told Mr Summers that he had 'got a temp', and Mr Summers accepted this without any further questioning or verification. In evidence to the panel, Mr Harney said that he kept a careful note of the hours his wife worked and paid her at the end of each week according to the appropriate hourly rate plus overtime premium. He paid her in cash from the cash box, intending, he said, to return the money from his own pocket after the end of the month when he received his normal salary payment. The audit investigation had begun, however, before he could replace any of the money he had taken.

7. Mr Harney admitted that he had taken this action knowing it to be in breach of the council's financial regulations. The proper procedure would have been for either Mr Summers or himself to have sought permission from an appropriate superior officer to employ temporary staff over and above whatever provision had been made in the budget of the sports centre. Mr Harney admitted that he knew he was breaking financial regulations in taking the action he did, but argued that he had done so only as a last ditch attempt to ensure that the sports centre remained open to the public and had, by approaching Mr Tudor, sought

to go through the 'proper channels' only to be rebuffed. He strenuously denied that he had made any attempt to defraud the council.

8. Mr Wickham had all this evidence placed at his disposal as a result of a long interview with Mr Harney on 12 March, in the presence of his NALGO representative. Mr Wickham then decided that Mr Harney would have to be dismissed from his post as assistant manager at the sports centre. In his letter of dismissal to Mr Harney dated 14 March, he said: 'This has been a very difficult decision to take, but a breach of financial regulations, no matter how well-intentioned it might be, cannot be condoned. I accept, however, that you had no intention of defrauding the council. I am therefore prepared to offer you an alternative post in the recreation division, here in the city hall, at one grade below that of your post at the Boreham Road Sports Centre.'

9. Members of the appeals panel questioned Mr Wickham about this letter. He was asked if his confidence in Mr Harney's integrity as an employee had irretrievably broken down. He replied 'yes'. He was then asked why he offered Mr Harney an alternative post, albeit one that did not involve any responsibility for handling cash. He replied, 'Because I felt that the evidence was finely balanced and I wanted to be as fair as possible to Mr Harney.' He added that there was nothing improper in Mr Harney's decision to employ his own wife at the sports centre on a temporary basis. His error was in failing to consult his superiors and then seeking to conceal the decision.

10. In evidence to the panel, Mr Harney said that it was wrong to 'cut corners', but he believed that what he had done was in the best interests of the council, bearing in mind that had he closed the centre at peak times because of lack of staff the council itself would have lost hundreds of pounds in income from admission fees. He could not, he said, accept Mr Wickham's offer of alternative employment since to do so would leave him with a stain on his reputation. He wanted nothing less than complete reinstatement and exoneration.

Questions for discussion

1. Comment on the way in which management has handled this matter.
2. What decision should the appeals panel take?

CASE 12: Jack Ellis

1. Jack Ellis has worked for Broadacres County Council since 1965. He has occupied a variety of manual jobs, but most recently has been employed as an attendant in one of the council's multi-storey car parks. As such he was not responsible for collecting any parking fees. The appropriate coins were fed into a machine by car park users who

obtained parking tickets in exchange. His record as a council employee was extremely good. He had no offences of any kind on his record, was never late and very seldom absent.

2. It is the council's policy to carry out snap audits on all their slot machine installations in car parks. The machines in the car park at which Mr Ellis was employed were the subject of a snap audit in April 1980. The audit revealed a deficit of £1.75. Mr Ellis was asked if he could suggest any reason for this deficit. He said that he had no idea how it had arisen. Shortly afterwards a technical expert examined the ticket machine and found that it had been tampered with. Mr Ellis then admitted that he had extracted £1.75 from the machine in small amounts over the preceding three weeks.

3. He was immediately summoned by the council's deputy chief executive, who was ultimately responsible for car parks, and asked if he had any explanation. He said that he had been having 'a bad time' at home and that between the beginning of February and the end of March:

(a) His wife had gone off somewhere with a man he had hitherto regarded as his best friend. He had not seen or heard from her since.
(b) His eldest daughter had told him that she was pregnant and was unsure who the father was. She had then taken an overdose of barbiturates and been taken to hospital, where she was still recovering.
(c) His youngest son had been caught by the police in charge of a motor cycle without insurance or a driver's licence and had been fined £50, which he could not pay.
(d) He himself had been off work for a few days suffering from shock as a result of being knocked down by a car. He was crossing a busy thoroughfare when the car hit him. He landed on the car bonnet and was fortunate to escape with a few superficial cuts and bruises.
(e) He had received a letter from the Broadacres CID to the effect that his eldest son was being held in custody and charged with various sexual offences.

4. The deputy chief executive burst out laughing and congratulated Mr Ellis on his 'heart-rending story'. He pointed out, however, that Mr Ellis had admitted breaking into the machine and stealing £1.75. In the circumstances, he said, the council had no alternative but to dismiss Mr Ellis since theft was gross misconduct. He was, he said, genuinely sorry to lose such a good and loyal employee, but unless the council enforced its disciplinary procedure with some rigour it would command little respect and would not deter other employees who might be tempted into acts of dishonesty.

5. Mr Ellis appealed against the decision, in accordance with the council's procedure, to a panel of councillors. He was supported by a full-time official of his union (NUPE), Mr Durham, who argued that the circumstances of the case were exceptional. Mr Durham criticized the deputy chief executive for failing to investigate whether the extenuating events quoted by Mr Ellis actually occurred or not. Had he done so, he would have discovered that they were all factual. Mr Durham also argued that, while it was not the union's policy to support appeals in cases of admitted dishonesty, he felt that the judgment of any ordinary person would have been adversely affected by the combination of events described by Mr Ellis. He recommended that Mr Ellis be reinstated.

Questions for discussion

1. Comment on the way in which management has handled this matter.
2. What decision should the appeals panel take?

CASE 13: Stanley Booth

1. Stanley Booth has worked for Aire Valley Yarns Ltd as a despatch worker at their Bradford factory since September 1974. He has been an active member of the TGWU for many years and since 1978 has been shop steward in the despatch department. In this capacity he has had several clashes with his departmental manager, Jack Wright, and has acquired a reputation for being 'awkward', 'militant' and 'unreasonable'. One factor which may well have influenced his behaviour is that since 1979 his wife has been suffering from cancer. Very few of his work-mates are aware of this, however, and he has never discussed the matter with any member of the management.

2. In recent years there have been several disciplinary incidents at this factory arising from drinking during working hours and eight employees have been dismissed for drunkenness. In each case the evidence was clear-cut and the decision to dismiss was not contested by the TGWU convenor, Fred Ackroyd. On two other occasions final warnings have been issued. Tom Broughton, the senior shop steward on the night shift, was caught drinking during working hours, but successfully claimed that he was under great personal stress at the time. The other case was that of Donald Hamilton, who admitted being an alcoholic. Notices are displayed round the factory warning employees that if they are caught drinking on the premises or are found to be under the influence of drink they 'may be instantly dismissed'.

3. Prior to the events of September 1981 which led to Booth's dismissal, he had been personally involved in two disciplinary incidents connected with drink. The day before Christmas Eve 1979 he turned up

for a routine meeting with his departmental manager smelling of drink. On the second occasion in June 1980 he similarly appeared at a departmental meeting smelling of drink and in a particularly aggressive frame of mind. On both occasions he received informal warnings from Jack Wright, but nothing was put in writing.

4. In early September 1981 the factory security officer, Bob Evans, received information to the effect that quantities of finished cloth were being systematically stolen from the company and sold 'on the side' by a group of employees. Suspicion centred on the despatch department and, after consultation with the managing director, Evans decided to hold an internal inquiry. Some six employees in the department were interviewed by Evans, including Stanley Booth, and statements were taken from several employees in other departments. As a result of these inquiries, Evans decided that the police should be called in and immediately suspended four despatch employees on full pay pending the outcome of the police investigation. The four employees were Albert Clough, Mohammed Rashad, John Walmsley and Stanley Booth. On 18 September Clough, Rashad and Walmsley were all charged with theft and conspiracy to defraud and were summarily dismissed by the company. Booth was advised that no charges would be made against him and management told him to return to work on Friday 21 September.

5. The internal inquiry conducted by Evans had also revealed, however, that Walmsley, Clough and Booth had been seen drinking on several occasions over the past year in the despatch area during their tea breaks and lunch breaks. It was alleged that they had concealed themselves behind several bales of cloth, drinking whisky and playing cards. On his return to work Booth was immediately summoned to a meeting with Jack Wright, Bob Evans and Fred Ackroyd. At this meeting it was put to Booth that he had been drinking during working hours. Booth neither admitted nor denied the allegation. He replied that he had been suspended on suspicion of theft, not for drinking, and demanded to know the source of management's information. Wright said that the information had been given in confidence and the source could not be disclosed. He added that the witnesses who had offered information had insisted that their names should not be disclosed as they were afraid of reprisals by Booth and his cronies. Booth replied that this was 'pure fantasy'. The TGWU convenor, Ackroyd, said that there was insufficient evidence to justify a conclusion one way or the other. Booth was told that his suspension would continue while further inquiries were made.

6. He was also called to another meeting on 2 October at which Wright and Evans were present. Ackroyd intended to be present, but was instead obliged to sort out a dispute elsewhere in the factory. Evans

said that further evidence had come to light which established 'beyond doubt' that Booth had been drinking during working hours. Booth angrily demanded details of dates, times and names. He said he would not comment on the allegations until he knew the names of his accusers and was given an opportunity to cross-examine them. Management refused to disclose this information. Booth then said, 'you b------ have cooked this one up because you couldn't get me for theft; you've been trying to pin something on me for years. This is victimization and I demand to see my full-time officer.' Wright replied that if he had wanted representation he should have asked for it at the outset of the meeting. He then told Booth that he would recommend his dismissal to the factory manager, John Grant. On 5 October Booth received a letter signed by Grant dismissing him summarily for 'using and possessing alcohol on company premises contrary to regulations'.

7. An appeal has now been lodged on his behalf by the local officer of the TGWU and is to be heard by management.

Questions for discussion

1. If you were in the local union officer's position, what points would you emphasize in constructing your case in favour of Booth?
2. If you were in management's position, how would you defend your decision to dismiss Booth?
3. Which argument, on balance, carries the most conviction?

CASE 14: Fred McLaughlin

1. Fred McLaughlin is 54 years old and has been a process worker with United Compost Ltd for 20 years. The company manufactures a range of chemical fertilizers and employs about 250 people. Most of the labour force is employed on the production process and works on a continuous, rotating shift system. The remainder, including some maintenance men, work on the day shift only. Although generous premia are paid for night shift and weekend working, there is great demand for day shift jobs, particularly among older employees, who find unsocial hours an increasing physical strain. By custom and practice, a seniority rule determines both promotions to higher grades and transfers from shift working to day-work. There is no formal, written agreement to this effect, but the seniority rule has been followed for as long as anyone can remember. The production manager, Charles York, has recently become concerned about the loss of some of the best process workers to day jobs through the operation of the seniority rule and has on two occasions argued with the senior TGWU steward, Alan Cox, about the rigidity of the rule. Nevertheless, in both cases York ultimately accepted that custom and practice should prevail.

2. Three joiners, two electricians and one painter are employed on day-work. York, who is under increasing pressure from the board to reduce costs, has for some time been of the opinion that there is insufficient work on day shift to justify this level of manning, but he has not so far discussed the matter with the trade union. Last Friday one of the joiners suffered a major heart attack, as a result of which the company decided to retire him prematurely on the grounds of ill-health. York knew that the painter, Geoffrey Williams, was also an experienced carpenter and decided that, since Williams was underemployed as a painter, he could without difficulty take over the vacant post of joiner. Accordingly York interviewed Williams and offered him the job. Williams was very pleased to accept the offer, particularly since the joiner's job was one grade higher than that of painter.

3. Williams assumed that York had cleared his promotion with the trade union and was therefore surprised by the reaction of Alan Cox. Cox was extremely angry and told Williams that on seniority McLaughlin should have got the joiner's job. He had been approached by McLaughlin only the previous week and had confirmed to him that he would get the next vacancy on the day shift. Cox therefore went to see York and demanded that custom and practice be followed. He further insisted that the workload of joinery and painting could not be done by three men. York replied that Williams was better qualified for the job than McLaughlin, who would need special training before he could become a joiner. He further insisted that as production manager it was his prerogative to decide manning levels and that in his view there was no need for three joiners and one painter.

4. Cox then said that his members would take further action unless management adhered to the seniority rule. York said that the rule must be interpreted with a degree of flexibility and common sense, or it would have to be abandoned. The discussion was then adjourned. Yesterday, at a special meeting of the union branch, a resolution was unanimously approved calling for a general withdrawal of labour with effect from 2.00 pm today unless management agreed to let the vacancy be filled by the senior shift worker, McLaughlin. It is now 1.00 pm and a meeting between Cox, Rushton (personnel officer), York and McLaughlin has been convened to attempt to resolve the problem.

Questions for discussion

1. Comment on the way in which management has handled the problem.
2. If you were in management's position, what strategy would you adopt for today's meeting?

CASE 15: Aire Valley Yarns Ltd: dismissal of Jim Gill

Background

1. Jim Gill joined Aire Valley Yarns, Leeds, in 1975 and for the next five years worked as a day shift chargehand. In November 1979 he was promoted to carding/spinning foreman on the night shift. At the time of this promotion he was 36 years of age. The production manager, Mr Thomson, who had engaged him as chargehand, believed that he had performed this job competently and would be capable of doing a supervisor's job. Gill did not, however, have a formal appraisal prior to his promotion as the company had not introduced an appraisal system at that time. Gill expressed reservations about his suitability for promotion, but he was informed by Thomson that any gaps in his knowledge or experience would be filled by training and development courses.

2. An appraisal system was implemented as from 1 January 1980, and in April Gill was appraised. The results were not satisfactory and it was noted that in many respects his performance was below the standard required. Between April and September he received numerous verbal warnings. Then, in September, he received the following final warning from Mr Thomson:

Aire Valley Yarns Ltd
Leeds
11 September 1980

Dear Mr Gill,
You have now held the position of night shift foreman for 10 months. In April 1980 a performance appraisal was carried out and you were rated a '4a' performer (which is less than the required standard, but not unreasonable for six months in a new job).

It is my duty to inform you that your job performance since April has not improved and in many respects has deteriorated, and consequently you are now issued with a formal warning. In addition, it must be made clear that unless a very positive improvement is made within the next two months, there will be no alternative but to terminate your employment with this firm.

You may be assured that every opportunity and assistance will be offered to you in the hope that your job performance will preclude the necessity of discharging you from our employment, and, in order that you may put greater effort into the areas with which we are dissatisfied, they are stated below:

(a) Allowing operatives longer than standard breaks.

(b) Stopping shift up to 20 minutes earlier than standard.

(c) Recording lower than actual machine speeds (up to four ypm) which falsely inflates wage levels as well as endangering certain machine motors.

(d) Low output caused by poor deployment and control of operators. Over the last two months the output per man hour has had an average efficiency of only 79 per cent, compared with an average performance of 109 per cent, and consequently the incentive cost has been higher than other shifts — 0.688 pence per lb produced.

(e) Industrial relations in recent months on the night shift have been appalling compared with the rest of the factory, and we must assume that you bear some responsibility for this situation. It is clear from the data explained above that you have tended to ignore or even condone malpractices, and this approach has led to a lack of respect for you which has manifested itself in abnormal industrial misconduct.

(f) Waste control is obviously very loosely managed, and sometimes two-thirds of a day's waste is created during the night shift.

(g) Concerning your personal situation, you once attended a

meeting half an hour late and appeared to be intoxicated. On three occasions you have failed to arrive at work without informing anyone in advance and later admitted that this was the result of alcoholic intoxication.

Yours sincerely,

H Thomson
Production manager

3. Following this final warning, Gill (who had not hitherto been a member of any trade union) attempted to join ASTMS, but his application was rejected. No reason was given by the local branch for this decision.

4. In December 1980 Gill was appraised once again by Mr Thomson. His overall rating was given as '5' (unsatisfactory) and the following comments were made on his appraisal form: 'The production performance of Jim's shift is poor and has been so throughout the year. Jim received a final warning for his performance in September 1980 and since then there has been a slight improvement, but he has not yet shown an ability to motivate his shift and control it. There is definite evidence to suggest that agreed quality control procedures have at times been ignored. Labour relations are very poor. There have been several industrial relations problems on this shift, resulting in stoppages. These problems have been badly handled by Jim. Jim's attendance record leaves much to be desired. His general attitude at meetings is totally unacceptable.'

Mr Thomson decided that Gill's development potential was 'not predictable'. It was also stated, however, that no development courses or activities had been planned for him after his April 1980 appraisal. This lack of provision was explained by the shortage of staff on the night shift and by the company's decision to curtail the use of external courses for financial reasons. Mr Thomson added, however, that over the next year he planned to give Gill some on-the-job training 'with maximum supervision'. The production director added a comment in writing to the effect that if Gill did not reach the required standard by 21 February 'he *must* be dismissed'. Mr Thomson interviewed Gill on 23 January 1981 and discussed the contents of his appraisal with him.

5. About this time Gill applied to join the TGWU. Management heard of this application 'on the grapevine' and realized that a problem could arise. When ASTMS negotiated a recognition and procedure agreement with Aire Valley Yarns in 1978 it was clearly laid down that this union

had bargaining rights for all staff up to senior management level. This in no way allowed for a staff employee to be formally represented as a member of ASTMS by an official of any other union. It was conceded by management, however, that Gill could be represented by the TGWU in any disciplinary proceedings not as a TGWU member, but as an individual employee with a legal right to be represented by a shop steward, a union official, or simply a 'next friend'. Relations in the Leeds plant between ASTMS and the TGWU had always been strained. Officials from these two unions habitually refused to sit down with each other at the same negotiating table. The origin of this bad feeling lay in the failure of the TGWU/ACTSS to obtain bargaining rights for Aire Valley Yarns staff in 1975. Management was well aware of this problem. Nevertheless, by the beginning of February 1981 management had failed to inform ASTMS branch officials of the likelihood that the TGWU would represent Gill in disciplinary proceedings.

The disciplinary incident

6. For some three months prior to February 1981 management had been aware that some of the disciplinary problems on the night shift had been the result of drunkenness. Early in 1981 the production manager, with the agreement of the TGWU branch secretary, posted a notice warning employees that anyone reporting for work in an unfit state because of drink or found drinking alcohol on the premises would be dismissed.

7. On the morning of Saturday 7 February Mr Thomson was informed by telephone that two night shift employees, messrs Ross and Cromarty, were asking to see him. Thomson arrived at the factory at 11.30am and had a meeting with Ross and Cromarty, accompanied by two shop stewards on the night shift (Sweeney and Barker), at which an alleged walk-out by four night shift workers the previous night was discussed. The four workers concerned were Ross, Cromarty, Argyle and Hamilton. Mr Thomson concluded the meeting by saying that more investigations would have to take place. After this meeting, however, Thomson heard from the night shift chargehand, Mr Blood, that the shift foreman (Gill) had agreed with the plant engineer (Mr Smith) that Ross and another operative named Cameron were physically incapable of work the previous night and should be sent home.

8. Mr Thomson interviewed Gill the following Monday morning and asked him why Ross and Cameron had not been sent home. Gill admitted that he had agreed with Smith that they should have been suspended and sent home. He had not taken disciplinary action, however, because of threats of physical violence that had been made against him by Ross, Argyle, Hamilton, Cromarty and Cameron. Thomson decided that in view of Gill's disciplinary record he would have to be

suspended from duty pending further inquiries.

9. Management made further inquiries on the same day and then called in the TGWU shop stewards to inform them of their findings, which were:

(a) Messrs Ross and Cameron must have come to work in an unfit state.

(b) No evidence of incapability because of drink was found in respect of Cromarty, Argyle or Hamilton, but they still stopped work that night and by doing so rendered themselves liable to suspension.

10. With the agreement of the TGWU stewards telegrams were sent to Ross, Argyle, Cameron, Cromarty and Hamilton telling them not to report for work on Tuesday night shift (10-11 February) but to report to Thomson's office on the following day. When they did so they were interviewed individually by Thomson and the personnel officer in the presence of a TGWU steward. In the course of this meeting:

(a) Hamilton and Argyle both admitted to having had a drink before starting work on the evening of Friday 6 February, but denied being incapable. They both admitted walking off the job that night. They were both suspended for one night without pay and given a final warning.

(b) Cromarty denied having had a drink, but admitted to having left work with the others. He was also suspended for one night and given a final warning.

(c) Ross admitted to having had 'a few drinks' that night but denied being incapable. He admitted, however, having left work that night. He and Cameron were suspended on full pay pending further investigations.

11. After these disciplinary decisions had been taken Thomson telephoned the personnel manager, Mr Pullen, explaining the latest developments and informing him that Mr Brown, the district officer of the TGWU, had asked to meet the production manager, the personnel manager and the production director to discuss the Gill case (Gill was still under suspension). This telephone conversation was, however, overheard by the branch secretary of ASTMS, who happened to be in an adjoining room. Immediately after the conversation had ended the ASTMS secretary informed Thomson that he had overheard the conversation and would have to report it to his branch chairman. The branch chairman subsequently told Pullen that if the TGWU was allowed to represent Gill it would be a breach of the recognition agreement between ASTMS and the company. If this happened, the branch chairman said, he would have no option but to refer the matter to national officer level.

12. On Thursday 12 February Mr Brown of the TGWU met Mr Lockerby (production director) to discuss the Gill case. It emerged from this meeting that management was thinking in terms of demoting Gill to chargehand status. Brown opposed this action on the grounds that Gill had been intimidated by some of the operatives. No decision was taken at this meeting regarding Gill's future with the company.

13. On the morning of Friday 13 February Thomson received copies of statements made by two witnesses to the incidents which allegedly occurred on the night of 6-7 February, namely Messrs Blood and Smith. These statements are reproduced in Appendices I and II. A statement by Messrs Sweeney and Barker is given in Appendix III and relates to the evidence concerning alleged drinking by Gill on the night of 6-7 February.

14. In the afternoon of Friday 13 February Thomson interviewed Cameron and Ross. Cameron was interviewed first in the presence of Messrs Sweeney and Barker. He was informed that management now had sufficient proof (in the form of written statements) to the effect that he was incapable of work on the night of Friday 6 February. He was asked if he had anything to say, but said nothing. He was then informed that because of the evidence the company had no alternative but to dismiss him. He was informed of the company's appeals procedure and was given payment in lieu of notice. Ross was then interviewed along the same lines and was also dismissed with pay in lieu of notice.

15. Thomson saw Gill the following Monday. No one else was present at the interview. Thomson states that he opened the interview by giving Gill copies of the statements by Smith and Blood. Gill, however, states that Thomson did not show him these statements, but merely referred verbally to Blood's allegation that he had been drinking and said that the company now had 'conclusive evidence' that he was drunk during the early hours of the morning of 7 February. Gill, however, denied the allegation that he had been drinking. When confronted with empty beer cans, an empty whisky bottle and fragments of broken glass, Gill remarked that such 'evidence' proved nothing. He reiterated that he had given the men pass-outs under duress. He added that he had asked the plant engineer, Smith, to stay in the department 'just in case things got rough', but that Smith had insisted on going home, saying that it was not his problem. Thomson said that, in view of Gill's past record and the fact that he had already had a final warning, the company had 'no alternative' but to dismiss him. The decision was confirmed in a letter dated 27 February:

Aire Valley Yarns Ltd
Leeds
27 February 1981

Dear Mr Gill,

Further to your interview on 16 February with Mr H Thomson, and in accordance with the disciplinary procedure, this letter is to confirm your dismissal from our employment for reasons of gross misconduct and failure to meet the standard required by your position as night shift supervisor.

Detailed reasons for dismissal as related to you by Mr Thomson are as follows:

(a) That you, by your own admission, drank spirits during your shift on Friday 6 February 1981.

(b) Your failure to suspend five other employees who were considered incapable through consuming alcohol before or during the shift; this was after refusing assistance from another manager and emphasizing to him that you would send the individuals home yourself. You later admitted that you realized you should have sent the particular employees home.

(c) Your previous record of written and verbal warnings and your recent unsatisfactory performance appraisal.

Your P45 and all monies due to you, which include a month's salary in lieu of notice and your holiday entitlement, will be forwarded as soon as possible.

R Pullen
Personnel manager

16. Both Ross and Cameron appealed against Thomson's decision and their appeals were heard by Messrs Lockerby and Pullen on 8 March. Both appeals were rejected. The following week there was a four-hour stoppage of work on the night shift in support of Ross and Cameron. On 12 March Mr Brown wrote to Mr Lockerby intimating that the trade union was very dissatisfied about the way in which the dismissals of Ross, Cameron and Gill had been handled. He threatened there would be an official withdrawal of labour on the night shift at Leeds until management agreed to discuss the matter. A meeting has been called for 22 March. Present are:

For the company: Mr Lockerby (production director); Mr Thomson (production manager); Mr Pullen (personnel manager)

For the trade union: Mr Brown (district officer); Mr Thorne (convenor, Leeds factory).

Messrs Gill, Ross, Cameron, Smith and Blood are available for consultation if required.

Appendix I

Statement made by Fred Smith on incidents which occurred in the Leeds factory on Friday 6 February 1981:

'On Friday 6 February at approximately 10.30 am I came into work to investigate complaints made by the operators on No 1 line in the factory. On reaching the third floor, I went to No 1 card where Joe Blood was working. While speaking to Joe Blood about the machine problems reported, I saw Andy Ross with his coat on and he approached me stating that he wasn't going to run the card. When I smelt his breath, I told him he wasn't fit to run the card but that he couldn't just walk out of the factory.

In my opinion Ross was not fit to work in the factory at all, as he was walking unsteadily and smelt very strongly of drink, in addition to which his face was very florid. I then made my way to find Jim Gill, the foreman I knew to be on duty, and just at the point when I was leaving the third floor, I met Gill coming in. I told Gill that in my opinion Ross was not fit to work as a result of intoxication.

At the same time as mentioning this to Gill, I offered to deal with the matter myself, but he intimated that he, as the foreman on duty, was entitled to deal with the matter. After this statement I offered to wait in the gatehouse in case there was any trouble, but again Gill refused this assistance. Finally I told him that I would remain at home on call beside the telephone in the event of any trouble occurring as a result of this. Before leaving the factory I was given a complete assurance by Gill that he intended to send all the men home. I warned him that not all of the men were under the influence of drink, and that he should be careful and deal mainly with persons thought to be incapable of work through drink.

At 1.00 am I telephoned from my home to the factory to make inquiries about the situation, but was unable to reach anybody. I found out later that the gateman was on his rounds at the time of my call.

Allegations have been made by Ross that I instructed him to clean up waste rather than run a machine. This I categorically deny. I told Gill that under no circumstances should he allow Ross near the machine, and the most that he should be allowed to do until the matter was discussed between me and Gill was cleaning up waste.'

Fred Smith

13.2.1981

Appendix II

Statement made by J Blood concerning incidents which took place on Friday 6 February 1981:

'My first knowledge of this matter was at 10.00 pm when I went to get the men to start work. Andrew Ross was obviously drunk. I could tell this by the way he talked, and the way that he staggered about the shop. At 10.05 I went to get Jim Gill to inform him about Ross. When I returned at approximately 10.10, Ross had actually started work on the machine. He complained that he couldn't do the work, that he wasn't capable of doing the work and suggested that he should go home. I said that was the best idea for him — to put his jacket on and just go down the road.

At approximately 10.20 pm Cameron came on the scene, sent up to me by Jim Gill. On seeing Cameron it was obvious that he was drunk, even more so than Ross. He was staggering and his speech was very slurred. I would state clearly that he was 'pie-eyed'. I then went down to the first floor and asked Gill the reason why Cameron had been sent up. Had Gill, in fact, sent him up from the first floor to get him out of the way? I informed him that under no circumstances was I allowing Cameron to continue working as I already had enough trouble with Ross. On returning to the third floor, I found that Ross already had his jacket on ready to go home, but at that time Fred Smith arrived and he commenced a discussion with Ross. After this discussion Ross decided to commence work on the carding machine. Approximately 10 minutes after being on this machine, which previously had been running perfectly satisfactorily, Ross was in considerable trouble.

Thereafter some work was done by the operatives, although on one occasion Cameron and Ross were on the verge of fighting with each other. The spinning frames by this time were running badly with most ends going up the pneumafil pipes.

At approximately 12.30 am Ross disappeared, and I later found out that he had attempted to leave the premises, but the gateman had asked him for a pass-out, which Ross did not have.

On further investigation, I found him in Gill's office where pass-outs were being written for Ross, Argyle, Hamilton and Cromarty. Although the pass-outs stated that they left the premises at 12.45 am, they did not in fact leave the factory until approximately 2.30 am. During most of this period they were to my knowledge arguing with Gill in the rest room.

It is worth noting that at approximately 3.00 am that morning

Gill offered me a drink from a bottle of vodka. From memory it was called Rasputin vodka and I specifically remember him telling me that it cost £4.99 pence a bottle. In the course of the night he had been drinking and he told me that he had consumed a bottle of this vodka during that shift. He told me this at 6.00 am, just before we left the factory. Gill also told me that he had disposed of the empty bottles through the toilet window and these bottles should be lying in the canal adjacent to the factory. I noticed that his speech was rather indistinct and that his eyes and nose were running.

I now regret not having given Mr Thomson the full information I have just stated concerning Jim Gill last Saturday morning when the issue was first raised.'

J Blood

Chargehand

13.2.1981

Appendix III

Statement made by J Sweeney (shop steward) and S Barker (shop steward):

'We searched the area under the toilet window and the surface of the canal on the morning of Friday 13 February. An empty quarter bottle of whisky and several empty beer cans were lying underneath the window. There were fragments of glass on the toilet window ledge. Several bottles of various shapes and sizes were seen to be lying on the surface of the canal.'

J Sweeney

S Barker

The quarter bottle of whisky and five empty beer cans, together with several pieces of broken glass, were produced in evidence in front of Mr Thomson, Mr Smith and Mr Blood on Friday 13 February.

Points for the management case

1. It is admitted that while the training and development promised for Gill were not provided, this was beyond the control of the production manager. The cutbacks in training also affected several other employees in comparable positions to Gill's, and he was neither victimized nor unfairly treated. The plain fact is that by February it was clear to management that Gill was unsuitable for the job of foreman. While management clearly shares part of the responsibility in so far as it offered him promotion in the first place, such mistakes cannot be tolerated indefinitely and an inadequate performer must be either demoted or dismissed.

2. The way in which Gill handled the incident of 6 February clearly illustrates his incapability as a foreman. Thomson's letter to Gill of 11 September 1980 refers to his tendency to condone malpractices and to the lack of respect for him on the part of other employees. Even if there was intimidation, which is by no means certain, Gill's own weakness as a foreman must be largely to blame.

3. If Gill was intimidated, why did he not summon the gateman for assistance? Why did he not telephone Smith, who was on call? Why did he not ask assistance from Blood, who was on the premises at the time? Why did he not send both Ross and Cameron home at the beginning of the shift, as Smith advised him to do? All the evidence seems to indicate that Gill was completely overwhelmed by the situation in which he found himself, but which a competent foreman would have handled with little difficulty.

4. There is no apparent reason why Blood, the chargehand, should have fabricated evidence of drunkenness or drinking on Gill's part. Thomson's letter of 11 September refers to Gill's drinking, while intoxication on the night of 6 February might help to account for his inaction when the disciplinary problem with Ross *et al* arose. The fact that the empty vodka bottle has not been found does not in itself invalidate Blood's evidence. The statement by Sweeney and Barker suggests that the missing bottle may well have been one of those lying in the canal.

Points for the trade union case

1. Management has admitted that Gill's suitability for promotion to the job of spinning foreman was not subject to any systematic investigation or appraisal. As a result, management must bear most of the responsibility for Gill's subsequent performance, especially since the training and development which Gill had been promised never materialized.

2. Without adequate training for his new responsibilities, Gill was

thrown in at the deep end. Even the on-the-job training 'with maximum supervision' never materialized. Bearing in mind the production director's comment on Gill's December 1980 appraisal, it could be said that by the beginning of February 1981 management had already decided to dismiss him and that the events of February gave them a convenient excuse to do so.

3. Management was aware that there had been a problem of indiscipline and drunkenness for three months prior to 6 February. Yet no steps had been taken to resolve this problem and it was left in the hands of a new and untrained foreman. It can only be concluded that the production manager knew that sooner or later there would be a major disciplinary incident on the night shift and had decided that Gill would be the scapegoat.

4. A number of unexplained problems arise from management's version of the events of 6 February. First, the only evidence that Gill drank spirits comes from the chargehand, Blood, who, curiously, did not submit a written statement of evidence until one week after the alleged incidents occurred. Did this gap allow management to 'refresh' Blood's memory? Blood also alleged that Gill had been drinking vodka, yet no empty vodka bottle was found either on or outside the factory premises. Second, Gill says he requested help from Smith but Smith refused. Smith, on the contrary, claims that he offered to assist but Gill declined. The real truth will probably never be known, but given that drunkenness was a common problem on the night shift it seems strange that Smith should suddenly be anxious to take firm disciplinary action. If he was so concerned about the situation as he claims, why did he not return to the factory after his abortive telephone call at 1.00 am?

5. While a more experienced foreman would obviously have handled the situation better than Gill, there is no proof that Gill did not do his best in the circumstances. There is no proof that he was drunk, no proof that he did not request assistance from Smith, and no proof that he was not intimidated into signing the pass-outs. He should be reinstated and should then receive some sympathetic counselling about his career development with the company.

CASE 16: Aire Valley Yarns Ltd: dismissal of Harold McIntyre

1. Mr Harold McIntyre was employed at the Dewsbury factory of Aire Valley Yarns Ltd from January 1972 until his dismissal on 12 November 1980. He was employed throughout this period as a fork-lift truck operator in the warehouse and warehouse yard. His job was to move pieces of woven material by means of the fork-lift truck and under the instructions of his supervisor. He is 42 years of age and has

been a member of the TGWU since he joined the company.

2. At about 11.45 am on the morning of Friday 31 December 1979, while the factory was operating (but McIntyre was not due to work), he and two other men walked into the factory in an obviously inebriated condition. They entered the ladies' cloakroom in the packing department and caused a considerable commotion. The factory security officers were summoned and the three men were forcibly ejected from the premises. Of the three men involved McIntyre was the only one employed by the company and on 3 January 1980 he received a written notice of dismissal from the factory manager.

3. Following strong representations by the TGWU convenor at the Dewsbury factory to the effect that the offence occurred on New Year's Eve when some employees tend to drink too much, and, because of McIntyre's good record to date, the company commuted the dismissal to a one-week suspension without pay. This notice was accompanied by the following written warning:

  (a) You will never again report for work under the influence of drink.
  (b) Any future breach by you of any works rule will result in your immediate dismissal.

4. No further difficulties arose until the summer months of 1980. On several Saturday mornings when he was supposed to be working McIntyre failed to turn up. On two other occasions his foreman, Mr Cooper, detected the smell of alcohol on his breath. For each of these offences McIntyre was given verbal warnings by Mr Cooper. No more disciplinary trouble involving McIntyre occurred until the present dispute which arose on Friday 12 November 1980. At 3.00 pm in the afternoon Mr Cooper observed the fork-lift truck being driven by McIntyre in reverse up the ramp connecting the warehouse loading bay platform to the warehouse yard. Having reached the platform McIntyre continued to drive the fork-lift in reverse, thereby knocking over five stacks of pieces which were awaiting loading on to a company vehicle. He continued to drive in reverse for several yards after the stacks had been strewn all over the loading bay platform.

5. When Mr Cooper arrived on the scene McIntyre was standing by the fork-lift with his hands in his pockets, apparently contemplating the damage done by the fork-lift truck. Mr Cooper was heard to say, 'You silly b - - - - -, what the hell do you think you're doing? Are you drunk again? Clear that mess up.' McIntyre then told Cooper to 'get stuffed'. Cooper thereupon repeated his instruction to McIntyre to assist in restacking the pieces by hand, otherwise he would take disciplinary action. McIntyre replied, 'I'm not paid to pick up pieces with my hands. Get someone else to do it or better still do it your b - - - - - -

self.' Cooper, highly incensed at this reply, thereupon told McIntyre to collect his pay and dismissed him. Cooper then instructed two general labourers to restack the pieces. While they were engaged in this operation Cooper informed the departmental manager, Mr Scott, and the assistant factory manager, Mr Beattie, of the details of the incident. The factory manager, Mr Lock, being away on a management development course at the time, Mr Beattie sent McIntyre a dismissal note, signed by both himself and Mr Scott stating: 'You are dismissed as of 3.10 pm for misuse of company equipment while under the influence of alcohol.'

6. When Mr Cooper returned to the warehouse at about 3.45 pm he found that only a few of the pieces had been restacked and that the two labourers were sitting on the edge of the loading bay doing nothing. Before Cooper could question them as to their failure to complete the task of restacking, the TGWU convenor at Dewsbury, Mr Fraser, approached him to ask why McIntyre had been dismissed. Cooper refused to discuss the matter and ordered the two labourers to continue their work or 'collect their cards'. Fraser replied that no more work would be done in the warehouse until the reason for McIntyre's dismissal was explained. He also questioned Cooper's right to sack anyone without reference to higher authority. Cooper replied that he could dismiss any employee for gross misconduct and added that unless Fraser and the two labourers immediately returned to work he would dismiss them as well. Thereupon Fraser led a mass walk-out from the warehouse and no work has been done there since.

7. Five days later the personnel manager of Aire Valley Yarns received a formal note from the district officer of the TGWU demanding that McIntyre be reinstated without loss of pay. The note stated that a refusal by the company to reinstate would have 'unfortunate repercussions' on industrial relations at Dewsbury. As a result of this note management has convened a meeting at the Dewsbury plant for 22 November. Present are:

For the company: Mr Pullen (personnel manager); Mr Lock (factory manager); Mr Beattie (assistant factory manager)
For the trade union: Mr Brown (TGWU district officer); Mr Fraser (TGWU convenor, Dewsbury).

Messrs Cooper and McIntyre are available for consultation if required.

Aire Valley Yarns Ltd: disciplinary procedure

General
1. The parties agree on the need to establish a procedure to ensure fair treatment to employees who become liable to disciplinary action because of failure to meet standards in regard to conduct, attendance, timekeeping and job performance.
2. Penalties for breaches of discipline will be graduated according to the seriousness of the offence and an employee will not, except in cases of gross misconduct, be dismissed for a first offence.

Disciplinary procedure: gross misconduct
3. In a case of gross misconduct, the supervisor will refer the matter to the factory manager, who has the authority to dismiss if he considers the case has been proved. If, however, the factory manager is not immediately available, the supervisor has the right to suspend the employee, on average earnings, pending a decision. He will confirm the suspension in writing to the employee. A decision will be made within 24 hours and communicated in writing to the employee concerned.
4. Gross misconduct may include:

   (a) Physical violence to another person.
   (b) Theft.
   (c) Fraud (including clocking offences).
   (d) Drunkenness or using, possessing or introducing intoxicating liquor.
   (e) Immoral behaviour.
   (f) Deliberate physical damage to the company's goods, plant, equipment and buildings.
   (g) Deliberate damage to the possessions of other employees whilst on company business.
   (h) Refusal to obey a reasonable instruction from a superior.

Disciplinary procedure: misdemeanours

Informal warning
5. The normal action in the first instance of a failure to meet the normal standards of work and conduct is an informal warning from the supervisor. Consideration should be given of whether a breach of discipline is the result of a misunder-

standing, carelessness or wilfulness.

Formal warning
6. A repetition of a similar failure to meet the standards will justify a formal warning from the departmental manager, who shall record a brief account of the incident and action to which the employee will be liable for any subsequent failure. This warning and subsequent failures must be made in writing to the individual and a copy placed on his personal dossier. The warning will remain in force for six months or such longer period as specified in an individual case, but at the end of the period the warning will be cancelled and removed from the man's record providing that his conduct has been satisfactory in the meantime.

Further disciplinary action
7. An employee may be dismissed or suspended without pay if, after receiving due notice and despite adequate warning, he still fails to reach the prescribed standards. He may only be summarily dismissed for gross misconduct. In other cases warranting dismissal the company will give notice of the termination of employment or will give payment in lieu of notice. The decision to dismiss or suspend must be confirmed in writing to the individual.

Right to be represented
8. Except in the case of an informal warning by a supervisor, an employee has the right to be represented by his trade union representative at each stage of the disciplinary procedure.

Right to appeal
9. An appeal by an employee against disciplinary action will follow the normal negotiating procedure, except that, in the case of dismissal or suspension without pay, the appeal shall be heard within two working days and shall be dealt with by the personnel director on behalf of the company.
10. Unless the appeal is lodged within two working days, it will be assumed that the employee has accepted the decision.

Points for the management case

1. McIntyre was given a written warning in January 1980 that future consumption of alcohol during working hours would entail instant dismissal. This warning was not contested by the trade union at the time. Cooper detected the smell of alcohol on McIntyre's breath on the afternoon of the incident in question and deduced that his irregular and dangerous operation of the fork-lift truck was caused by drink.

2. McIntyre's refusal to clear up the mess he made in the loading bay was a clear case of gross insubordination. The request from Cooper was perfectly reasonable in the circumstances.

3. The company specifically reserves the right to dismiss employees on the spot for gross misconduct. This was obviously a case of gross misconduct and, in the absence of the factory manager, the assistant factory manager was perfectly correct in acting as he did in support of the foreman.

4. The fork-lift truck driven by McIntyre was subsequently inspected for mechanical faults and none was found.

Points for the trade union case

1. The company's written warning to McIntyre of 3 January 1980 was too severe in that it made him liable to be dismissed on the slightest pretext at any time thereafter. The very fact that Cooper tacitly ignored the letter of this warning when giving McIntyre oral reprimands for the same offence a few months later implies that the foreman recognized the undue severity of this written warning. Indeed, despite the fact that Cooper suspected that McIntyre had been drinking, he still permitted him to continue operating the fork-lift.

2. The dismissal note sent by Messrs Beattie and Scott on 12 November stated that the cause of the dismissal was deliberate misuse of company equipment while under the influence of drink. The company took no steps, however, to validate the accuracy of Cooper's assumption that McIntyre was in fact drunk.

3. Beattie and Scott acted in breach of procedure in dismissing McIntyre without apparently trying to contact the factory manager first. There is nothing in the procedure which states or implies that an assistant factory manager can act on behalf of his superior when the latter is still accessible for decision-making purposes. The correct procedure would have been to delay taking any action until the factory manager returned and the appropriate trade union officials had been consulted. Moreover, it is quite clear that it was the foreman, Cooper, who dismissed McIntyre in the first instance. Beattie and Scott simply rubber stamped Cooper's action without taking the trouble to ascertain the real facts of the situa-

tion. Under the company's disputes procedure, the foreman has no authority to dismiss, even where gross misconduct is involved.

4. McIntyre was not being insubordinate in refusing to restack the pieces. He honestly believed that it was no part of his duties as fork-lift truck operator to move pieces by hand. The general labourers who subsequently started to restack the pieces should have been called to do the job in the first place. McIntyre had no real intention of being insubordinate and was provoked by Cooper's aggressive manner.

5. Unfair Dismissal

It is generally agreed after 10 years' experience that the impact of statutory protection against unfair dismissal has fallen far short of what was originally intended. It was hoped that by providing employees with a right of complaint to an industrial tribunal, the remedy for which would be either reinstatement or financial compensation, their job security would be enhanced. This, in turn, would encourage employers to improve their own voluntary practices and procedures. As 'specialist industrial juries', industrial tribunals would dispense quick and effective justice, thereby developing a body of case law which reasonable employers would take into account when operating their own disciplinary procedures. It has long been evident that these intentions have for the most part not been fulfilled and that, despite a widespread belief to the contrary, employers still enjoy a broad discretion to dismiss employees who are in some way unsatisfactory or (in the case of redundancy) for whom insufficient work exists.

Of the 30,000 or so complaints of unfair dismissal which are likely to be heard this year, over half will not even reach an industrial tribunal. Of this number, about half will be settled 'out of court' with the help of ACAS and the other half will simply be withdrawn by the applicants. Of the minority of cases which actually proceed to a hearing, only about one in three is likely to be won by the employee. In the overwhelming majority of those cases which go in favour of the employee, the remedy will be financial compensation. In recent years less than 2 per cent of successful claims have resulted in the employee being reinstated despite the fact that many more *want* their jobs back. Compensation payments have also been modest, with £500 being fairly common and very few four-figure settlements.

Why do so few applicants win their case? One reason lies in the tribunal system itself. Although tribunal hearings are far less formal than court proceedings, they still rely on the adversarial principle of examination and cross-examination. Knowledge of case law and presentational skill are essential. In short, an applicant who cannot afford to be represented by a lawyer is likely to be at a disadvantage and currently only about one-third of applicants are so represented, compared with over half of the respondents. Another and much more important reason, however, lies in the adoption by tribunals of *managerial* standards in determining the fairness of a given dismissal. In the early days tribunals were enjoined to strike a balance between the needs of the employer's business and the employee's need for fair treatment. Since about 1976, however, the balance has shifted decisively in favour of the employer's interests. As the EAT declared in *Cook* v *Thomas Linnell & Sons* (*1977*): 'Although employers must act reasonably in dismissing an unsatisfactory employee, it is important that the operation of unfair dismissal legislation should not unreasonably impede employers in the efficient management of their business.'

The emergence of an increasingly managerial perspective on unfair dismissal has not sat easily with the original conception of tribunals as 'specialist industrial juries'. The EAT has repeatedly instructed tribunals *not* to put themselves in the employer's shoes and say whether *they* would have dismissed the employee or not. The prevailing doctrine is that in many circumstances there is a range of responses which a reasonable employer might adopt and that, provided the response does not fall outside this range, the decision cannot be challenged by a tribunal. The question which tribunals must ask themselves is whether the employer behaved reasonably, and this must be determined in the light of the circumstances as they appeared to the employer at the time of the dismissal. Tribunal decisions have been overturned by the EAT because the tribunal has 'misdirected' itself by asking the wrong questions. An employer does not have to *prove* that an alleged offence had been committed or that an employee was incompetent or that he was redundant. All the employer needs to show is that there were *reasonable grounds* for believing that such was the case.

As a result, the role of tribunals and the appellate courts has increasingly become one of reviewing the procedure which the employer followed rather than investigating the substance of the decision itself. Employers would argue that a tribunal is seldom in a position to assess the substantive fairness of a managerial decision. If, for example, an employer genuinely believes an employee to be incompetent and can point to some evidence which is consistent with this belief, how can any tribunal maintain that the belief was mistaken? In these circumstances, all that a tribunal can do is to satisfy itself that the rules of procedure which management adopted were fair and reasonable. Over the years, however, there has been an unmistakable dilution of the standards which a reasonable employer is expected to achieve. Giving an employee the right to state his case, for example, was once regarded as a standard rule to be followed in all but the most exceptional circumstances. Now, however, it is legitimate for an employer who has not observed this rule to argue that 'on the balance of probabilities' the failure to give the employee the right to state his case made no difference to the final outcome. In such circumstances, all that a tribunal can do is in effect ask itself whether, in retrospect, the employee received 'his just deserts' (ie whether the dismissal was fair to the employee), not whether the employer acted fairly at the time the decision to dismiss was taken. Procedural unfairness, in short, does not necessarily mean that a dismissal will be found to be unfair.

A very recent case, however, suggests that the EAT may now be more responsive to this criticism. In *Williams* v *Campair Maxam Ltd* (*1982*) the EAT adopted a much more rigorous standard of fairness which, unless it is overturned by the Court of Appeal, will certainly influence future case law. While reiterating the point that there is a range of 'reasonable responses' which an employer might take, the EAT emphasized the role of industrial tribunals as 'industrial juries' which must bring specialist knowledge to bear in deciding the fairness or otherwise of a decision to dismiss. To decide whether an employer's action falls within the range of reasonable responses, a 'properly instructed' tribunal must know the principles which, in current industrial practice, a reasonable employer would be expected to adopt. A tribunal which shows itself to be unaware of these principles will, said the EAT, be held to have acted 'perversely'. In the *Campair Maxam* case, therefore, the EAT has sought to halt and even reverse the steady drift away from the original conception of the tribunals' role as disseminators of good practice. Tribunals have, in effect, been reminded that the statutory test for unfairness is directed towards the behaviour of the employer, not to the question of whether the employee got his 'just deserts'.

A significant trend in the case law on constructive dismissal may also be regarded as an attempt to strengthen the current standards of fairness. The enunciation by the Court of Appeal of a strict contractual test for constructive dismissal was initially seen as portending a significant reduction in successful claims and as a potential gateway through which unscrupulous employers could escape the test of 'reasonableness'. The subsequent tendency of the EAT to regard breaches of *implied* contractual terms by employers as important, however, clearly infers that the reasonableness of the employer's behaviour will, in practice, be carefully weighed in claims for constructive dismissal. Behaviour by an employer which is likely to damage the relationship of trust and confidence which must exist between employer and employee, for example, will break an implied contractual term.

Despite these trends, the sympathy which tribunals, the EAT and the Court of Appeal have shown for the employer's problems and needs helps to explain why only a minority of applicants press their case to a tribunal hearing and why only one in three of these actually wins his case. The cases which follow have been selected with a view to illustrating these underlying trends, as well as the more recent developments, in the law on unfair dismissal.

CASE 17: Higgins v Dimwick & Co Ltd

1. Mr Higgins was employed by Dimwick & Co Ltd as a polisher from 1977 until his dismissal in November 1980. He was also treasurer of the employees' Christmas club and in this capacity he made weekly collections of subscriptions to this club. On 12 November he was making such a collection when another employee, Mr Grassman, claimed that Mr Higgins had given him incorrect change. Mr Higgins denied this allegation and some heated words were exchanged. Mr Higgins asked if Mr Grassman was calling him a thief, to which Mr Grassman replied, 'Yes I b - - - - - - well am.' Thereupon blows were exchanged. Mr Higgins used a broom handle in the course of the struggle which followed.

2. The chargehand stopped the fight and told both men to report to the personnel officer, Mr Atkinson. He interviewed them separately and alone. Each man alleged that the other had begun the fight and was wholly to blame. Employees who had witnessed the incident were interviewed and statements were taken from them. As a result of these interviews and the statements taken from other employees, Mr Atkinson decided who was responsible. Both men were suspended for the day and the following morning Mr Higgins was called into Mr Atkinson's office and, in the presence of his shop steward, was summarily dismissed for gross misconduct.

3. Mr Higgins appealed against this decision and on 16 November the appeal was heard by Mr Knight, the personnel manager, and Mr O'Brien, the production manager. On this occasion Mr Higgins was accompanied by the union convenor. Mr Grassman and the other witnesses were not present at the meeting. Mr Higgins gave his explanation of the incident and was then told to withdraw. The appeals panel then saw Mr Grassman, questioned him, and then considered their statements, together with those of the witnesses, without either party being present. Mr Higgins was not given copies of the written statements of the witnesses nor was he allowed to cross-examine Mr Grassman. The decision to dismiss was confirmed. Mr Higgins then complained to an industrial tribunal.

4. In evidence to the tribunal Mr Higgins argued that the procedure adopted by the company had put him at a disadvantage. He had not heard Mr Grassman's evidence and had not been able to cross-examine. If the procedure had been fairer, the company might have come to the conclusion that Mr Grassman was equally to blame for the fight. In its evidence to the tribunal the company argued that giving the protagonists the chance to cross-examine each other was not essential to natural justice. In support of this argument the company's representative quoted the decision of the EAT in *Khanum* v *Mid-Glamorgan Area Health Authority* (*1978*): 'There are only three basic requirements

which have to be complied with during the proceedings of a domestic disciplinary inquiry: first, that the person should know of the nature of the accusation made against him; second, that he should be given an opportunity to state his case; and, third, that the investigating or appellant body should act in good faith.' All three of these requirements, said the company, were met in this case.

Question for discussion

What would an industrial tribunal be likely to decide?

CASE 18: Carter v Longsite Engineering Co Ltd

1. Mr Carter was employed as a maintenance fitter by the company from 1975 until his dismissal on 15 August 1978. He and another fitter, Mr Johns, worked in a small section of the plant together. Initially they got on reasonably well, but by early August of 1978 relations were rather strained. On 7 August Mr Johns arrived for the start of the day shift some five minutes late. This provoked an argument, after which the two men refused to speak to one another for several days.

2. The incident which led to Mr Carter's dismissal occurred at 9.30 am on 13 August. Mr Johns was asked to go to one of the production lines in the main factory which had broken down. To do the necessary repair work he needed a particular set of tools which Mr Carter was using at the time. It would appear, however, that Mr Carter was reluctant to let Mr Johns have the tools, so Mr Johns attempted to take them forcibly. The men came to blows. Mr Carter inflicted most of the blows, but neither man sustained any serious injury. Mr Johns had a little minor bleeding from his face. The foreman soon arrived on the scene and stopped the fight.

3. The section manager, Mr Taylor, suspended the two men so that the matter could be investigated. Having conducted an inquiry, Mr Taylor acted in accordance with the company's procedure and dismissed both men. Both men appealed and, in due course, the matter went to the works manager, Mr Ash. Both men were called to give evidence, along with several witnesses. Mr Ash listened to all the evidence and came to the conclusion that Mr Carter had been the aggressor and that Mr Johns had only used violence in self-defence. As a result, Mr Johns was allowed to return to work following a further period of one week's suspension. Mr Carter, however, was dismissed.

4. Mr Carter claimed that the dismissal was unfair. He argued that in the circumstances it was unreasonable to discriminate between Mr Johns and himself. Both he and Mr Johns were to blame. Either *both* should have been dismissed or *both* reinstated. Neither of them had any

previous disciplinary offences on their records. Mr Fisher, a shop steward who knew both men very well, said that of the two Mr Johns was more likely to become aggressive than Mr Carter.

Question for discussion

What would an industrial tribunal be likely to decide?

CASE 19: McCabe v Soft-Tread Tyres Ltd

1. Mr McCabe worked as a labourer for Soft-Tread Tyres Ltd from 1976 until his dismissal in 1978. On 3 August 1978 Mr Gilmour, the works manager, reported to the police that a dozen radial-ply tyres had been stolen from the premises the previous evening. Later that day the police discovered some tyres in a disused warehouse a short distance from the factory premises. Mr Gilmour identified them as the missing tyres. He was subsequently informed by the police that Mr McCabe and two other men had been charged with breaking into the premises and stealing the tyres. They had all been in custody overnight. The firm's records revealed that Mr McCabe had been off work since early July because of an industrial accident. There were no previous disciplinary offences on his record.

2. The company's disciplinary procedure laid down that, in the case of ordinary misconduct, a verbal warning and a final written warning should be given before an employee was dismissed. In the case of gross misconduct, however, instant dismissal was the penalty. In Mr Gilmour's opinion, the theft by an employee of his employer's property was obviously gross misconduct.

3. Although Mr Gilmour had authority to dismiss employees, it was his practice to refer cases of gross misconduct to the production director, Mr Sinclair, and to the personnel manager, Mr Shires. This was done in McCabe's case and the decision taken by Messrs Sinclair and Shires was to dismiss. Mr Shires wrote to Mr McCabe, dismissing him for gross misconduct, on 16 August. Mr Sinclair felt that, while an employee would in normal circumstances be interviewed before a final decision was taken, the circumstances in McCabe's case were exceptional. The police had found McCabe at or near the place where the tyres had been hidden and the tyres had been identified as the company's property. McCabe had been charged with theft, along with two other men who were not employees of the company.

4. Mr McCabe claimed that he had been unfairly dismissed. In evidence to the industrial tribunal he argued, first, that since he had pleaded 'not guilty' to the theft charge the company should have suspended him until his trial had taken place and, second, that he had not had an opportunity to state his case. He further maintained that if the

company had conducted a proper inquiry, it would have realized that he played only a minor part in the theft. He also claimed that he had visited the factory on 6 August to collect an income tax rebate and had told Mr Gilmour that he had been charged with theft but was innocent. He said that Mr Gilmour had advised him to see Mr Sinclair on 10 August. He said that he had attempted to see Mr Sinclair on 10 August, but that the latter was not available. He admitted, however, that after receiving his letter of dismissal on 17 August he did not appeal against the decision or seek another meeting.

5. Mr Sinclair in evidence to the tribunal said he was unaware of any request by Mr McCabe for a meeting prior to his dismissal but that, had he requested one, it would have been arranged. Mr Gilmour denied that Mr McCabe had visited the factory at any time between 3-17 August. In any event, he said, no useful purpose would have been served by interviewing Mr McCabe since he had already pleaded 'not guilty' to the charge and would presumably have continued to deny any knowledge of the theft. Management was also doubtful whether it would have been proper for them to investigate a matter which was already *sub judice*.

Question for discussion

What would an industrial tribunal be likely to decide?

CASE 20: Mills v Great Northern Stores Ltd

1. Mrs Mills was employed as a full-time cashier at the company's Barnsley store. At the time of her dismissal in January 1982 she had seven years' service with no previous disciplinary problems. Her duties as cashier were to operate one of four tills on the sales floor. After ringing up each sale she was required to give the customer a duplicate receipt. The till also recorded the amount of cash at the beginning and end of each working day. Every till roll was regularly checked by the office manageress in the store. It was a contractual term of employment for all cashiers that all cash must be recorded through the till immediately on receipt. Any breach of this rule was regarded as gross misconduct which would render the employee concerned liable to instant dismissal.

2. For some time prior to January 1982 the store management had been concerned about a steady loss of money from the tills and the company's store detectives had been called in to carry out routine surveys on two occasions. Nothing irregular, however, had been noticed. On 19 December 1981 two store detectives visited Barnsley again and made test purchases at all four till points. One of the detectives took five items to Mrs Mills' till point. Two of these items, costing £4.50 and £2.25, were not recorded on the till and Mrs Mills failed to provide

a receipt. When the till record was checked at the end of the day, the office manageress found that the total cash taken did not exceed the total shown on the till roll, the inference being that the sum of £6.75 had not reached the till.

3. Following this routine check, the results of which were reported to the store manager, Mr Rawlings, the store detectives visited the Barnsley store again on Tuesday 11 January 1982. On this occasion both made purchases at Mrs Mills' till point. A total of four items was involved, three of which were handled properly but the fourth item, costing £3.60, was not. The detective reported that Mrs Mills had operated the till in a way which entered workings on the till roll. No receipt was given.

4. Mr Rawlings was then away at head office and did not receive the detectives' report until Friday 14 January. He then consulted the office manageress, who reported that the total cash recorded as taken from Mrs Mills' till on that day did not exceed the total recorded on the till roll. Mrs Mills was off with a bad cold on 13, 14 and 15 January and returned to work on Monday 17 January. Mr Rawlings, accompanied by the staff manageress, Miss Baxter, interviewed Mrs Mills for over an hour on that day. She was asked repeatedly for an explanation for her failure to operate the till correctly on both 19 December and 11 January. She replied that she could not remember the items in question. She pointed out that on both occasions the store was very busy because of the pre-Christmas rush and the January sales respectively, and that she could not be expected to remember small items, especially as so much time had elapsed. She then said that she had not recovered from her cold and did not feel well.

5. Mr Rawlings eventually closed the interview and said that, as she could offer no explanation, she would be dismissed immediately for gross misconduct. Mrs Mills consulted her union representative and lodged an appeal under the company's procedure. The grounds for her appeal were, first, that a delay of six days and four weeks respectively had elapsed between her dismissal and the two occasions on which the alleged misconduct happened. Second, it was argued that the store manager had failed to remind her of her rights under the company procedure to be accompanied at an interview by a union representative or 'next friend'. Third, it was argued that she should not have been interviewed when she felt unwell. The appeal was conducted through an exchange of letters and was rejected by the area manager.

6. Mrs Mills then complained to an industrial tribunal. Her counsel argued that the EAT decision in *British Home Stores* v *Burchell (1978)* requires an employer who suspects misconduct to satisfy three tests. First, management has to show that it genuinely believed that the employee had committed the offence of which he or she was charged.

145

Second, it has to show that there were reasonable grounds to sustain that belief. Third, it has to show that a reasonable investigation was made into the circumstances. Counsel argued that the company had failed to pass the second and third tests. The delay between the alleged offences and the interview was unreasonable, she was not allowed representation and she was not feeling well.

7. Counsel for the company argued that there was unchallengeable evidence from the test purchases that Mrs Mills had committed a serious breach of till regulations and that, whatever the procedural short-comings, it was reasonable for the company to act on the information it had. Counsel further argued that the six days' delay was virtually unavoidable in the circumstances and that neither the absence of union representation nor the fact that Mrs Mills said she was unwell made any difference to the final outcome since there was no possible explanation she could have put forward.

Question for discussion

What would an industrial tribunal be likely to decide?

CASE 21: Hayman v Broadacres County Council

1. Mr Hayman was employed by Broadacres County Council for 28 years as a schoolmaster. The last eight years of his career prior to his dismissal in 1978 were spent as head of the geography department at Fern Bank, a large comprehensive school. He had been transferred to Fern Bank by the Council's education department in 1960 following a conviction for indecency. Up to that time he had taught in a small rural school some 30 miles away. This conviction also resulted in the permanent removal of his warrant as a scout master.

2. No further difficulties occurred until February 1978 when Mr Hayman was convicted by the local magistrates of an offence of gross indecency with another adult male in a public toilet. He pleaded guilty and was fined £50. Following the publicity which Mr Hayman's case attracted, the special sub-committee of the council's education committee considered the matter.

3. The sub-committee took into account the following evidence before making a decision. First, it considered the recommendation of the Fern Bank governors that Mr Hayman should be severely reprimanded, but that he should continue in his present appointment with a final warning. Second, it considered the submission of the education department that Mr Hayman had homosexual inclinations which he was not always able to control. There was, however, no evidence that any resulting acts or relationships had involved any pupils at the school.

No further evidence was offered concerning his sexual interests or activities. Third, the sub-committee considered the evidence of the headmaster of Fern Bank, who said that he did not wish to take responsibility for Mr Hayman's continued employment at the school. He also said that, if Mr Hayman was now applying for his present post and all the relevant facts had come to light, he would not be appointed.

4. The sub-committee also considered the opinion of the Minister for Education given in accordance with the Schools Regulation Act of 1959. Under the terms of this Act the Minister is empowered to decide whether a teacher convicted of a criminal offence is unsuitable for further employment as a teacher. The Minister wrote to the Council saying that Mr Hayman would 'not be deemed unsuitable for continued employment as a teacher.'

5. The special sub-committee conducted a full inquiry and heard submissions from both sides. Mr Hayman was supported by his trade union official, who argued that:

(a) There was no evidence of any incident suggesting a risk to pupils.
(b) Even if it was not practicable to continue Mr Hayman's employment at Fern Bank, the council should have made efforts to find him a job, even of an administrative kind, elsewhere.

6. On 12 April 1978 the sub-committee decided to dismiss Mr Hayman, 'the reason being his admitted conduct which was the subject of his conviction at the magistrates' court in February 1978 for an act of gross indecency.' His dismissal took immediate effect, but in the light of his long service he was paid a sum equivalent to his salary to the end of August 1978 and his superannuation was protected. Mr Hayman then complained to an industrial tribunal that he had been unfairly dismissed.

Question for discussion

What would an industrial tribunal be likely to decide?

CASE 22: Crawford v Broadacres County Council

1. Mrs Crawford was employed as a typist in the typing pool of the Broadacres County Council's social services directorate from January 1976 to July 1979, when she was dismissed for absenteeism. Her attendance record for the first two years or so of her employment was satisfactory, but it then began to deteriorate. In the quarter to 30 September 1978 she was absent for 25 per cent of working days; in the quarter to 31 December 1978 she was absent for 29 per cent of working days; in the quarter to 31 March 1979, she was absent for 20

per cent of working days, and in the quarter to 30 June she was absent for 32 per cent of working days. All these absences were covered by medical certificates from her doctor. These certificates indicated that she had at various times suffered from dizzy spells, anxiety, virus infections, migraine, cystitis and dyspepsia.

2. Under the council's disciplinary procedure, 'persistent absenteeism beyond the agreed level' is defined as an offence which could, if repeated, lead to suspension and ultimately to dismissal. The level of absence agreed with the trade unions for this purpose was 10 per cent. Mrs Crawford received her first (verbal) warning on 20 July 1978, and further (written) warnings were issued on 13 October 1978, 12 January 1979 and 10 April 1979. On each occasion she was interviewed by a senior officer of the council in the presence of her NALGO representative. The last written warning she received (10 April 1979) stated: 'Your current level of absenteeism of 20 per cent is totally unacceptable. It must improve to 10 per cent within the next month. A failure to reach this target may result in your dismissal from the council's employment. This is your final warning.'

3. Before the decision to dismiss was taken, the directorate personnel officer consulted the council's medical adviser, Dr Jacobson, who examined Mrs Crawford's medical certificates. Dr Jacobson found that no useful purpose would be served by examining her as she had not had any illnesses which he could subsequently verify and ethically he could not contradict another doctor's medical certificates. He could not, however, see any common link between the illnesses and said Mrs Crawford was not, apparently, suffering from any chronic illness.

4. Finally Mrs Crawford was absent, again certificated, from 15 June to 8 July 1979. When she returned to work on 8 July she was told to report to the principal secretary who, in the presence of her NALGO representative, dismissed her summarily. The decision to dismiss had been taken prior to Mrs Crawford's return to work, although both she and her union representative were invited to speak. Neither of them advanced any extenuating circumstances. Mrs Crawford subsequently claimed that she had been unfairly dismissed.

5. In its evidence to the tribunal the council argued that the reason for Mrs Crawford's dismissal was her persistent absence from work, which had continued despite several formal warnings. It was argued on behalf of Mrs Crawford that her absences were supported by medical certificates and that, if the council suspected that these certificates had not been issued in good faith, it should have investigated the matter.

Question for discussion

What would an industrial tribunal be likely to decide?

CASE 23: Crooke v Grubthorpe Metropolitan District Council

1. Mr Crooke was employed by the Grubthorpe County Borough Council from 1955 until local government reorganization in 1974, by which time he occupied the post of clerk of works in the engineering division. In 1974 he transferred to the successor metropolitan district council and was appointed senior engineer (drainage) in the direct works organization. He was then 54 years of age.

2. During 1976 it became evident that Mr Crooke's health was deteriorating. His sickness and absence record for the year was as follows:

- 23 March to 31 May: absent because of mild stroke
- 31 May to 31 July: absent because of general debility
- 31 July to 31 August: absent because of general debility
- 1 September to 30 September: absent because of anxiety and depression

All these absences were certificated.

3. In July Mr Crooke's superiors in direct works became concerned about his absences. He occupied a fairly important post in the drainage section, and his continued absence was causing difficulties for other staff and impeding their efficiency. On 9 July the chief personnel officer, Mr Feather, wrote to Dr McKay, the district community physician, requesting a report on Mr Crooke's state of health: 'Mr Crooke has now been absent for some time because of a stroke. His duties entail a fair amount of field work and travelling as well as normal office work. As he is now 56 years of age, I should be grateful for your opinion on whether we would be justified in retiring him prematurely on grounds of ill-health.'

4. Dr McKay asked Dr Woodward of the area health authority to examine Mr Crooke with a view to a possible premature retirement. Mr Crooke and Dr Woodward had known each other for many years and the meeting took the form of a five-minute discussion. There was no physical examination, nor was Mr Crooke told that he was being considered for early retirement. Dr Woodward then wrote a report to Dr McKay, part of which read as follows: 'Since local government reorganization, Mr Crooke had found the physical and mental demands of his job increasingly beyond his capacity. Although he has now recovered from his stroke, he seems lacking in self-confidence and has visibly aged. I cannot, therefore, recommend that he be allowed to return to work in his present condition. I have discussed the matter with his own GP, Dr Rice, and we believe that early retirement would be the best solution for Mr Crooke.'

5. Having received Dr Woodward's report, Dr McKay wrote to Mr

Feather on 25 July: 'I asked Dr Woodward to examine Mr Crooke and have now received his report. There is no doubt in his mind that Mr Crooke should be retired on the grounds of ill-health and I must concur with his judgment.' Mr Feather did not ask to see Dr Woodward's report and there was no further communication with Mr Crooke until 1 August, when he received formal notice of termination of employment by letter from Mr Feather: 'In view of your continued absence from work this year, it has been necessary for the council to request its medical adviser to consider the state of your health in relation to your future employment with the council. We have now received his report, which recommends that you be retired immediately on the grounds of ill-health. The council accepts this recommendation and, as a result, you will retire from our employment with effect from 30 September 1976.' Details of Mr Crooke's pension entitlement were enclosed and he was given a lump sum of £4500.

6. In October 1976 Mr Crooke complained to an industrial tribunal that he had been unfairly dismissed. In evidence to the tribunal Mr Crooke said that he had been treated in a manner which he found degrading and demoralizing and which had contributed to his state of depression and anxiety. He said he had never been consulted about his early retirement and that he was unaware that his own doctor had been consulted. He further argued that he should have been given the opportunity to challenge Dr Woodward's report and that, in any event, this report was not based on a thorough examination. He contended that the council had, in effect, decided to dismiss him before they received Dr Woodward's report and that this was unfair.

7. The council argued that it is not the function of employers or industrial tribunals to turn themselves into medical experts and question the opinions and advice they receive from qualified medical practitioners. Mr Crooke's continued absence by reason of ill-health was impeding the efficiency of his department and the council's medical adviser recommended early retirement. The council felt obliged to accept that recommendation. No useful purpose would have been served by allowing Mr Crooke to contest Dr Woodward's recommendation, since it would have involved making a medical judgment which a layman was unqualified to make.

8. The tribunal also considered the evidence of Dr Rice, Mr Crooke's own doctor: 'Mr Crooke has been my patient since 1966. Until 1974 his health was good. Between April 1974 and April 1976 I saw him professionally on 22 occasions. He complained of a variety of symptoms, most of which were the result of acute anxiety. His condition gradually worsened until on 23 March 1976 he was admitted to hospital after a mild stroke. No evidence of any organic disease was found and his symptoms were held to be the result of stress and strain

at work. Since then he has gradually responded to treatment by anti-depressant drugs.'

Question for discussion

What would an industrial tribunal be likely to decide?

CASE 24: Lees v Great Northern Stores Ltd

1. Mr Lees entered the company's employment on 1 March 1980 as a warehouseman at their Blackpool store. When he completed the appropriate application forms he had to answer certain questions about his health. In answer to the question, 'Have you ever suffered from any serious illness?', he wrote 'No'. In answer to the question, 'Do you suffer from any serious disability or handicap?', he wrote 'No'. He was then given a medical examination by the store doctor who again asked him for details of any accidents, operations or illnesses he had suffered. He replied that he had had his appendix removed in 1974, but that otherwise he never had any problems. He failed to disclose that he was an alcoholic. The doctor then passed him medically fit for employment.

2. In August 1980 Mr Lees took two weeks of his annual holiday entitlement and visited a Dr Dawson, a specialist in the treatment of alcoholism and other addictions. As a result he spent 10 days in a rehabilitation centre near Lancaster and, after his return to work, underwent a course of treatment prescribed by Dr Dawson. He still failed to disclose his problem to the company and misled Dr Dawson into believing that he had. In October Dr Dawson rang up the store manager, Mr Butler, to advise him that the course of treatment had been successful and that Mr Lees' addiction had been cured. Mr Butler was naturally surprised to learn that Mr Lees had been an alcoholic.

3. Mr Butler then consulted the store doctor, who said that if he had known that Mr Lees was an alcoholic he could not have recommended him for employment and that he could not advise the company to retain an alcoholic in its employment. The doctor considered an alcoholic to be a potential danger both to himself and to others and, in the light of the high incidence of relapse among 'cured' alcoholics, Mr Lees would have to have additional supervision. Mr Butler then consulted his area manager, who said that it was company policy to dismiss employees who had knowingly falsified their employment application forms.

4. Mr Butler then saw Mr Lees, in the presence of his union representative, and told him that he had discovered he was an alcoholic. Mr Lees first denied that he had ever had a drink problem and then claimed that Dr Dawson had cured him. He argued for a chance to prove that he

was no longer an alcoholic. Mr Butler replied that he had wilfully misled the company when asked questions about his health record and that he would have to be dismissed. He was given two weeks' pay in lieu of notice. Mr Lees then complained that he had been unfairly dismissed.

5. Counsel for Mr Lees argued that the employers should have investigated the matter much more thoroughly. They should have consulted Dr Dawson and discussed the matter sympathetically with Mr Lees. Had they done so, they might have come to the conclusion that Mr Lees could have been retained in their employment. Counsel for the company argued that he had obtained employment by deception, that it was entirely reasonable for them to refuse to employ an alcoholic, and that nothing that Dr Dawson could have told them would have made any difference.

Question for discussion

What would an industrial tribunal be likely to decide?

CASE 25: Brook v ABC Wholesalers Ltd

1. The company owns a chain of depots in the North of England which supply a wide range of goods to retailers. Mr Brook joined the firm in 1970 at the age of 36 as an area representative. He specialized in household goods, hardware, furnishings and kitchen equipment and in October 1974 he was promoted to area sales manager.

2. As area sales manager he was based in Bolton and was responsible for three large depots in central Lancashire. Well over half the total turnover of these depots was in foodstuffs and beverages, of which he had had no previous experience. Although he had performed very well as an area representative and had in fact been nominated 'most successful salesman' in the company in 1973, it soon became apparent to the sales director that he was not doing well in his new job.

3. In the year to 1 April 1974, the last full financial year before Mr Brook took over, the three Bolton area depots achieved a combined turnover of £5.75 million, with a reported net profit of £650,000. In 1974-75, however, turnover fell to £5.2 million and net profits to £475,000. In 1975-76 turnover fell to £4 million and net profits to £325,000. In July 1975 the sales director, Mr Pearson, visited Bolton and had an 'informal chat' with Mr Brook about his performance. Mr Brook pointed out that prior to his appointment he had never been involved in the food side of the business and confessed to being 'a bit at sea' with it.

4. As a result of this meeting Mr Pearson arranged for Mr Tapsell, the

company's senior food merchandiser, to advise Mr Brook on the technical aspects of the food and drink business. In the course of the next few months Mr Tapsell paid three visits to Bolton and sought to help Mr Brook improve his performance. The sales position, however, continued to deteriorate and in January 1976 Mr Pearson saw Mr Brook and told him that, unless the downward trend was reversed within three months, his future with the company would have to be 'seriously considered'.

5. On 5 April 1976 Mr Brook was summoned to head office in Manchester and told by the managing director, Mr Glover, that he could no longer continue as area sales manager. Mr Glover offered him a job as an area representative in West Yorkshire at a 'personally protected' salary (ie no loss of earnings). Mr Brook, however, declined this offer, first, because it would have entailed an 'unacceptable' loss of status and, second, because it would have involved heavy travelling costs from his home in Bolton to West Yorkshire. In these circumstances the board of directors decided that they had no alternative but to dismiss Mr Brook.

6. Mr Brook then lodged a complaint of unfair dismissal. In evidence to the industrial tribunal he argued:

(a) That a period of 18 months in the job was an insufficient period of time in which to prove himself, particularly in view of his lack of experience in the food trade.

(b) That the fall-off in the trade of the depots for which he was responsible was largely caused by the general economic recession which began in 1974 and continued well into 1976.

(c) That the company had by April 1976 obviously made up its mind to dismiss or demote him and that he was never given a proper opportunity to state his case of appeal against the decision to dismiss.

7. In its evidence to the tribunal, the company contended that:

(a) An extended trial period for Mr Brook was out of the question in view of the seriousness of the fall-off in the trade of the Bolton depots.

(b) Mr Brook had been made aware of the company's dissatisfaction with his performance at an early stage and had been given appropriate assistance. Having failed to show the required improvement, it was fair and reasonable for the company to dismiss him.

(c) While the company as a whole had suffered from the recession, the decline of 50 per cent in the net profits and of 30 per cent in gross turnover was considerably worse than the average for the company as a whole. The company was, therefore, entitled to conclude that Mr Brook was responsible for the exceptionally poor performance of his area.

(d) By April 1976 the directors had lost all confidence in Mr Brook as an area sales manager, although they were quite prepared to continue his employment in the less demanding job of area representative. In the circumstances this offer was fair and reasonable and Mr Brook's refusal to accept it left the board with no alternative but to dismiss him.

Question for discussion

What would an industrial tribunal be likely to decide?

CASE 26: Broxtowe v Gripewater Groceries Ltd

1. The company operates a national chain of retail grocery stores. For management purposes, the organization was sub-divided into 12 regions, each headed by a regional manager. Mr Broxtowe joined the company in 1954 at the age of 22 and was gradually promoted through the hierarchy until, in 1978, he was made manager of the north western region covering Lancashire, Cheshire, and Cumbria.

2. Early in 1981 the board of directors decided that, as a result of the economic recession, staffing and administrative overheads would have to be reduced. As a result, the chief accountant, advised by the personnel manager, was told to reorganize the management structure of the company to achieve substantial savings in costs. It was envisaged that there would have to be some compulsory redundancies. In February 1981 the chief accountant submitted a report which proposed that the number of regional units be reduced from 12 to six. This plan entailed the elimination of a total of 40 regional posts, including auditors, sales managers, clerical staff and regional managers.

3. The board adopted these proposals and instructed the personnel manager, Mr Morland, to implement them as soon as possible. In identifying those who were to be declared redundant, Mr Morland adopted the criteria of capability, mobility and adaptability. The company did not recognize any trade union for bargaining purposes, nor did it have any redundancy procedure or customary arrangement. In the case of the regional managers, Mr Morland did not attempt a complete reshuffle, but sought instead to determine redundancies on a one-to-one basis between neighbouring regional managers.

4. Under the reorganization, the north western and north eastern regions were merged to form one northern region. The manager of the north eastern region, Mr Wills, had only eight years' service with the company, compared with Mr Broxtowe's 26 years. On managerial grounds, however, Mr Morland decided that Mr Broxtowe should be dismissed. Mr Morland felt that Mr Broxtowe, although by no means

incapable, was not a 'high flyer' like Mr Wills and was not of the same managerial calibre. He also felt that the older man (Mr Broxtowe was 49 and Mr Wills was 36) would be less adaptable. Finally, he took into account the fact that Mr Broxtowe's wife was a semi-invalid, which meant that he would be reluctant to leave Manchester, where he had lived for the last 16 years, and move to Leeds, the new headquarters of the northern region, where Mr Wills was already based.

5. On 28 February Mr Broxtowe was summoned to head office and told that he was to be dismissed by reason of redundancy. He was given three months' gross pay and additional cash payments, amounting in total to £7000. Mr Broxtowe, on his own evidence, was 'dazed and humiliated' by the decision, of which he had had no prior warning. There had been no previous discussion about his future with the company and he said he had no idea that he would be made redundant. Although he said he knew that major changes were 'in the offing', he had assumed that as a long-serving and capable manager his job would be secure. He claimed that he had been unfairly dismissed because the company had failed (a) to take account of the 'last in, first out' principle and (b) to establish that he was incapable or inefficient.

6. In evidence to the tribunal, the company argued that although Mr Broxtowe was not 'culpably inefficient', he was not of the same standard as Mr Wills and that, given the need to reduce the number of regional managers by 50 per cent, it had no alternative but to retain the services of those who had most to give the company. It regretted the lack of consultation, but maintained that in the circumstances consultation would have made no difference to the final decision.

Question for discussion

What would an industrial tribunal be likely to decide?

CASE 27: Spencer v Amalgamated Breweries Ltd

1. Mr Spencer was employed as a bottle-washing supervisor from September 1977 until his dismissal in October 1980. Throughout most of his period of employment he was one of three bottle-washing supervisors at the company's Norwich bottling plant. A three-shift system operated at this plant and one supervisor was employed on each shift. There were, however, a number of technical problems with the bottle-washing plant which led to frequent breakdowns and impeded efficiency.

2. In February 1980 the production director drafted in a small team of plant engineers and work study officers from the company's headquarters in order to investigate and report on these recurrent problems. They found that some of the plant was obsolete and needed to be

replaced. Once this had been done, they believed that the shift system could be discontinued and that, as a result, only one bottle-washing supervisor would be needed. The production director immediately began to implement these recommendations and in September 1980 the new equipment was installed.

3. Shortly before these changes were made, one of the three supervisors, Mr Grimes, left the company and was not replaced. Soon afterwards, at the end of August, Mr Spencer had to go into hospital for a minor operation. As a result, when the new machinery was installed only one supervisor, Mr Stacey, was in post. Mr Stacey had joined the firm in October 1979 and was generally regarded as energetic and efficient. At 28, he was 15 years yonger than Mr Spencer. It soon became clear to the management at Norwich that only one supervisor was needed and that Mr Stacey should have the job. When Mr Spencer returned to work early in October, therefore, he was given notice of termination of employment by reason of redundancy. He claimed that the dismissal was unfair.

4. In evidence to the tribunal the company said that it had no customary or agreed redundancy procedure. It had selected Mr Spencer because of the way in which the former had done his work in the past. Mr Spencer had not, they said, kept the plant as clean as he should have done and had not shown enough enthusiasm for his work. In May 1980 he had been reprimanded by the production manager, Mr Webster, for lateness in arriving on shift. Mr Spencer had apologized and admitted that he was at fault. The company also argued that Mr Spencer seemed to be in poor health. Mr Spencer, however, replied that he had had to have his appendix removed in September 1980, but that otherwise he was completely fit. No further evidence was submitted on this point by the company.

5. The company further argued that there were no suitable vacancies for Mr Spencer in any other section of the Norwich plant. The only vacancy they had was for an electrician, which Mr Spencer was not qualified to fill. Mr Spencer, however, argued that as the longest-serving supervisor he should not have been selected for redundancy. Before the redundancy arose he had, he said, never been taken to task about his allegedly unsatisfactory performance and had never been warned that unless he improved he would be dismissed.

Question for discussion

What would an industrial tribunal be likely to decide?

CASE 28: Green v Moonweave Ltd

1. Moonweave Ltd manufactures seat covers for various vehicle

assembly firms. It operates a three-shift system, but the employees who work on the various shifts are not required to rotate between shifts. The contract of each employee specifies which of the three shifts he is employed to work on. Mr Green joined the firm in August 1976 and always worked on the night shift at their Nottingham factory.

2. In October 1979 the company experienced a sudden and serious decline in the demand for its products. In part this reflected the general fall in the demand for motor cars, but more particularly resulted from a prolonged strike at the company's major customer. This strike made it necessary for Moonweave to put its factories on a three-day week. When the strike ended on 17 October Moonweave was told by this customer that in future its requirements for seat covers would be reduced by 30 per cent. During the strike Moonweave had built up an abnormal stock of seat covers which it needed to reduce when the strike ended. It sought to persuade the customer not to reduce requirements so drastically, but had little success.

3. The company decided, therefore, to reduce output by abolishing the night shift. In certain sections of the Nottingham factory it was necessary for technical reasons to operate the machinery for 24 hours a day, but this was not the case in Mr Green's section. Management decided and announced on 23 October that all the employees on the night shift in Mr Green's section, except for a skeleton staff of three long-serving employees, would be declared redundant. On 24 October Mr Green received notice of termination of employment by reason of redundancy, effective from the end of the same week, 27 October. The total number of employees made redundant in Mr Green's section was 25 out of 28, including the foreman.

4. Mr Green then claimed that his dismissal was unfair. He argued that on previous occasions when the company had declared redundancies (though these were rare), it had followed the 'last in, first out' principle. He pointed out that there were several employees on the two day shifts with less service than he had and who should have been dismissed before him. He also argued, and the company accepted, that there was no discussion or negotiation on the redundancies with trade union representatives in the plant. The company argued, however, that the decision had to be made at great speed and that, in the absence of an agreed redundancy procedure or customary arrangement, it was not unreasonable to concentrate the redundancies on the night shift. If all three shifts had been treated alike, the company argued, it would have had to dismiss some employees from each shift and then 'fill up' with the remainder of the night shift. This would have caused unreasonable disorganization on the other two shifts.

Question for discussion

What would an industrial tribunal be likely to decide?

CASE 29: Haddon and Others v Grimtex Yarn Spinners Ltd

1. Mr Haddon and six colleagues were employed as spinners in the company's Kidderminster plant. For several years they had worked on a three-shift system which, because of its premium rates of pay, was very attractive to the employees. In 1977-78 there was a sharp decline in the company's business, as a result of which management imposed a freeze on recruiting and took one machine out of production on each shift. When the level of demand continued to decline, however, the board decided that, in order to reduce output by one-fifth, there would have to be a move to two-shift working which would in turn give rise to redundancies.

2. During 1979, however, business improved and the company shelved its proposed abandonment of three-shift working and withdrew its notice of redundancy. The improvement was short-lived and by September 1979 demand was falling once again. Management decided that the move to two-shift working could no longer be postponed. It was agreed with the trade union that, with effect from 30 September 1979, a two-shift system would be worked. All employees who had previously worked on the three-shift system, including Mr Haddon and his colleagues, would continue to receive their old (ie three-shift) rates of pay until 30 January 1980. Thereafter there would be a downward adjustment of earnings. Mr Haddon and his colleagues protested to their union official and to the production manager that this would mean working a greater number of hours for less pay. Nevertheless they operated the new system until 30 January 1980.

3. On 23 January the spinners held a meeting at which they expressed their opposition to the changes which were due to come into effect after 30 January, when their average earnings would fall by £5 a week. The meeting resulted in a decision to ban overtime and work to rule. On 30 January there was a general stoppage of work which lasted nearly one week. On their return to work several spinners, including Mr Haddon, handed in their notice on the grounds that they were not prepared to accept a reduction in their earnings of £5 per week. The resignations took effect on 14 February. They then claimed, first, a redundancy payment and, second, that they had been constructively dismissed.

4. It was argued on behalf of Mr Haddon *et al* that it was obvious in September 1979 that the requirements of the business for employees to carry out the work that these men were doing had ceased or diminished or were expected to cease or diminish. It was obvious in September 1979 that there was a fall-off in demand for the company's products and that a redundancy situation was in prospect. It was argued that Mr Haddon *et al* were actually dismissed in September when they were told that their three-shift contracts of employment had come to

an end. In the period between 30 September 1979 and 30 January 1980, the employees were, in reality, simply taking advantage of S84 of the Employment Protection (Consolidation) Act of 1978, and were following their statutory trial period under a new contract. At the end of the trial period the men were entitled to terminate their new contracts and hold that they had been dismissed at the end of September.

5. It was also argued on behalf of the applicants that there was a dismissal at the end of January when the employees decided to go because they were not prepared to accept the terms which the company was seeking to impose on them. These terms were, it was claimed, imposed unilaterally by management without the agreement of the employees concerned. Accordingly, the employer was alleged to have committed a fundamental breach of the employees' contracts, entitling them to resign and claim constructive dismissal.

6. The company argued that there were no redundancy circumstances in the spinning department between the spring of 1979 and the end of January 1980. The mere changeover from three-shift to two-shift working did not in itself constitute a redundancy situation. Although no employees were recruited during this period, none was dismissed by reason of redundancy. Moreover, the employees were mistaken in concluding that because they were unhappy with the anticipated reduction in wages they could, therefore, regard their contracts as being at an end, entitling them to resign. In reality, there was a variation in their terms and conditions, of which the company had notified them after consultation and agreement with their trade union.

Question for discussion

What would an industrial tribunal be likely to decide?

CASE 30: Hardy and Bishop v Bleak Moor Engineering Ltd

1. Messrs Hardy and Bishop were employed as chargehands by the company at their Oldham factory. Mr Hardy had been with the company since 1968 and Mr Bishop since 1971. In October 1979 the company negotiated a post-entry closed shop agreement with APEX in respect of all clerical, technical and supervisory grades, including that of chargehand. When the agreement was concluded, 70 of the 96 employees covered by it already belonged to APEX. Messrs Hardy and Bishop were two of the 26 employees who did not belong to the union.

2. Under the terms of the agreement, employees who were on the pay-roll as of 1 October 1979 and did not wish to join APEX could not be compelled to do so. Anyone employed after that date, however, would

be required to join the union within three months of their taking up their post. The agreement also exempted those who objected to trade unionism on religious grounds. In the months following the introduction of the closed shop, APEX representatives in the factory succeeded in persuading 24 of the remaining 26 employees to join the union. Only Messrs Hardy and Bishop still refused to join.

3. In October 1980 the company decided that, because of the sharp fall-off in business, redundancies would be necessary. An announcement was made to this effect and discussions began with the three manual unions in the plant and with APEX. The general attitude of APEX to selection for redundancy was to insist on the principle of 'last in, first out'. In workplaces where, however, the union operated closed shops its policy was to ensure that non-union employees were selected for redundancy before APEX members. Initially, the company argued that the 'last in, first out' principle should be applied, subject to variations in cases of poor performance or misconduct. Eventually, however, management conceded that non-union employees should be selected first.

4. In the case of the chargehands, the firm's initial view was that there would have to be four redundancies, but they were persuaded by APEX to reduce that number to three. Messrs Hardy and Bishop were selected for redundancy, together with an APEX member, Mr Jay, who was the 'last in' of the remaining chargehands. On 9 November all three employees received formal written notice of termination of employment by reason of redundancy, having been told verbally a few days before that they would be dismissed. Prior to their dismissal Messrs Hardy and Bishop had sought a meeting with Mr Owen, the personnel manager, who allegedly said that the company was morally wrong to depart from the 'last in, first out' principle. Nevertheless, the company stood by its decision.

5. Messrs Hardy and Bishop claimed that they had been unfairly selected for redundancy. In evidence to the tribunal, they argued that had the 'last in, first out' principle been applied, Mr Bishop would have ranked seventh and Hardy eleventh for the purpose of redundancy selection in the chargehands' grade. They further argued that they had believed that they could not lawfully be dismissed for refusing to join the union. The company, they said, had not made it clear to them before the redundancies arose that by not joining the union they were putting their jobs at risk. They also claimed that they had not been properly consulted by the company prior to being selected for redundancy.

6. In evidence to the tribunal the company argued that Messrs Hardy and Bishop must have known that if there were redundancies they, as non-unionists, would be at risk. Indeed, the union's recruitment

campaign in the Oldham factory in the months following October 1979 had laid great emphasis on this point. They had had ample opportunity to join the union but, alone among the chargehands, had refused to do so.

Question for discussion

What would an industrial tribunal be likely to decide?

CASE 31: Fox v Laze Around Holidays Ltd

1. Mr Fox was employed as an entertainer at the company's holiday village at Scapa Flow. The village itself has about 200 self-catering caravans and is open from April to October. There are nine permanent staff at the village, including the general manager and three maintenance men, and an additional 12 seasonal staff are normally employed during the summer. Mr Fox was appointed to the job of seasonal entertainer at Scapa Flow on 15 March 1979, and expected that his employment would end on 30 September 1979. However, his letter of appointment stated that the position would be reviewed at the end of the summer with a view to making the job permanent. In fact his employment was continued throughout the winter months as a general odd-job man and barman. He was told that he was now on the permanent staff.

2. In the 1980 season Mr Fox again worked as an entertainer and at the end of the season reverted to the kind of maintenance and barwork he had done before. However, on 10 January 1981 he received a letter of summary dismissal, together with one month's salary in lieu of notice and an *ex gratia* payment of two weeks' pay. Shortly afterwards Mr Fox applied for the job of entertainer at the holiday village for the 1981 season. Initially, he was told that the job would be advertised and that he could apply. In March 1981, however, the company's personnel manager wrote to him to say that they had decided to appoint a leisure supervisor instead of an entertainer and that this would be a lower grade job unsuitable for someone of Mr Fox's experience. Mr Fox then made a complaint of unfair dismissal.

3. In evidence to the tribunal the company argued that the principal reason for the dismissal was redundancy. It had envisaged that during the winter of 1980-81 Mr Fox would be working on the new, enlarged bar facilities in the village for which planning permission was sought. The planning application was, however, refused in January 1981 so that there was no work for Mr Fox to do. The company also argued that it was obliged to reduce the operational costs of running the Scapa Flow holiday village. The staffing budget for 1980-81 had been exceeded and it was this fact, together with the refusal of planning permission, which led the company to dismiss Mr Fox. The company

accepted that it did not consult Mr Fox before dismissing him, but maintained that such consultation would have made no difference.

4. Counsel for Mr Fox argued that pressure to reduce costs, unsupported by any other evidence relating to the company's profitability, does not necessarily justify a dismissal by reason of redundancy. He also argued that, if the company had consulted Mr Fox, it might have appreciated that dismissal was unjustified in the circumstances, or at least the outcome might have been different.

Question for discussion

What would an industrial tribunal be likely to decide?

CASE 32: Parkinson and Others v Oxenford Services Ltd

1. Mr Parkinson and four colleagues were employed by Oxenford Services Ltd at the latter's premises near Abingdon. Some 200 staff are employed at this establishment, and the majority of them belong to ASTMS, which is recognized by the company for the purpose of collective bargaining. During 1981 the company was badly affected by the economic recession. In the third quarter of the year it recorded a trading deficit of £75,000 and in the final quarter a deficit of £150,000. In early November the company asked for volunteers for redundancy and 40 employees volunteered. By the end of the month, however, the prospect of a continuing decline in trade induced the company to put the entire workforce on a four-day week.

2. In January 1982 a new managing director, Mr Edwards, was appointed by the parent company with instructions to restore the financial health of the business. He considered a range of options, including complete closure, and decided to pursue a policy of 'slimming down' and complete reorganization. As a first step, the number of departmental managers was reduced from five to three. The three surviving managers were told to merge the two redundant departments with their own and then decide which employees they wanted to retain and which should be made redundant.

3. Shortly afterwards, on 27 January, there was a meeting between Mr Edwards and the local full-time official of ASTMS, Mr North. Mr Edwards said that there were to be 50 redundancies and that he intended to ask for volunteers. Mr North agreed to volunteers being sought. Nothing was said about the steps which management would take if the appropriate number of volunteers was not forthcoming, but Mr North expected that there would be a further meeting to discuss the matter.

4. In the meantime, the three departmental managers proceeded to

select those employees who were to staff the merged departments. Mr Parkinson and his four colleagues were in the department managed by Mr Frampton. In evidence to the tribunal Mr Frampton said that in drawing up his list of who should stay and who should go, his judgment was influenced mainly by his own subjective assessment of the capabilities of the employees concerned. Length of service *per se* was not taken into account. When Mr Frampton and the other two departmental managers had completed their respective lists, they submitted them to Mr Edwards who, since he did not know any of the employees concerned, automatically approved them.

5. The next communication with ASTMS took place on 12 February, when Mr North was told that there had been insufficient volunteers for redundancy (10 in number) and that, as a result, some 40 compulsory redundancies were about to be announced. Mr North requested a list of the employees who were to be made compulsorily redundant, but this was refused. Management wrote to each of the employees concerned the following day, giving them their statutory notice, four weeks' salary and redundancy payments well in excess of their statutory entitlement. Mr Parkinson and his four colleagues were among the 40 selected for redundancy and claimed that they had been unfairly dismissed.

6. In evidence to the tribunal, counsel for the company argued that the business was in a 'survival situation' and management had to take drastic action. It was reasonable, he said, for management to retain the services of those employees who were regarded as most likely to ensure the long-term viability of the company. Since the employees had known for some time that there were to be redundancies, no further warning was necessary. In any event the extra four weeks' salary which each redundant employee received gave them additional time to look for alternative employment. The company did not consider transferring the employees concerned to lower paid jobs since, on the selection criteria adopted, the same employees would have still been selected for redundancy.

7. Counsel for the employees argued that proper criteria for selection had not been applied and that there had been inadequate consultation with the employees concerned.

Question for discussion

What would an industrial tribunal be likely to decide?

CASE 33: Godfrey v Horton Transport Ltd

1. Mr Godfrey was employed by Horton Transport Ltd at its Hull depot from 1965 until his dismissal in January 1980. At the time of his dismissal he was 54 years of age. He was originally employed as a

fork-lift truck driver and was promoted to chargehand in the stacking department in 1968. In 1971 all chargehands employed by the firm were retitled 'supervisors' and were given certain additional responsibilities. Mr Godfrey was not enthusiastic about this promotion and shortly afterwards, when the firm asked for volunteers for redundancy, he applied for a severance payment. His application was, however, refused.

2. In persuading Mr Godfrey to accept his promotion, the company gave him a verbal assurance that he would not be moved out of his existing department and that he would not be given any additional duties. When, in 1976, the company gave all its supervisors written job descriptions, he objected to one of the paragraphs which stated that he could, at the discretion of management, be required to supervise any other section and perform any appropriate duties. After discussing the matter with the personnel officer he received written confirmation of the fact that in 1971 he had been given a verbal assurance that he would not be moved out of the stacking department or given extra duties.

3. In October 1979 the company decided to reorganize its Hull depot in order to reduce costs. As a result of the reorganization a very small section known as the 'DB' section was left unattached to any other department. Following discussions between the depot manager and trade union representatives, it was decided to amalgamate the 'DB' section with the stacking department. The 'DB' section was physically close to the stacking department and employed two women and one man on day shift. The discussions between management and the trade union did not, however, include Mr Godfrey, who was very unhappy about the proposed change.

4. Over the next few weeks there were prolonged and intensive discussions with Mr Godfrey. Both the personnel officer and his own shop steward tried to persuade him to accept the proposal, even on a three-month trial basis. Mr Godfrey, however, raised several objections. First, he said that he was already at full stretch and could not cope with additional work or responsibility. Second, he did not wish to supervise two women. Third, the additional strain might cause his health to break down again (he had had a nervous breakdown in 1977). Finally, he maintained that the proposal was contrary to the agreement he had had with management since 1971, confirmed in 1976.

5. Management sought to overcome the difficulty by persuading a supervisor in the traffic department — Mr Sloan — to accept responsibility for the 'DB' section. With some reluctance, Mr Sloan agreed to this suggestion. Mr Godfrey, however, approached Mr Sloan and told him that he would feel 'humiliated' if he, Sloan, accepted responsibility

for the 'DB' section. Mr Sloan then withdrew his acceptance. Management considered demoting Mr Godfrey to the shop floor but no vacancies existed and demotion would in any case have been contrary to the custom and practice of the workplace.

6. By the end of December 1979, therefore, management decided that the issue would have to be resolved one way or the other. On 10 January 1980 the personnel officer wrote to Mr Godfrey stating that he would either have to accept supervisory responsibility for the 'DB' section or be dismissed. When Mr Godfrey again refused, management dismissed him with three months' pay in lieu of notice.

7. In support of his claim of unfair dismissal Mr Godfrey argued that he had a contractual right not to have additional duties forced on him and that management had broken his contract of employment. The company argued, in reply, that the reorganization was necessary in the interests of the business and that Mr Godfrey's refusal to accept this very modest increase in his responsibilities was unreasonable in the circumstances.

Question for discussion

What would an industrial tribunal be likely to decide?

CASE 34: Burke v North End Builders Ltd

1. Mr Burke was employed as a labourer by North End Builders Ltd from January 1979 until his resignation in June 1980. It was part of his terms of employment that if he worked overtime he would have time off in lieu. He was a member of the local darts team and on 27 May asked the site foreman if he could have part of the afternoon off to travel with the team to their next match. The foreman refused this request, saying that there was too much work to be done. Mr Burke, however, left the site at 3.00 pm and went off with the darts team.

2. The following day Mr Burke was dismissed by the foreman for leaving the site in defiance of instructions. Mr Burke appealed against this decision, under the company's procedure, to the regional manager. On 5 June the regional manager decided to allow the appeal and commuted the penalty to five days' suspension without pay.

3. This decision left Mr Burke in some financial difficulty. He was at the time living with his 'common law' wife and their six children. His take-home pay, after tax and other deductions, was £46.50 per week. He had no savings on which he could draw, but he had an accrued holiday pay entitlement of £109.50. His loss of five days' pay meant that he had no money to finance the family budget. He

obtained £7 from social security but this sum was insufficient, so he telephoned the company's welfare officer and asked for an advance on his accrued holiday pay. He was told, however, that it was not company policy to pay holiday pay unless the holiday itself was actually taken. He then asked for a loan of £40 to tide him over his week on suspension. The welfare officer replied that the company could not make a loan to that extent.

4. Mr Burke then saw the site personnel officer and told him that he had to have his holiday pay. He said: 'I don't want to leave but if that is the only way I am going to get my holiday pay so that I can make ends meet then I shall have to leave.' On 11 June he collected his holiday pay and left. He then claimed that he had been constructively dismissed.

Question for discussion

What would an industrial tribunal be likely to decide?

CASE 35: Wilson v Broadacres County Council

1. Mr Wilson joined Broadacres County Council in 1965 as an assistant finance officer in the revenues division. By 1973 he had been promoted to senior finance officer, a post he retained until his resignation in 1979. Up to the end of 1978 his superior officer in the revenues division was a Mr Collingham, with whom he got on very well. Towards the end of 1978, however, Mr Collingham was replaced by Mr Smales and thereafter relationships deteriorated. It soon became apparent that Mr Smales was not satisfied with Mr Wilson's general performance and by March 1979 relations between them were strained.

2. About this time Mr Smales, in consultation with the chief revenues officer, decided that the workload in Mr Wilson's section of the revenues division was heavy enough to justify the appointment of an assistant to Mr Wilson. It was decided within the divisional management team that the new assistant should be a Mr Bell. Mr Wilson himself, however, was not consulted about this appointment and first learned of it when Mr Smales brought Mr Bell into the department and introduced him. Mr Wilson protested strongly about the way in which this appointment was being handled. He wrote a memo to the chief revenues officer in which he argued that the normal rule should be followed, ie that the post should be advertised across the entire directorate of finance. This procedure was in fact followed, but, because it was generally known that Mr Bell had been 'earmarked' for the post, there were no other applicants and in mid-March Mr Bell was appointed. Mr Wilson felt that it was grossly inconsiderate for Mr Smales to select his assistant without involving him in any way.

3. Mr Wilson took some leave shortly afterwards and returned on 10 April. On 15 April he was summoned to Mr Smales' office where Mr Smales, in the presence of the directorate personnel officer, Mr Breeze, read out to him a long, critical statement concerning his performance. The statement ended with a formal warning that his performance would be reviewed at the end of three months and a decision made as to whether to proceed to the final warning stage of the council's procedure.

4. In the normal course of events Mr Wilson would have progressed to the next point on his incremental pay scale in April. However, he was told by Mr Smales that he would receive his increase if, and only if, his performance over the next three months improved to a level which would justify this increase. When Mr Wilson took a week's leave in May, Mr Smales said to him, in relation to his coming back, something about 'if there's still a job for you'.

5. When Mr Wilson returned from leave he found that his office had been taken over by Mr Bell. He had in fact been told before he went on leave that he would be moving to a new office, but when he returned he found that this office was still being redecorated and would not be ready for a day or two.

6. On 2 June Mr Wilson wrote a brief note to the directorate personnel office giving one month's notice of termination of employment. Mr Smales then asked Mr Wilson to come and see him. He asked Mr Wilson why he had resigned and was told that he, Wilson, had a better job to go to. Mr Wilson added, 'What you are doing is probably right for the division but I want no part of it.' Mr Smales asked him to change his mind, but he adhered to his resignation. The council then paid him his salary in lieu of notice and he left.

7. Mr Wilson subsequently lodged a complaint of constructive dismissal.

Question for discussion

What would an industrial tribunal be likely to decide?

CASE 36: Lowe v Bullman's Brewery Co Ltd

1. Mr Lowe joined Bullman's Brewery in 1976 as a mobile relief barman, but within a few weeks he was transferred to the Knowsley Arms, a large hotel owned and managed by the company, as a bar steward. He also assisted the hotel manager with the supply of bar snacks. In May 1978 the company decided to appoint a bars manager at the Knowsley Arms and advertised the post within and outside the company. The advertisement stated that: 'The bars manager will be responsible for the efficient running and trading performance of the

hotel bars. Duties will include cleaning the bars area, washing up and control of bar stocks. Other duties will be assigned when the post-holder is not on bar duty. The working week will be 38 hours, although additional hours may be worked at overtime premia. The successful applicant will be experienced in the licensed and catering trades and will have a working knowledge of stock control.'

2. The weekly rate of pay offered in the advertisement was higher than that which Mr Lowe was then receiving as a bar steward. As a result he applied for the job and was successful. In a letter dated 24 May 1978 the company confirmed his appointment as follows: 'Your rate of pay takes into account the fact that you will be required to work a 38 hour week, which will be primarily related to the preparation and operation of the bars and will include weekends, evenings and bank holidays. Your actual hours will be arranged in advance by the hotel manager or his assistant. When you are not required for bar duty, the hotel manager will assign you to other catering duties in the hotel.' Mr Lowe accepted these terms and for the next two years he worked as bars manager at the Knowsley Arms.

3. As bars manager he had a responsible job which he enjoyed. He was responsible for the stocks of drink and food sold over the bars and the general operation of the bars. By its very nature the job was largely free of immediate supervision and Mr Lowe enjoyed a fair amount of day-to-day autonomy. The hotel manager did not, however, find him a particularly easy employee to deal with and occasionally there was friction between them.

4. In May 1980 the company decided that the hotel needed a complete facelift and that its facilities should be changed. Between May 1980 and April 1981 the ground and first floors of the hotel were rebuilt so that in place of three drinking bars and a small dining room there were three major eating areas with relatively small 'inset' bars. As a result of this change, Mr Lowe had considerably less work to do as bars manager. The hotel's business moved heavily towards the food and catering side and most of the drink trade was henceforth supplied with meals. Mr Lowe spent only about half his time managing the bars; the other half was spent 'helping out' on the catering side.

5. Mr Lowe was not at all pleased with this development, especially as he had not been consulted about it in advance. He resented the amount of catering work he was now expected to do, particularly as it involved work of a type he found demeaning to his status as a manager. This involved manual work in the hotel kitchen, including washing some cooking utensils and lifting heavy packs of food. On several occasions he refused to do duties in the kitchen to which he had been assigned by the hotel manager, but the latter wanted to avoid a personal confrontation and took no disciplinary action. Eventually, in January 1982 Mr

Lowe resigned from his employment with the company and claimed that he had been constructively dismissed.

6. In evidence to the tribunal Mr Lowe argued that in 1978 he had been appointed primarily as a bars manager with an obligation to fill in time on other duties, including catering. By the middle of 1981, however, he felt he was being employed more as a catering assistant or even a kitchen hand than as a bars manager. He argued, therefore, that the company was trying to make him work under a different contract of employment from the one under which he had been originally employed. As he had not agreed to the changes, he said that he was entitled to regard himself as dismissed.

7. The company argued that under the contract agreed with Mr Lowe in May 1978 it was entitled to ask him to perform duties in addition to those of bars manager. After April 1981 the changes which, for good business reasons, they had made to the Knowsley Arms had reduced the amount of work available to him as bars manager. They were contractually entitled to call upon him to do other available work on the catering side and in doing so had committed no breach of his contract.

Question for discussion

What would an industrial tribunal be likely to decide?

CASE 37: Robson v Grimditch Mutual Insurance Ltd

1. Mrs Robson was employed from 1957 until 1980 by a Mr James, who ran a small insurance broking business. During this period of 23 years she was employed under a contract which described her as 'assistant manager and accounts supervisor'. Her immediate subordinate was a Mrs Green, who was accounts clerk. Mrs Robson spent most of her time as personal assistant and secretary to Mr James and delegated the bulk of the work on accounts to Mrs Green.

2. At the beginning of 1980 Mr James sold his business to Grimditch Mutual Insurance and retired. Grimditch offered to continue Mrs Robson's employment on terms 'no less favourable in any respect' than those on which she was employed by Mr James. Mrs Robson accepted this offer.

3. Between the time at which the sale of Mr James's business was agreed and the assumption of formal operational control by Grimditch, Mr James, without consulting the new owners of the business, gave all his employees a 10 per cent increase in pay. When Grimditch took over and discovered what had happened, the management decided that Mrs Robson was overpaid and asked her to accept a reduction in her

earnings. Mrs Robson took legal advice and refused. The company then let the matter drop.

4. The next cause of friction between Mrs Robson and her new employers arose shortly afterwards, in February 1980, when Mrs Green was made redundant and dismissed. The company asked Mrs Robson if she would increase her hours from 25 to 40 per week to absorb Mrs Green's former duties. Mrs Robson again consulted her solicitor and refused. The company did not pursue the matter.

5. Another incident occurred towards the end of March. Under Mr James, Mrs Robson had normally 'balanced the books' at the end of every working day or, on odd occasions, Mr James had done it himself. One day Mrs Robson found Mr Richards, the company secretary of Grimditch, 'balancing up' and was told that henceforth this would be the normal procedure. Mrs Robson took this as a personal insult and accused Mr Richards of trying to 'elbow her out'. After this incident, the managing director of Grimditch issued her with a written warning concerning her future conduct.

6. In April the company issued Mrs Robson with a new contract of employment. Her job title was changed to 'secretary and accounts clerk', first, because Mrs Green's redundancy meant that there was no longer a subordinate accounts clerk and, second, because Grimditch saw her duties as secretarial rather than managerial in character. Mrs Robson refused to accept the new contract. Early in May she was handed a new contract in which her original job title was fully restored.

7. Early in May the company introduced new and more up-to-date accountancy procedures. These procedures were explained to Mrs Robson and she was told that, as a result, she would be spending more of her time on the accounts and less on secretarial and managerial duties. She was given a new job specification which reflected this change in the balance of her work. Mrs. Robson, however, felt that she was being given more work than one person could reasonably handle. On 7 May her solicitors wrote to the company saying that Mrs Robson would not accept the new job specification.

8. On 13 May Mrs Robson was interviewed by the managing director and the chief accountant. They told her that they had consulted ACAS and that if she did not accept her new job description she would be dismissed. On 14 May Mrs Robson's solicitors wrote to the company saying that she would not attend work again and would complain to an industrial tribunal alleging constructive dismissal.

9. In evidence to the tribunal, counsel for the company argued that none of the company's actions, taken either in isolation or together, amounted to a repudiatory breach of contract. The company had sought to persuade Mrs Robson to accept reasonable changes in the

nature and balance of her responsibilities in accordance with the needs of the business. Only when it became clear that she had no intention of accepting any change, no matter how reasonable, in her contract or job description, did her employer give her an ultimatum. Counsel for Mrs Robson argued that these events, taken together, amounted to a breach of an implied term in the contract that the company would not, without reasonable and proper cause, conduct itself in a manner calculated or likely to destroy or seriously damage the relationship of confidence and trust between the parties.

Question for discussion

What would an industrial tribunal be likely to decide?

CASE 38: Hameed v Calderdale Foods Ltd

1. Mr Hameed worked at the company's Halifax plant, which produces pickled onions, from 1969 to 1980. In 1978 he was appointed supervisor of the despatch department. A large proportion of the workforce at the plant are Pakistani and it has long been the company's practice to appoint an appropriate number of Pakistanis to supervisory positions.

2. Early in 1980 Mr Hameed returned to Pakistan for a month to visit relatives and in his absence a Mr Khan was appointed to his post on a temporary basis. The works manager, Mr Gregory, was very impressed with Mr Khan's performance as despatch supervisor and found him more cooperative than Mr Hameed. Shortly after Mr Hameed's return to work on 1 March the foreman in the production department left the firm and Mr Gregory had to find a successor. He decided that he would confirm Mr Khan as despatch supervisor and transfer Mr Hameed to the post of production foreman.

3. Mr Gregory told Mr Hameed that his new post was a promotion, carrying a higher salary than he had received as despatch supervisor. Mr. Hameed accepted that this was a promotion. He refused the offer, however, on the grounds that the onion fumes would cause him great personal discomfort and would lead to the recurrence of a sinus ailment from which he had suffered in the past. However, he refused to consult either his own doctor on this matter or the company's doctor.

4. On 14 March Mr Khan assumed the post of despatch supervisor and there was a major row on the shop floor between Mr Gregory and Mr Khan on the one hand and Mr Hameed on the other. Mr Gregory admits that he was very annoyed at Mr Hameed's continued refusal to undergo a medical examination and used intemperate language. Mr Hameed subsequently sent a long list of grievances to the company which was never answered. On 21 March, after a further sharp exchange with Mr Gregory, Mr Hameed resigned and claimed that he had been

constructively dismissed.

5. In evidence to the tribunal it was argued on behalf of Mr Hameed that, since the employer had clearly broken his contract of employment, the dismissal was constructive and, therefore, unfair. It was argued on behalf of the company that the loss of the production foreman had made a reorganization of some kind inevitable and that management had done all that any reasonable employer could be expected to do. If the dismissal was constructive it was, in the firm's submission, still fair.

Question for discussion

What would an industrial tribunal be likely to decide?

6. Race and Sex Discrimination

For employment purposes it is illegal to discriminate against anyone by reason of their race, colour, nationality, ethnic origins, sex or marital status. Complaints to an industrial tribunal may arise when an employee fails to get a job for which he or she had applied, or fails to obtain promotion, or is dismissed. The claimant must be able to show that the reason for his treatment was discrimination by reason of his race, sex, colour, etc. Once a *prima facie* case has been established, the evidential burden of proof shifts to the employer. If, however, the employer can show that the reason for the treatment complained of was non-discriminatory, the claim must fail.

The law distinguishes between *direct* and *indirect* discrimination. Direct discrimination occurs when an employer treats someone less favourably on the grounds of race, sex, marital status, etc than he treats or would treat someone else. Indirect discrimination occurs when an employer applies a condition or requirement which appears to affect everyone equally, but, in reality, disadvantages blacks, women, married people, etc. It is not necessary that an employer should have a discriminatory intention in order to be guilty of unlawful discrimination. It is enough if the effect of his actions is that someone is treated less favourably on the prohibited ground.

To establish a *prima facie* case in a claim of direct discrimination, the claimant must show that he or she suffered unfavourable treatment in comparison with the treatment which someone of a different race, colour, sex or marital status had or would have received. In many cases, however, the central question is one of *degree*. To what extent have racial or sexual grounds led to the less favourable treatment complained of? The American approach has been based on the 'but for' test, ie if the answer to the question is that the claimant would not have suffered less favourable treatment *but for* the fact that he or she was black, married, etc the claim will be upheld. In Britain, by contrast, the courts have adopted a more stringent test. In *Seide* v *Gillette Industries Ltd* (*1980*), the EAT ruled that for a claim to succeed the claimant must show that the *activating cause* of the employer's behaviour was racial. In other words, it is not enough for the claimant to show that unlawful discrimination merely 'played a part' in the employer's decision. He must show that it was the activating cause of, or at least a substantial reason for, the decision.

In cases of alleged indirect discrimination the claimant must show that the employer applied a condition or requirement with which he or she could not comply, that it was to his or her detriment, and that only a comparatively small proportion of those in the same racial, sexual or marital category could comply with it. Once the claimant has surmounted these hurdles, the onus rests on the employer to show that the condition or requirement was justifiable in the circumstances. The existing body of case law suggests that this burden is by no means easy to discharge. In *Steel* v *The Post Office (1978)*, the EAT held that a condition or requirement which would otherwise be discriminatory cannot be 'justifiable' under the law unless it is directly related to the needs, not merely the convenience, of the business. Even then a tribunal must weigh the business necessity of the requirement against its discriminatory effect, the implication being that in some circumstances the latter may outweigh the former. It is, however, the facts of the individual complaint which matter. This means that a discriminatory rule might be justifiable even if other reasonable employers apply different rules or the same employer applies different rules in other locations.

The cases included in this section have been chosen to illustrate some of the points of substance which have emerged from recent tribunal decisions.

CASE 39: Patel v Brudderfax Clothing Co Ltd

1. Mr Patel, who is a Pakistani, has been employed by Brudderfax Clothing Co Ltd as a press-packer since January 1978. Until May 1979 he was employed on a two-shift basis and for much of this time worked alongside a Mr Thwaites on the same shift. During June 1978 Mr Thwaites made a remark to him which was anti-Pakistani in character. He made similar remarks to Mr Patel on various occasions in July, August and September 1978. On the last of these occasions, 17 September, Mr Thwaites' remarks made Mr Patel very angry and, as he was also feeling unwell, he left the factory and went home without permission.

2. His absence resulted in an investigation of the incident by the shift manager, Mr Jackson, who decided to issue written warnings to both Mr Thwaites and Mr Patel. Mr Thwaites was warned that his provocative behaviour must cease, or he would receive a further warning. Mr Patel was warned that he must not leave work without permission and that, if he did so, he would receive a second warning. He was further advised to refer any further provocation from Mr Thwaites to the shift manager

and was asked not to 'over-react' if such provocation arose.

3. Shortly afterwards, in October 1978, Mr Patel was transferred from the shift on which Mr Thwaites worked to the other shift, on which he worked alongside a Mr Richards. On 24 April 1979, the shift manager saw Mr Patel and told him that Mr Richards had requested a transfer to another section. Mr Richards wanted to move because he could no longer tolerate the climate of hostility which existed between Mr Patel and certain other employees in the press-packing section. He added that he found some of Mr Patel's personal habits unacceptable and irritating.

4. Mr Jackson then discussed the matter with Mr Patel and other employees and reported to the production manager, Mr Huckerby, that there was 'considerable friction' between Mr Patel and other press-packers. He recommended that Mr Patel should be removed from the double-day shift section and go on to single-shift working. This would mean a slight loss of pay for Mr Patel, but it would ensure that he was brought under the wing of more experienced supervision. As a result, Mr Huckerby decided that Mr Richards' application would be refused and Mr Patel transferred to single-shift working.

5. Mr Patel then registered a formal grievance about the decision and claimed that both Mr Richards and Mr Huckerby were prejudiced against him. Following this complaint he was seen by the personnel officer, Mr Wigham, on 8 May. The latter emphasized that the object of the transfer was to avoid further trouble. After this meeting, Mr Patel's transfer took place. He took the grievance, however, to the next stage of procedure and, in company with his shop steward, saw Mr Gunning, the production director. After hearing Mr Patel's allegation of prejudice, Mr Gunning decided that it was right to transfer him to put him under better supervision.

6. Mr Patel continued to pursue his grievance through procedure to the final stage, when he saw Mr Rothwell, the managing director, on 17 May. Mr Rothwell investigated the matter and found that the employees in press-packing held strong and opposing views of who was the aggrieved party. Both Mr Thwaites and Mr Richards quoted occasions on which Mr Patel had said and done things which had led to tension and argument. They claimed that Mr Patel was tending to imagine, quite wrongly, that things were being said about him behind his back and that people were against him when they were not. Mr Rothwell came to the view that it was practically impossible to decide who was to blame. He concluded, however, that since Mr Patel objected so strongly to going on the single shift, he should be reinstated on the double-day shift as long as all parties agreed not to indulge in provocative behaviour.

7. Mr Patel accepted Mr Rothwell's suggestion and agreed to discontinue his grievance. He resumed work on the double-day shift on 24 May.

However, on 14 June he informed Mr Rothwell that he was still being provoked by racialist remarks and that, since he had now exhausted the internal grievance procedure, he had no alternative but to complain of racial discrimination to an industrial tribunal.

8. At the tribunal hearing, counsel for the company argued that the decision to transfer Mr Patel was taken not on racial grounds but as a sensible move to resolve a difficult human relations problem. If the allegation that Mr Thwaites was racially prejudiced against Mr Patel and was provoking him had been substantiated, the company would have taken disciplinary action against him. Mr Richards could not be said to be racially prejudiced since he was prepared to be transferred to another section or even risk his job rather than have anything more to do with Mr Patel. The problem, the company argued, was one of personalities rather than one of race.

9. Counsel for Mr Patel argued that the decision to transfer him rather than Mr Richards was discriminatory. He further argued that it was no defence to say that it was done with good intent or in the interests of good management. One of the reasons why Mr Patel was transferred, with loss of earnings, was that he was a Pakistani and had been subject to ill-treatment by a fellow employee for racial reasons. The company was therefore guilty of discriminating against him on racial grounds.

Question for discussion

What would an industrial tribunal be likely to decide?

CASE 40: Shaheed v Metropolitan Borough of Cleckleydale

1. Mr Shaheed, who was born in the Punjab and is 42 years of age, has been employed by Cleckleydale Council since 1968 as a community relations officer. Since 1973 he has been a senior community relations officer, the post above him being that of principal community relations officer. Since 1976 the superior post has come vacant on three occasions and on each occasion Mr Shaheed applied for the post. On none of these occasions has he been successful. He has also applied for six other posts within the council at principal officer level, but again without success.

2. His work with the council involves regular contact with community organizations, especially those representing Punjabis, as well as liaison with other departments of the authority and, on occasion, elected members of the council. The community relations unit in which he works comprises a principal community relations officer, a senior community relations officer, three community relations officers and one secretary/administrative assistant. The community relations unit

is part of the council's corporate planning department, which is ultimately responsible to the chief executive.

3. The council does not operate a formal appraisal procedure for its employees, but on several occasions since 1973 the head of corporate planning, Mr Gregson, has told Mr Shaheed that he is suitable for promotion within the council and that he has done an excellent job. In 1977 Mr Gregson recommended him for promotion to the post of principal community relations officer when it came vacant but, although he was shortlisted, a Mr Spicer was appointed. Mr Spicer had previously occupied a senior post with an inner London borough. In 1979 Mr Spicer left the authority for a more senior post in Liverpool and Mr Shaheed again applied for the vacancy. Again he was shortlisted, but came second to a Mr Poynton, who previously held a more junior appointment with a neighbouring authority.

4. In October 1981 Mr Poynton suffered a heart attack and decided to take premature retirement. The post was advertised internally and externally and attracted 27 applications. Nine of the applicants were shortlisted, including Mr Shaheed and a Mr Crawford, who worked in the research section of the corporate planning department as a community analyst and statistician. He had five years' service with Cleckleydale Council and his post was graded SO2 compared with Mr Shaheed's grade of PO1(1), which was the next grade up.

5. The interviews for the post were held on 9 and 10 December 1981. The interviewing board consisted of the head of corporate planning (Mr Gregson), the principal manpower officer (Mr Fox), the deputy chief executive (Mr Wilson), the chairman of the corporate planning sub-committee (Councillor Hyde) and his deputy chairman (Councillor Brearley). Mr Crawford was already personally known to Mr Fox and the two elected members, whereas Mr Shaheed was known well only by Mr Gregson. After the interviews the board placed Mr Crawford first and Mr Shaheed third, and Mr Crawford was duly appointed. Mr Shaheed was very angry at the result and complained to an industrial tribunal that he had been discriminated against on racial grounds.

6. In evidence to the tribunal the council argued that Mr Crawford had been chosen in preference to Mr Shaheed for two reasons: first, his academic qualifications were much superior to Mr Shaheed's and, second, his performance at the interview was also better. They denied any prejudice against Mr Shaheed on racial or any other grounds. Counsel for Mr Shaheed argued that academic qualifications were less important in this post than a proven ability to communicate with and represent the interests of ethnic minorities. Although Mr Crawford was familiar with the statistical aspects of the immigrant community he had had little personal contact with them and spoke no foreign language. The council responded to this argument by saying that they felt Mr

Crawford, at 32, had more potential for development than Mr Shaheed and that his linguistic deficiencies could be remedied by courses, etc. The board members firmly denied that their choice had been motivated by racial factors.

7. When asked why Mr Shaheed had not been successful in his applications for six other posts within the council since 1976, the authority's representatives replied that in three cases he had been shortlisted but the selection panel had decided that he was 'not suitable' without offering any further comment.

Question for discussion

What would an industrial tribunal be likely to decide?

CASE 41: Winston v Cohen's Turf Accountants Ltd

1. Mr Cohen has an off-course betting shop situated in the Chapeltown area of Leeds. He employs seven people, four of whom are women. Although, when vacancies occur, he normally prefers to recruit employees with previous work experience, occasionally he advertises for school-leavers. In either case, he applies to the main job centre in Leeds, which sends him a list of potential employees for interview. For the past two years, however, Mr Cohen his stipulated that he does not wish to employ school-leavers or youths who live in Chapeltown itself. His reason for so doing is that, from past experience, local youths tend to attract their own unemployed friends from the same area, who tend to hang around the shop in gangs and deter potential customers from entering the premises. The Chapeltown area of Leeds contains a large number of West Indian residents.

2. Mr Winston, who was born of West Indian parents and has lived in Chapeltown all his life, left school in July 1979 and 'signed on' at the job centre. On 15 August he saw the manager, Mr Grundy, who indicated that Mr Cohen had a vacancy for a school-leaver. Mr Grundy telephoned Mr Cohen and told him that he had an applicant for the vacancy who might be suitable. At some point in the conversation Mr Cohen asked where the applicant lived and, when he was told the address in Chapeltown, immediately said he was not interested. He added: 'These lads who live within walking distance of my shop attract half the unemployed in the neighbourhood. They hang around and make a lot of noise. It puts my customers off.' Mr Grundy then said that, to avoid future misunderstanding, he would add the words 'no locals' to any job vacancy card which he prepared for Mr Cohen. This was then agreed.

3. Mr Winston was sitting in Mr Grundy's office while this telephone conversation took place and said he was very upset that he would not even be given an interview with Mr Cohen. He said he would not have

minded had he been interviewed for the job and then rejected, but he felt that to be automatically excluded simply because he lived in Chapteltown was extremely unfair. He told Mr Grundy that he was going to lodge a complaint of discrimination on racial grounds.

4. In evidence to the tribunal, counsel for Mr Winston said that the great majority of the city's West Indian population lived in Chapeltown, where they outnumbered the white population. An embargo on the employment of Chapeltown residents would therefore exclude the majority of the West Indian population. Counsel for Mr Cohen denied any intention to discriminate against Mr Winston or any other applicant on the grounds of colour or race. He maintained that a white applicant from Chapeltown would have received exactly the same treatment. He also pointed out that he himself was Jewish and that he was fundamentally opposed to any form of racial or religious discrimination. His embargo on local applicants was simply intended to protect his own business.

Question for discussion

What would an industrial tribunal be likely to decide?

CASE 42: O'Neal v Delgardia

1. The applicant, Mrs O'Neal, is a married woman with three young children and lives in Harpenden. Her husband is employed by the local council as a refuse collection supervisor. From 1974 to 1980 she worked four nights a week as a barmaid at the Four Feathers, a large steakhouse in Harpenden. While she was at work either her husband or her sister took care of the children. She was a satisfactory employee, but by 1980 the long hours of work were beginning to affect her health. Frequently, she did not get home until well past midnight. In August 1980 she, therefore, resigned and began to look for a job with fewer hours.

2. On 20 August she saw an advertisement in the window of a restaurant in Harpenden called 'Mario's Pizzateria' which read 'Waitresses wanted. Day or evening work. Apply within.' She immediately went in and saw the restaurant manager, Mr Gambretti. She told him that he could obtain a reference from the Four Feathers and they agreed that she should start work at the restaurant on Friday 24 August at 6.30 pm and that, subject to satisfactory performance, she would be engaged to work on Friday and Saturday evenings from 6.30 pm to 10.30 pm.

3. Mrs O'Neal worked on the evening of 24 August as arranged and about 9.00 pm Mr Gambretti told her that she was entirely satisfactory. He further told her that he had taken up her references, which were also very good, and intimated that she would be employed on a

permanent basis. Later the same evening, however, the owner of the restaurant, Mr Delgardia, arrived and saw Mrs O'Neal. He asked her if she had any children and she told him she had three, aged four, six and seven respectively. Mr Delgardia then saw Mr Gambretti and reminded him that his policy was not to employ women with young children. He told Mr Gambretti that Mrs O'Neal would have to go.

4. Mr Gambretti then saw Mrs O'Neal, apologized and said it was impossible for him to give her any further employment because it was Mr Delgardia's policy not to employ women with dependent children. The reason, he said, was that in Mr Delgardia's view women with small children were 'totally unreliable' as employees in terms of their time-keeping and attendance. Mrs O'Neal replied that her attendance record in her previous employment had been excellent, as her reference must have made clear, and that in her view Mr Delgardia's rule was ridiculous discrimination. She subsequently complained that she had been discriminated against contrary to S6(1) of the Sex Discrimination Act 1975, such discrimination being on the grounds either that she was a woman (S1) or that she was married (S3).

5. S1 of the Act provides that : 'A person discriminates against a woman in any circumstances relevant for the purposes of any provisions of this Act if, on the grounds of her sex, he treats her less favourably than he treats or would treat a man.' S3 provides that an employer discriminates against a married person if the employer 'applies to that married person a requirement or condition which he applies or would apply equally to an unmarried person but which:

(a) Is such that the proportion of married persons who can comply with it is considerably smaller than the proportion of unmarried persons of the same sex who can comply with it.
(b) He cannot show to be justifiable irrespective of the marital status of the person to whom it is applied.
(c) Is to that person's detriment because he or she cannot comply with it.'

6. In evidence to the tribunal Mr Delgardia argued that he could not be guilty of direct discrimination under S1 because his policy was not to employ anyone, whether male or female, who had small children. He further argued that, while fewer married than unmarried women would satisfy his requirement that employees should not have small children, this requirement was 'justifiable' under S3 on the grounds that it was necessary for his small business. He was running a small restaurant where, if one waitress did not turn up for work, he would be missing one-third of his staff and would be unable to find a replacement at short notice. Counsel for Mrs O'Neal argued that there was no evidence

that Mr Delgardia's policy was directed at anyone other than women with dependent children. No man with dependent children had ever applied for a job at his restaurant.

Questions for discussion

What would an industrial tribunal be likely to decide?

7. Notes for Tutors: Analysis of Cases

The following notes cover each of the cases contained in this book and are intended primarily for the guidance of tutors. They represent the present writer's personal opinions and should be regarded simply as an aid to stimulating group discussion. None of the solutions suggested in the course of these notes is put forward as *the* solution and it is freely conceded that alternative analyses of at least some of the case histories in this book could be more convincing than those put forward below. Nevertheless, if tutors regard them solely as aids to discussion they will no doubt serve their purpose. The commentaries on the unfair dismissal and discrimination cases reflect the state of tribunal case law at the time of writing.

CASE 1: Great Northern Stores Ltd

1. The origins of the industrial relations problems facing the company lie partly in the shortcomings of management's approach to employee relations, partly in the company's organization structure and partly in its declining market position.

  (a) The board of directors obviously take a 'unitary' view of the organization, in which no legitimate conflicts of interest are perceived or admitted. The interests of management and workers are believed to be identical, and thus any conflict which does arise must be the result of faulty communication. The communications network within the company, however, contains several weaknesses. As a result senior management is not aware of what is going on at store level. No steps have been taken to ensure that store management is properly equipped to deal with employee relations problems for the simple reason that the existence of *collective* problems is not admitted.

  (b) The organization structure compounds these philosophical weaknesses by impeding the lines of communication between head office and stores. On the commercial side the company is over-centralized: too many decisions which could be taken at store level are taken in head office, with adverse effects on the morale and motivation of store management. Conversely, too little professional advice and expertise is available to store management in the field of staff relations. As a result of these structural problems the company is not able to respond quickly to internal crises or external challenges.

(c) Some of the raw material of conflict has been provided by the company's increasing economic difficulties. Management's response has concentrated on cost-cutting which has, in turn, put greater pressure on staff at store level. Remuneration increases have not, however, compensated staff for higher productivity.

2. The first option is to maintain the current strategy, ie to encourage the growth of the staff association and refuse to recognize any of the trade unions with membership in the company. The main advantage of this strategy is that it seems to accord with the wishes of roughly half the staff. The main disadvantage is that the two (potentially) most powerful bargaining groups within the company — the warehousemen and the computer staff — have already been organized by the TGWU and ASTMS respectively. Both groups are in a position to press their claims for recognition, by direct action if necessary, and do not seem willing to accept the staff association. The stage is set for a prolonged and bitter conflict for membership between the staff association on the one hand and the three trade unions (ASTMS, USDAW and the TGWU) on the other, which will have adverse effects on the climate of employee relations within the company.

An alternative strategy, therefore, would be to declare a moratorium on recognition claims (including that of the staff association) and invite ACAS to conduct another secret ballot. Whatever the result, the trade unions are more likely to regard it as an authentic expression of staff opinion than the company's own ballot. Another ballot will not in itself resolve anything, but it should provide a common point of departure. It now seems unlikely that the company will be able to avoid recognizing more than one trade union, whatever the fate of the staff association. The overriding need at the moment is for management to reduce tension and gain a breathing space for itself. Conciliation by ACAS offers the only practicable method of achieving this objective.

3. The board must use this breathing space to review its traditional approach to employee relations. Its future strategy must, realistically, be based on an acceptance of the principle of collective bargaining. This outcome was not inevitable, but the way in which the company has handled the dispute has made it so. The board will have to think hard about how the company is to organize itself for bargaining purposes. What, for example, should the bargaining *units* be? At what *level* within the organization is a given issue of substance going to be

bargained about? What *procedures* will be needed?

The board will also have to consider changing its organization structure so that store management is given more responsibility on the commercial side and is given more professional support in the employee relations field. The appointment of area personnel managers and the provision of systematic training in employee relations for store managers, staff manageresses and supervisors are two obvious steps which should be taken in the near future. Another useful innovation would be the establishment of a staff council in each store to act as a 'clearing house' for all grievances at store level. In short, the board will have to change its traditional style of management and encourage genuine two-way communication with store management and sales staff. Such innovations can, of course, only be realized over a long period, but the board must learn the lessons of the current dispute and begin the process of change as soon as possible.

CASE 2: The Huddersfield Abstinence Building Society

1. This case illustrates some of the difficulties which a trade union seeking recognition from a hostile employer may encounter. The purpose of section II of the Employment Protection Act 1975 was to put additional pressure − in the shape of ACAS − on those employers who, despite a clear demand for collective bargaining on the part of a substantial proportion of their workforce, still refused to concede recognition. What became known as the statutory recognition procedure was repealed by the 1980 Employment Act, having greatly disappointed those trade unionists who had initially expected to achieve, with the help of the law, significant penetration into companies and industries where the level of union membership was low. In practice the section II procedure was found to be too cumbersome and time-consuming to provide much practical help to trade unions. This case illustrates how *timing* can strongly influence the outcome of recognition disputes.

2. The society quickly realized that if it could stall the union's claim long enough, the momentum behind the latter's recruitment drive would soon begin to decline. Management rightly assumed that many employees are reluctant to join a trade union which has little or no prospect of obtaining recognition and bargaining rights. If such employees are going to join a union (or staff association), they will expect their interests to be represented in bargaining with management. In the present case BIFU had to win a quick victory or none at all. By not only playing for time but using this time in order to set up a counter-organization, management first halted the growth of BIFU membership and then sent it into reverse. Faced with these tactics, the union's only response was to involve ACAS. Yet even if ACAS should decide to undertake a formal inquiry into BIFU's claim for recognition, by the

time this gets under way it is likely that the level of BIFU membership will have declined still further. In short, it seems increasingly improbable that BIFU will obtain any kind of recognition from the society.

3. The main problem which the society now faces is that of ensuring that the staff association is seen to work effectively in the interests of the employees. The secret ballot suggests that while support for BIFU is declining, APEX has now established a significant foothold in the organization. Although the 'actual' plus the 'potential' level of support for APEX (as revealed by the ballot) is still far too low to justify the concession of even limited or joint bargaining rights, if the staff association is seen to be nothing more than a 'sweetheart' organization it is possible that a significant number of employees will join APEX. The society would then have a second recognition dispute on its hands.

4. It follows that the society must now accept that its traditional relationship with its own employees has been permanently changed by the present dispute. The staff association will represent the employees and will, presumably, bargain collectively on their behalf on all major terms and conditions of employment. To the extent that it carries out these functions effectively, the association will assume many of the characteristics of a trade union and, by the same token, the society will have to come to terms with the fact that the old days of unilateral decision-making by management have gone for good. How far the directors of the society appreciate the significance of this change remains to be seen.

CASE 3: Redwood Garden Tools Ltd

1. Only in a very superficial sense is this an inter-union dispute. The first task for the conciliator must be to try and produce some agreement on why relations have reached their present impasse. The contradictions and ambiguities in management's approach to bargaining arrangements at Bilston must obviously take a large share of the blame. Remedial action could and should have been taken at a much earlier stage. It is equally clear that the AUEW has little influence over the strikers and that any formula which is not acceptable to the latter is unlikely to produce a lasting solution.

2. Having assessed the significance of interpersonal conflict within section C, the next task is to explore the possibilities for 'normalizing' relations without transferring either setters or chargehands to another department. If this is impossible then ASTMS will demand a substantial *quid pro quo* in return for their agreement — if indeed they can be persuaded to agree at all — to the transfer of their members out of section C. Such a *quid pro quo* would almost certainly involve a full and formal recognition by both the company and the AUEW of the

right of ASTMS to represent chargehands. It would also involve an accelerated transition to full staff status for the chargehands.

3. The fundamental problem facing all three parties, however, is that of balancing short-term gains against long-term objectives. If the company's main aim is to secure a resumption of work it can simply accept the current AUEW formula and gamble that ASTMS will be unable to take effective counter-measures. This will probably get the setters back to work at the cost of destroying what little remains of management's authority within section C and also of poisoning future relations with ASTMS. For the AUEW the problem is one of defending its customary representational role in respect of chargehands against what is obviously a long-term threat from ASTMS. The difficulty facing the AUEW is that the chargehands themselves evidently see ASTMS as a more appropriate bargaining agent. The difficulty facing ASTMS is that the chargehands are not as coherent or powerful a workgroup as the setters. Both unions must be anxious not to 'lose' the argument at Bilston in case this is used as a precedent elsewhere.

CASE 4: Bullman's Brewery Co Ltd

1. This is a company which has been allowed to run gently downhill for a considerable period of time. Indeed, had the business not been protected against the full rigours of competition by the tied house system it would almost certainly have been swallowed up years ago. As such it faces problems common to many semi-moribund businesses and most of the proposed strategic plan will have to be implemented if it is to survive.

2. The new management, however, faces a dilemma. On the one hand, it would be a relatively easy task to cut costs and eliminate the strongest, most militant section of the workforce 'at a stroke' by closing the Toxteth brewery and making all the employees redundant. On the other hand, such a course of action would almost certainly provoke a vigorous response from the workforce, attracting unwelcome publicity which might in turn adversely affect sales in Liverpool. It might also help to 'radicalize' the rest of the workforce by confirming the (no doubt) widespread suspicion that Grand Central's management is about to introduce a much more rigorous cost-conscious philosophy which relegates human considerations to the bottom of the list of management objectives.

3. Management would, therefore, be well-advised to make a genuine effort to communicate with the workforce at Toxteth, including their militant shop steward, and explain to them the realities of the company's declining position. It should then invite suggestions as to how the Toxteth brewery might become more efficient and thereby

remain in production. If no constructive proposals are forthcoming, a decision to close the plant would not be seen in quite the same unfavourable light as it would otherwise be. It is more probable, however, that Page and his union will suggest some course of action whereby the brewery could be kept open for at least a trial period. If this involves an acceptance on their part of reduced manning levels and more flexible working practices, management must obviously give it serious consideration.

4. One of the main points which this case underlines is that if management seriously intends to regenerate a declining business, it will need the full cooperation and commitment of the workforce and its representatives. This will be difficult to achieve if the workforce believes that management has already decided to close down all or at least a substantial part of the business and is going through consultation exercise for purely cosmetic purposes. It follows in the present case that management must encourage the TGWU to put forward counter-proposals and then give serious and genuine consideration to such proposals, even if most are ultimately rejected. The other two organizations involved, NALHM and the staff association, will certainly expect their suggestions to be carefully considered. Whatever happens to the Toxteth brewery, management will need the full cooperation of representatives and officials of all three employee organizations in implementing the recovery plan. It is important, therefore, that the closure of Toxteth (if that is ultimately decided upon) should not damage management's relations with any of them.

CASE 5: Cleckleydale Metropolitan Council

1. This case illustrates the limitations of trade union power in circumstances where new technology is being introduced and employment is contracting. It has often been argued that trade unions exercise a veto over technological change and that the main reason why Britain has been slow to adapt new processes lies in the short-sightedness of the trade union movement. The present case, however, is much closer to reality in suggesting that, where union resistance is encountered, it is usually related to the way in which new technology is introduced. If the terms and conditions are right, there is no union veto on new technology. What is 'right' will obviously depend on the circumstances, but the present case suggests that management can sometimes achieve its objectives without making unduly expensive concessions to the trade unions.

2. The bargaining power which a union can bring to bear to ensure that its members share in the benefits of technological change partly depends on the skills which are required by the new technology. In the present case, the skills needed to operate word processing equipment

187

can be acquired relatively quickly by employees accustomed to routine typing work. The weakness of the trade union's position was clearly exposed in 1978 when, regardless of its formal opposition, clerical staff in the directorate of technical services accepted the new technology on the terms and conditions offered by management. From then on management was in a good position to introduce the new technology with or without union consent throughout the rest of the organization. Indeed, it is possible that, had it not been for the council's need to reduce manpower costs during 1979-80 and its corresponding need for union cooperation, management would have gone ahead and extended the new technology unilaterally.

3. Yet despite the opportunity presented by the current situation for NALGO to improve the terms and conditions under which new technology is to be applied, it is evident that the balance of bargaining power still lies in management's favour. Although the union has secured a pledge that there will be no compulsory redundancies, and has thereby protected individual employees, it is very doubtful if it will succeed in preserving the existing level of employment. Experience casts doubt on the fashionable belief that new technology will create as many jobs as it displaces. In the present case, it is difficult to see how the council, facing the need to make further substantial reductions in its revenue spending, will be in a position to create new jobs even if it promises to do so. The revenue savings derived from the introduction of word processing equipment will almost certainly be applied to mitigating the effect of further spending cuts on service levels. While this may well help the council to preserve some jobs which would otherwise be lost, it will by no means lead to the creation of new jobs.

4. Moreover, the creation of new jobs is essentially a *trade union* objective. The primary concern of most *employees*, by contrast, is to ensure that their *own* employment is protected and that their terms and conditions are, if possible, improved. If management and union fail to agree on the terms on which the new technology is to be extended, management may well be successful in convincing employees that the most effective method of protecting their own employment is to accept the new equipment. In these circumstances the role of the trade union is likely to be both limited and defensive.

CASE 6: Burntisland Heating Co Ltd

1. This exercise, like the Aire Valley Yarns case, illustrates several important problems which can arise when some form of change is being introduced into an organization. Here we have several factors which are likely to generate conflict. First, management seems to have little awareness of the labour relations 'culture' of the factory. Too much

emphasis is being placed on the formal enunciation of managerial rights and too little on the need to explain and 'sell' the proposed changes to the workforce. The presentation of the management case was extremely inept, particularly since the craft stewards, the main force of opposition to the proposals, were not present at the initial meeting called by the managing director.

2. The realism of the changes themselves seems questionable. Where management is seeking to introduce more efficient working practices in a plant where, as a result of past managerial weakness, a strong, informal structure of customary practices has been allowed to develop, one obvious danger is that the strength of the resistance on the shop floor will be underestimated and over-ambitious targets adopted. Is it realistic in these circumstances, for example, to insist on *total* flexibility? Is it also realistic to insist that all earnings will henceforth be geared to productivity, regardless of other, more traditional criteria in wage bargaining such as the cost of living and comparability? Is it sensible to assume that such radical changes will be willingly accepted by the workforce when so little effort has been made by management to explain why they are necessary and no attempt made to discuss objections from the shop floor?

3. Rigidity on one side of the bargaining table frequently encourages the other side to adopt the same attitude. Bearing in mind that, despite all the mistakes made by management, the craft stewards entered into serious negotiations on the flexibility provisions and, taking into account the lack of an agreed yardstick for measuring productivity gains, management's outright rejection of the stewards' claim on 2 May seems short-sighted and provocative. If management had been sufficiently sensitive to the problems which the craft stewards were experiencing in selling the agreement to their members, they would have given the stewards something to 'take back'. In the event, the rigidity of management has simply resulted in a change for the worse in the craft union leadership in the plant, making the prospects of reaching agreement even more remote.

4. It makes little sense for management to insist dogmatically on the observance of a given principle, only to retreat from that principle in practice. For example, management has refused to concede the craft unions' demand for separate bargaining facilities, yet it has implicitly accepted the demand by conducting separate negotiations with the craft unions over the efficiency agreement. Management, furthermore, quite deliberately closed down the plant and announced that it would not negotiate 'under duress', as though it was prepared to withstand a long strike. The decision, taken barely two weeks later, to re-open negotiations on the craft unions' terms without any offer by them to resume work must therefore leave management with a major credibility problem.

5. Any employer who embarks on a course of imposing changes in terms and conditions of employment, including working practices, on a reluctant workforce must ultimately be prepared to withstand a prolonged stoppage, with the possibility of complete closure, if he is to retain credibility. In some circumstances where, despite adequate opportunity for negotiation, workforce representatives still refuse to accept reasonable and necessary changes, an employer may well be justified in taking this extreme course of action. In the present case, however, the breakdown of negotiations and the consequent stoppage could almost certainly have been avoided if management had approached their admittedly difficult task with a greater sense of realism and a greater willingness to communicate with ordinary workers and their representatives. When the present dispute is resolved, one suspects that it will be on terms far less favourable to management than would have been the case if a different approach had been adopted.

CASE 7: Aire Valley Yarns Ltd

1. This exercise illustrates some of the problems which commonly arise from the introduction of changes by management in customary rules, payment systems and working practices. In this case the new management made the error of putting together a major package of changes in terms and conditions without seeking either to identify potential sources of opposition on the shop floor or involve, even informally, any workers' representatives in the process. However beneficial such changes may be to the workers in the longer term, management seems to have overlooked the simple fact that there are always strong vested interests in any *status quo*. The maintenance fitters are the main stumbling block to the SSA and obviously see it as a threat to their traditional status in the factory. The only way in which management will overcome their resistance is by persuading them that the new job-evaluated wage structure fully recognizes their significance within the factory.

2. The exercise also underlines the limitations of formal, written statements of managerial rights and functions. There is little doubt that management's actions are sanctioned by both the SSA and the works rules agreement, although the timing and sequence of what management did leaves them vulnerable to the trade union claim that they were not acting in good faith. Managerial rights, whether written or unwritten, can only be exercised in the final analysis with the consent of those employees who are affected by them. Managerial discretion is, therefore, in practice limited both by the need to observe custom and practice and to give adequate prior warning of any changes. Another point is that, when management sets out to get rid of 'inefficient' working practices, it will usually be seeking to change habits and rules which

have in the past been tolerated or even encouraged by management itself. In workplaces where the level of labour productivity is low, much of the responsibility frequently lies with shortcomings in management rather than in the outdated trade union rule book of popular mythology.

3. The *timing* and *presentation* of change by management are obviously crucial. In the present case not only has too little effort been put into explaining the necessity for change but the redundancy situation has been allowed to become associated, at least in the minds of the fitters, with the new agreement. Management would have been better advised to leave the issue of the fitters and the job evaluation scheme in abeyance until the threat of further redundancies had been removed. By failing in the first instance to allay the employees' fears that the factory might be completely closed, and then using the closure threat as a bargaining weapon, management has probably played into the hands of those workers in the Leeds plant whose sole aim is to maximize their own redundancy payments rather than cooperate in an attempt to ensure the long-term survival of the company.

4. At the meeting of the JNC convened for 29 March, the management side must be aware, first, of the need to re-establish some kind of dialogue with the AUEW and particularly with the representative of the fitters. The recent arrest of AUEW pickets will simply have inflamed feelings and made the prospects for an agreement more remote. The second problem for management is that the trade union side may well have difficulty in maintaining a united front. There is an obvious temptation for management to try and split the TGWU from the AUEW, which, given the present circumstances, would not be hard to do. An open breach between the two unions, however, may simply serve to polarize opinion even further and reinforce the determination of the AUEW membership to fight the issue through to the end. The plant cannot be restored to normal working without the support of the AUEW and it is on this objective that management should concentrate.

CASE 8: CCS Construction Ltd: dispute at the Duckhaven power station construction site

1. (a) First, the strike organizers are liable under S16 of the Employment Act 1980 for secondary picketing. Up to 1980, statute law laid down that it was lawful to picket in any location except outside a person's private residence provided that the picketing was intended to achieve certain purposes and took place in contemplation or furtherance of a trade dispute. The purposes of picketing, in law, have since 1906 encompassed 'peacefully obtaining or communicating information, or peacefully persuading any person to work or abstain from working'. As long as

a person was attending a picket line for these purposes and in connection with a lawful trade dispute, he would not be liable for any criminal offence. The 1980 Act, however, restricts picketing to the worker's own place of work. Only a trade union official (including a shop steward) is now permitted to picket a workplace in which he is not employed. Consequently, in the present case the SJSFPT flying pickets have clearly acted outside the law.

(b) The organizers are also liable to be sued by other construction firms whose sites have been closed down by the SJSFPT pickets. The action against them could be regarded as a 'sympathetic' strike and, as such, unprotected from liability in tort by S17 of the 1980 Act. The organizers of the action could therefore be sued for inducing breaches of commercial contracts. The various suppliers whose vehicles have been denied access to the Duckhaven site and other sites in the area would also have a similar claim against the strike organizers.

(c) The employers would have little difficulty in obtaining an interlocutory injunction from a court. The Employment Protection Act of 1975 provides that where an employer applies for an interlocutory injunction (ie an order requiring the defendants to discontinue their industrial action pending a full trial in a court of law) and the union official offers the defence that he was acting within the 'golden formula', the court must 'have regard to' the likelihood of the defence succeeding at the full trial. Even in cases where a golden formula defence would be likely to succeed, the judges retain a residual discretion to grant injunctions. In the present case, however, a golden formula defence would obviously fail and the employers would get their injunction. If the strike organizers ignored it, they would be liable to imprisonment.

2. The provisions of the Employment Bill 1982 would affect the workers' liability in two ways. First, the employers would be able to sue the SJSFPT as a corporate body rather than the strike organizers as individuals. In the present case, the liability of the union for the actions of its officials would be clear-cut since, far from repudiating them, the union's national executive committee has given the local strikers its full backing. CCS could therefore sue the SJSFPT in respect of the illegal secondary picketing carried out by its members, while the other firms affected by the picketing could sue the union for inducing breaches of commercial contracts. Second, the Bill proposes to change the definition of a 'trade dispute' to exclude disputes between 'workers and workers'. If the employer can show that in reality the dispute is between the SJSFPT and the other unions represented on the Duckhaven site, any protection offered by the 'golden formula' will be removed.

3. Whether the union is sued as a corporate body or the strike organizers are sued as individuals, it seems reasonably certain that the employers will win their case, should it come to full trial. Assuming, however, that an interlocutory injunction is obtained and the industrial action is immediately discontinued, the case is unlikely to be tried. This would obviously serve the interests of both the employer and the trade union. It is extremely unlikely that CCS would wish to re-engage the SJSFPT members who have been dismissed and although the task of recruiting new labour may delay the completion of the contract even more, this may be a price that management is prepared to pay. Nevertheless, the CCS management should not overlook the circumstances in which the dispute arose. There may be weaknesses in Blocket's management of the site which need to be investigated and rectified. In short, now that CCS has clearly shown all the trade unions with which it deals that it will not tolerate unlawful industrial action, it would be appropriate for management to take a more positive initiative in the interests of improving labour relations at the Duckhaven site.

CASE 9: Grebworth Metropolitan Council

1. (a) A court would almost certainly issue an interlocutory injunction in this case since there is *prima facie* evidence of unlawful picketing. Although there is no guidance in either the 1980 Act or the code of picketing on precisely what is an employee's 'place of work', it is extremely doubtful that the Sandybanks site would fall within any reasonable definition as far as DLO employees are concerned. McKinnon himself, however, as a trade union 'official' would be immune from suits for damages under this heading.

   (b) On balance a court would probably decide that this was not a lawful trade dispute within the meaning of S29 of TULRA. The council has in the past pursued a policy of excluding private contractors from housing work and found it to be impracticable. It has given the trade unions a guarantee that there will be no compulsory redundancies in the DLO as a result of the current policy of using private contractors. It has also undertaken to ensure that such contractors pay fair and reasonable wages. In the case of Muttley Brothers, an investigation failed to substantiate the allegation that the firm was in breach of this undertaking. In the circumstances, therefore, a court would ask itself whether the industrial action could be considered to be 'reasonably capable' of furthering the declared objectives of the DLO employees and would probably conclude that it could not. The statements attributed to Ross regarding the apparent desire of the TGWU to damage Muttley's business and the fact that no other union with members in the DLO is officially supporting the action would also be weighed in the balance.

(c) Muttley's argument that the repeal of S13 (3) of TULRA has left union officials open to liability in tort would also be accepted in the circumstances of this case. In *Hadmor Productions Ltd and Others* v *Hamilton* (*1982*), the House of Lords overturned a Court of Appeal decision which suggested that such a liability now exists. But in the *Hadmor* case it was held that a lawful trade dispute existed and S13 (1) of TULRA clearly protects union officials 'acting in contemplation or furtherance of a trade dispute' from actions in tort. In the present case a lawful trade dispute probably does not exist and the S13 immunities, therefore, do not apply.

2. It is certainly desirable that when an employer is faced with collective action which is being taken for malicious or punitive motives, or for some reason falling outside the legal definition of a trade dispute, he should be able to invoke a quick and effective remedy in order to prevent further damage to his business. The interlocutory injunction provides such a remedy. The main weakness in the 1980 Act, however, is the complexity of the provisions surrounding secondary action where a lawful trade dispute clearly exists. The government's most recent proposals for further legislation should remove these ambiguities.

3. The 1982 Employment Bill, when enacted, will affect the defendants' liability in several ways. First, it will make it possible for employers to sue trade unions for the actions of their 'officials'. In the present case, the TGWU has given unambiguous support to the actions of McKinnon and his fellow members and would therefore be liable for damages. Second, it is proposed to remove legal immunity from industrial action which is taken to force an employer to employ trade union members only. Third, the definition of a 'trade dispute' will be changed to narrow the scope of trade union immunities. It is proposed that trade disputes should relate *wholly* or *mainly* to the matters listed in S29 of TULRA rather than be simply 'connected with' those matters. This would ensure that industrial action taken for political or personal motives would not be protected from suits. It is also proposed to restrict trade disputes to disputes between an employer and his own employees. This would remove immunity from any action which was directed at any employer, such as Muttley Brothers in the present case, whose own employees were not in dispute with him. In short, the proposed legislation will open up new possibilities for employers who find themselves being damaged by industrial action and are prepared to sue the trade union responsible. However, the extent to which employers will, in practice, exploit these possibilities remains problematic.

CASE 10: Sally Brown

1. Management has made several glaring errors in its handling of this case. First, it was extremely unwise to promote her to the position of sales supervisor when her own manager opposed the idea and she herself was reluctant to accept promotion. This should have warned Morrison that something was wrong. Second, the odd pattern of behaviour which she subsequently adopted may well have been the result of stress arising from her role as supervisor. If either Blaine or Morrison had given some thought to the problem they might have requested a more detailed diagnosis from Dr Hargreaves. In the event Dr Hargreaves' recommendations were unhelpful in so far as they resulted in Miss Brown's resumption of work without in any way adding to management's understanding of her problem. Third, the store manager, Blaine, virtually abdicated his responsibility for ensuring that she was given a fair chance to come to terms with her supervisor's role and that she was given encouragement and support by management. Faced with some understandable irritation on the part of the staff, he seems to have made no attempt to persuade the staff to show more understanding and consideration. At no time did he have a one-to-one discussion with Miss Brown about her difficulties. If he found the task too difficult or embarrassing, Miss Crawley should have done it instead. In the event the only discussion which Miss Crawley seems to have had with Miss Brown was for the purpose of persuading her to accept a transfer. Had she been encouraged to discuss the matter on a private and personal basis, it is possible that a much more sensible and humane solution could have been worked out.

2. Difficult and sensitive problems of this kind should, wherever possible, be resolved without recourse to formal grievance procedures in which third parties may be involved. If, however, formal procedures are invoked, they should at least be followed and the principles of natural justice observed. This means that the employee concerned must be told in some detail the nature of the allegations against him or her and be given a full opportunity to state his or her case. The way in which the meeting of 4 June was handled by management fell far short of the minimum standard of fairness.

3. The first decision Morrison must make is whether there is a future for Miss Brown in the Sheffield store. Both management and staff want her out and it is possible that their attitudes have now hardened to a point where, if she were to return to work as a supervisor, further difficulties would soon arise. Another confrontation might be very damaging to her mental state as well as to staff morale and could result in the problem being brought to the attention of head office. One possibility is that she could be offered continued employment at Sheffield as an ordinary sales assistant on a personally protected salary.

By relieving her of the stress inherent in a supervisory role, this might induce a return to her normal 'pre-promotion' pattern of behaviour. Morrison should certainly discuss the idea with Miss Brown and the store management and consider the proposal in the light of their reaction. If all parties are in agreement, the problem may well be resolved.

It may be, however, that either Miss Brown or the store management or the staff would find the idea unacceptable. If this proves to be the case, Morrison will have to choose between transferring her to another store or offering her an early retirement package on the grounds of ill-health. Transferring her to another store as a supervisor would simply be 'exporting' the problem and would in itself resolve nothing. The only sensible option, therefore, would be to offer her early retirement on attractive terms.

CASE 11: George Harney

1. In this case management, in the shape of Mr Wickham, has demonstrated a very uncertain grasp of procedures and their uses. It is a well-established point of case law that the dismissal of an employee for a breach of the rules governing the handling of money is within the range of responses that a reasonable employer might make. The employer does not have to prove that the breach took place, nor does he have to prove that the employee had criminal intent. He merely has to show that he genuinely believed that an offence has been committed and that he has evidence to support this belief. Generally, if an employer, especially in the public service, argues that his confidence in the integrity and honesty of an employee has 'irretrievably broken down', dismissal is the only appropriate decision. In the present case, however, Mr Wickham has asserted, on the one hand, that his confidence has irretrievably broken down and yet, on the other, he has offered the employee another position at only one grade below that of his present post. He has also conceded that Harney had no intention of defrauding the council. The appeals panel is, therefore, entitled to ask itself whether a reasonable employer would lose all confidence in the integrity of the employee, and whether Wickham's actions were consistent with his own claim to have lost such confidence.

2. The panel is likely to decide that dismissal is an excessive penalty and it will be right to do so. Harney should be given a clear warning that a future breach of financial regulations may result in his dismissal but he should be reinstated as assistant manager at the sports centre. The panel should also point out to Mr Wickham the shortcomings in his approach to the matter. Finally, it is to be hoped that as a result of this case the council will find a more sensible method of dealing with temporary shortages of staff, and one which does not involve the employment of wives or relatives.

CASE 12: Jack Ellis

1. However improbable the combination of extenuating circumstances quoted in this case might appear to be at first glance, the deputy chief executive should not have reacted in the way that he did. Management is under a clear obligation in cases of this kind to undertake some investigation of all the relevant circumstances and the failure to check the validity of Mr Ellis's claims cannot be overlooked. Even if it is clear that an employee has committed an act of dishonesty, a reasonable employer should not refuse to consider whether the circumstances were such that the employee's judgment might have been seriously impaired. While management should always aim to preserve the credibility of its procedures, this does not mean that penalties must be rigidly and mechanically enforced regardless of the circumstances. In the present case, management should also have given weight to the employee's good service record with the council. A degree of sensitivity is not necessarily incompatible with the overall aim of procedural consistency. Accepting that it is sometimes difficult to decide where flexibility ends and inconsistency begins, this was clearly a case in which insufficient weight was given to the employee's plea in mitigation.

2. The decision to dismiss should therefore be set aside and the employee either reinstated or offered an alternative job in some other appropriate section of the council. However, despite the trivial amount of money involved and the extenuating circumstances which influenced the employee, the appeals panel should not overlook the fact that the employee committed a criminal act. He should, therefore, be formally warned that any repetition in the future will result in his dismissal.

CASE 13: Stanley Booth

1. The following points could be made on Booth's behalf by his union:

   (a) The way in which management conducted the meetings of 21 September and 2 October strongly suggests that they were determined to dismiss Booth at any price and the sudden appearance of the drink issue was, to say the least, very convenient for management. Prior to the meeting on 21 September, Booth had been given no indication that the case against him had shifted from one of alleged theft to one of alleged drinking. It was unfair to confront him with this charge without giving him time to prepare a defence.

   (b) It is contrary to the principles of natural justice that an accused man should be prevented from knowing in detail what is being said against him. Booth repeatedly asked for the source of the information against him and was refused. It is primarily for this reason that the trade union is supporting his appeal. The convenor

197

made relatively little comment at the meeting on 21 September because the only evidence which management put forward was hearsay. He anticipated that further inquiries would be made and validated statements by witnesses produced for all to see. However, it would seem that at the meeting on 2 October management furnished no fresh evidence, or at least none that could be validated in detail.

(c) Certain questions need to be asked about management's inquiry. Why, for example, have the names of the key witnesses been withheld? How many employees either refused to give information or gave evidence which contradicted the allegation? Why was the trade union not told that the inquiry was being conducted? The convenor knew that an inquiry of some kind was taking place but assumed that it was connected with the theft allegations, not with drunkenness.

(d) While the trade union has always supported disciplinary action against employees who have been shown to have broken the 'no drinking' rule, the rule itself states that employees '*may* be dismissed'. This implies that each case will be judged on its merits and, indeed, in recent years there have been at least two cases in which employees discovered drinking have not been dismissed. One was that of Tom Broughton, the senior night shift steward, who showed that he was under great personal stress at the time of his offence. The other was that of Donald Hamilton, who was an admitted alcoholic. In both cases the penalty was a final warning, not dismissal.

(e) There is some evidence that management were determined to 'make an example' of someone. If drinking was so well-established and regular in this department, why had the appropriate supervisor failed to notice it and take action long ago? This tends to reinforce the union's view that management turned a blind eye to the drinking in this section until it became expedient to notice it.

(f) There are no warnings on Mr Boyd's record card about drinking or indeed any other offence. It is beyond question that he is a good employee and a capable, if occasionally militant, union representative. The evidence seems to point to a deliberate decision by management to get rid of a shop steward whom they regard as a thorn in their side.

2. The following points could be made on behalf of management's case:

(a) The accusation of drinking on the premises did not seem to surprise Booth when it was first made on 21 September, and at no time did he actually deny it. Nor did the convenor, Ackroyd, deny it on his behalf. The present appeal is, in fact, the first indication of any support for Booth's case on the part of his trade union.

(b) The general rule that drinking is a dismissable offence is well known to all employees and has been consistently applied in recent years. There have only been two exceptions. The first was that of the senior night shift shop steward, Tom Broughton, who was found drinking during working hours, but had his penalty commuted to a final warning on appeal. In this case management accepted that Mr Broughton was suffering from great personal stress at the time and that this was a mitigating factor. The second case was that of Donald Hamilton who was suspended on suspicion of being intoxicated but who was a self-confessed alcoholic. He received a strong final warning. Both had already received two informal warnings about drinking.

(c) It is a well-established feature of dismissal case law that management does not have to prove that an offence was committed. Management need only have reasonable grounds for believing that an offence has been committed. In this case the grounds were reasonable and the allegation has not so far been refuted by Booth.

(d) Booth's status as a shop steward is relevant only in so far as the company has a right to expect, if anything, a higher standard of behaviour from accredited union representatives than from the rest of the workforce.

3. This case illustrates how easily management's motives can be misinterpreted when disciplinary procedures are not followed. While it is a well-established point of law that management does not have to prove that an offence was committed, only that it has reasonable grounds for believing such, this does not remove or limit the obligation which rests on every employer to observe the principles of natural justice. In the present case it would have been more in accordance with those principles if Booth had been given more detailed information about the accusation that he had been drinking. It would also have been more sensible, bearing in mind Booth's status as a shop steward, if management had postponed the final interview until either his union convenor or the district officer could be present.

4. Procedural inconsistency can also weaken management's position. In the present case, there were two previous occasions when there was a strong suspicion that Booth had been drinking, yet no formal warning was given to him. On both occasions members of management were in a position to take action on the basis of their personal knowledge of the incident. When they finally did decide to take action, however, it was on the basis of second-hand information from other employees and in circumstances which left them vulnerable to the charge of victimization.

5. If a procedure states that the penalty for drinking (or any other offence) *may* be dismissal, then there is a strong implication that management will consider each case on its merits and take into account any extenuating circumstances. In the present case the way in which management acted left a distinct impression in the minds of the union representatives, rightly or wrongly, that, irrespective of any weaknesses in the evidence against Booth, management was determined to get rid of him. In the circumstances the trade union's case is likely to carry the most conviction.

CASE 14: Fred McLaughlin

1. One fundamental point about customary rules and practices of the kind represented in this case is that to be effective they require the adherence of management as well as of workers and shop stewards. In the present case management, in the shape of York, has acquiesced in the operation of the seniority rule and, in so doing, has tacitly conceded that the power of management to determine manning standards unilaterally is, in practice, limited by the need to secure union agreement. If York was genuinely concerned about the operation of the seniority role, he should have approached Cox and explained why he wanted to modify the role and make it less rigid. There is no guarantee that Cox would have responded positively to this approach, but there would at least have been a possibility of a constructive dialogue on the problem. The way in which York has handled the matter has ensured a negative response from the union side.

2. The union is now concerned not only about the breach of the seniority rule, but also about the overt threat of job losses on the day shift. If management's main objective is to reduce manning costs, one possible way forward would be to seek to persuade the trade union that there was scope to introduce lower manning levels. This would obviously mean detailed discussions on individual workloads with Cox, but, assuming that management was able to provide some convincing evidence, the union would then be faced with the choice of either accepting the need for a suspension of the seniority rule and allowing Williams to 'double up' as joiner/painter or resisting the proposal to a point where, if cost pressures increase, management may be compelled to resort to compulsory redundancy. In such circumstances the need for a day shift might itself be seriously questioned. If the threatened strike goes ahead and business is disrupted, this could well precipitate a fundamental reappraisal of day-only working. Considerable emphasis must, therefore, be placed on this point in discussions with the union without giving the impression that management is merely sabre rattling. In those circumstances the union's enthusiasm for strike action might diminish, especially if York makes conciliatory noises about the failure to consult the union about the McLaughlin problem.

CASE 15: Air Valley Yarns Ltd: dismissal of Jim Gill

1. The principal reason for Gill's dismissal was his incompetence as a night shift supervisor, not that he was allegedly intoxicated on one particular shift. Disciplinary problems which arise from incompetence or incapability are often more complex and difficult to resolve than those which are caused by some form of misconduct. Indeed, it is arguable that an employee who is not performing up to standard has not really committed a disciplinary offence in the strict sense of the term at all. This is particularly so in cases where the employee's alleged incompetence is at least partly the result of a failure on the part of the employer to train him properly for his job, or provide him with appropriate assistance, or set him realistic and achievable targets. While an employee who is not performing satisfactorily must be given a clear warning to this effect, cases of alleged incapability need not be approached with quite the same procedural punctilio as ordinary cases of misconduct.

2. In the present case there is some evidence to suggest that Gill was not adequately trained for the post of night shift foreman, bearing in mind that his previous job with the company had been on the day shift. Despite the promise of 'every assistance' in helping him to achieve the desired standard, no training or development materialized. This was a particularly significant omission in so far as the 'man management' problems on the night shift were well known to all concerned. If, however, the provision of appropriate training and development had failed to secure the desired improvement, management would have been entirely justified in considering dismissal or demotion. There is a case for saying that, where an employee has been promoted to his level of incompetence, the first remedy to be considered should be demotion. In the present case this option does not appear to have been considered.

3. One potential spin-off from imposing legal penalties for unfair dismissal is that it should, in theory, encourage managements to take more care over recruitment and promotion decisions. The extent to which this has happened in practice, however, remains problematic.

CASE 16: Aire Valley Yarns Ltd: dismissal of Harold McIntyre

1. There is little point in management issuing warnings which it either cannot or will not enforce. Management's first mistake was to issue a warning ('any future breach by you of any works rule,' etc) which was far too wide and open-ended. In the event, the warning was not enforced by management, despite several opportunities to do so.

2. Foremen and supervisors must know the details of procedure agreements and must, in particular, be aware of what they can and cannot do

in the field of discipline and dismissal. In the present case it is obvious that Cooper exceeded his powers.

3. It is essential that management should conduct an investigation into the circumstances of the case. Had either Scott or Beattie done so, they would have realized that Cooper's behaviour contributed to the situation.

CASE 17: Higgins v Dimwick & Co Ltd

An industrial tribunal would be likely to find in favour of the employee, Mr Higgins. Although there was no doubt that Higgins was involved in a fight with another employee, the procedure adopted by the employers meant that he did not have the opportunity of knowing in sufficient detail what was being said against him as to who or what had provoked the fight. In the case of *Bentley Engineering Co Ltd* v *Mistry* (*1978*), the EAT held that: 'Natural justice . . . requires not merely that a man shall have a chance to state his own case in detail; he must know sufficiently what is being said against him so that he can properly put forward his own case. In order to satisfy the requirements of natural justice it may be, according to the facts, that what is said against the employee can be communicated to him in a written statement, or it may be sufficient if he hears what the other protagonist is saying, or it may be adequate in an appropriate case for matters which have been said by others to be put orally in sufficient detail. There is no particular form of procedure which has to be followed in any and every case. It is all a question of degree.'

CASE 18: Carter v Longsite Engineering Co Ltd

An industrial tribunal would be likely to find in favour of the employee, Mr Carter. In the similar case of *Bowie* v *British Leyland Ltd* (*1976*), a tribunal held that in circumstances where two employees are guilty of aggressive or violent behaviour, even if the evidence shows that one is more to blame than the other, it may well be unfair to dismiss one and not the other. In cases of this kind either both employees should be dismissed or neither dismissed. If, of course, the evidence clearly shows that one employee was the aggressor and the other merely the innocent victim, or alternatively that one deliberately provoked the other to use violence, then differential penalties may well be justified. The present case, however, does not fall into this category.

CASE 19: McCabe v Soft-Tread Tyres Ltd

An industrial tribunal would be likely to find in favour of the employer, Soft-Tread Tyres Ltd. In the similar case of *Carr* v *Alexander Russell*

Ltd (*1976*), a tribunal laid down the following guidelines which have not hitherto been challenged or significantly modified by a higher court: 'In cases involving dismissal on grounds of alleged or proven criminal acts, the test is whether the employers acted reasonably in the light of the circumstances known to them or which they ought reasonably to have known at the time the decision to dismiss is taken. It is up to the employers to make such inquiries as they properly can, but it is not their function to adopt the role of a court of law and attempt to establish the guilt or innocence of the person concerned. For establishing that employers acted reasonably, the standard of proof is the balance of probabilities.'

There is no obligation on an employer to wait until a case is brought to trial and decided before he himself can take a decision to dismiss. As long as he believes, on the balance of probabilities, that a criminal act has been committed and that the employee concerned has committed it, he may dismiss that employee. If the charges against the employee are subsequently disproved and the latter is declared innocent, this will not make the dismissal unfair. The employer is simply obliged to show that he acted reasonably in the circumstances known to him at the time.

Moreover, in cases where the police have already charged an employee with an offence, the employer is *not* obliged to give that employee an opportunity to state his case. The purpose of such statements is to augment the information at the employer's disposal and enable him to make a fair and reasonable decision. If an employee has already pleaded not guilty to a charge, he is unlikely to say anything which will add significantly to the employer's knowledge. This does not apply, however, to cases where the police have been called in, but have decided not to prefer charges. In such circumstances the employee should be given an opportunity to offer an explanation and put his case.

CASE 20: Mills v Great Northern Stores Ltd

An industrial tribunal would be likely to uphold the employee's claim. The purpose of an investigation by the employer in which the employee is allowed to state his or her case is to add to the employer's knowledge. If delays elapse such that an employee cannot reasonably remember the alleged misconduct and cannot, therefore, offer an explanation, the employer is hardly likely to add anything to his knowledge. Interviews should also take place when the employee is in a reasonable state of health — *Tesco Holdings Ltd* v *Hill (1977)*. It is also well-established that management should remind an employee of his or her procedural rights, including that of representation, without waiting to be asked. It is possible that in certain circumstances the employer's need to preserve security and prevent theft will be difficult to reconcile with the employee's entitlement to fair and reasonable treatment. In *Marley Homecare Ltd* v *Dutton (1981)*, the EAT suggested that, if test purchases show a suspected breach of till procedure, the employee concerned should be immediately suspended while further investigations take place. The hearing can take place as soon as the investigation has been completed and the employee's memory is still relatively fresh.

CASE 21 : Hayman v Broadacres County Council

An industrial tribunal would be likely to find in favour of the employer, Broadacres County Council. In recent years there have been several cases in which employees in public service have been dismissed for misconduct outside the workplace on the grounds that such misconduct has undermined the employer's confidence in their integrity as public servants. Tribunals are particularly sympathetic to the employer's viewpoint in cases where the employee concerned has direct contact with members of the public, including children (*Nottinghamshire County Council* v *Bowly* [*1978*]).

In cases of this kind there is a range of responses which a reasonable employer can take. The council could have found Mr Hayman a post elsewhere, but the fact that it did not choose to do so did not make the dismissal unfair. A reasonable employer could either dismiss or not dismiss. If the employer decides to dismiss the employee in circumstances of this kind, it must be demonstrated that the matter was approached 'fairly and properly', that a fair procedure was followed and that the employer's judgment was not clouded by prejudice. If the employer satisfies a tribunal on these points it is likely to find in his favour, notwithstanding that another employer might have decided not to dismiss.

CASE 22: Crawford v Broadacres County Council

An industrial tribunal would be likely to find in favour of the employer, Broadacres County Council. A distinction must be drawn between persistent absenteeism, whether supported by medical certificates or not, and absence from work because of serious and genuine ill-health. The former can reasonably be seen as a normal disciplinary matter, necessitating warnings and an opportunity for improvement. The latter is essentially a matter of capability rather than conduct and should be approached in a different way (see Case 23).

The guidelines appropriate to the present case have been laid down by the Employment Appeals Tribunal in *International Sports Co Ltd* v *Thomson* (*1980*): 'Where an employee has an unacceptable level of intermittent absences due to minor ailments, what is required, first, is that there should be a fair review by the employer of the attendance record of the employee and the reasons for it; and, second, appropriate warnings after the employee has been given an opportunity to make representations. If there is then no adequate improvement in the attendance record, in most cases the employer will be justified in treating the persistent absences as a sufficient reason for dismissal.'

The EAT has also made it clear that an employer is under no obligation to investigate the authenticity or genuineness of medical certificates before reaching a decision. Nor, in cases of persistent absenteeism resulting from minor ailments, is the employer obliged to carry out a formal *medical* investigation. In the present case, the employer consulted its medical adviser and followed his guidance. That is all that a reasonable employer need do. The council investigated the case and issued warnings; it did not simply rely on the mechanistic working of the '10 per cent rule'. This is a case in which a reasonable employer is entitled to say 'enough is enough'.

CASE 23: Crooke v Grubthorpe Metropolitan District Council

An industrial tribunal would be likely to find in favour of the employee, Mr Crooke. The EAT has laid down clear guidelines in *East Lindsey District Council* v *Daubney* (*1977*) which are applicable in the present case: 'Unless there are wholly exceptional circumstances, before an employee is dismissed on the grounds of ill-health it is necessary that he be consulted and the matter be discussed with him and that steps should be taken by the employer to discover the true medical position. Discussion and consultation will often bring to light facts of which the employers were unaware and which will throw new light on the problem. Or the employee may wish to seek medical advice on his own account which, brought to the notice of the employer's medical advisers, will cause them to change their opinion. If the employee is not consulted and given an opportunity to state his case, an injustice may be done.'

In the present case it is the total lack of consultation which makes the dismissal unfair. Although the medical evidence on which the decision was taken was barely adequate, the council would have been entitled to act on it if it had consulted Mr Crooke. Had it done so there was a possibility that he might have been persuaded to accept early retirement and no claim would have arisen. In some cases, the medical evidence may be so clear-cut that consultation will serve no useful purpose, but this was not such a case.

CASE 24: Lees v Great Northern Stores Ltd

An industrial tribunal would be likely to dismiss the employee's claim. Although another employer might have taken a more lenient view, it was well within the range of reasonable responses for an employer to decide to dismiss an employee who was an alcoholic and had concealed his addiction in order to obtain employment. In the circumstances no useful purpose would have been served by wider or more prolonged consultation. In *Walton* v *TAC Construction Materials Ltd* (*1981*) the EAT said: 'Whilst it is good practice that an employer look at the circumstances of the particular case, where it is shown on the balance of probabilities that such an investigation would have produced exactly the same result, the dismissal does not become unfair because of the failure to investigate.'

An *obiter dictum* in this case should also be noted, namely that there is not normally any duty on the employee to volunteer information about himself other than in response to a direct question.

CASE 25: Brook v ABC Wholesalers Ltd

An industrial tribunal would be likely to find in favour of the employer, ABC Wholesalers Ltd. This is another case in which a reasonable employer could make one of several responses. While it was open to the employer to give Mr Brook a longer trial period in his new post, the decision to offer him an alternative post and, ultimately, to dismiss him was not an unreasonable response in the circumstances. There is no suggestion that Mr Brook was not doing his best, but the company had given him all reasonable assistance and the performance of his depot was considerably worse than the company average. There must come a time when a reasonable employer has to 'cut its losses' and replace an incapable employee. As the EAT observed in *Cook* v *Thomas Linnell & Sons* (*1977*): 'Although employers must act reasonably in dismissing an unsatisfactory employee, it is important that the operation of unfair dismissal legislation should not unreasonably impede employers in the efficient management of their business.'

The fact that Mr Brook did not have a formal opportunity to present his side of the case is unlikely to affect the outcome. The critical questions to be answered in cases of alleged incapability are: first, 'Was the employee aware of the fact that his performance was considered unsatisfactory and was under review?'; second, 'Did the employee know what was expected of him in terms of performance standards?'; and, third, 'Was the employee aware that he would be dismissed if his performance did not improve?' In the present case there can be little doubt that Mr Brook was well aware of all three points. He had adequate time in which to justify his performance and seek to show that he was not responsible for the fall-off in trade.

CASE 26: Broxtowe v Gripewater Groceries Ltd

An industrial tribunal would be likely to uphold the employee's claim for unfair dismissal. In the similar case of *Farthing* v *Midland Household*

Stores Ltd (*1974*), an industrial tribunal said: 'Regardless of the nature of the employment, the principle must apply that the longer an employee goes on working for the same employer, the more dependent he becomes on him and the employer owes a corresponding moral duty to avoid dismissing that employee if reasonably possible. Only in cases of sufficient gravity should a senior employee have to be dismissed and this should be avoided if possible.' While it is doubtful whether any tribunal would go quite so far nowadays, the fact remains that in the present case the employer's decision to select Mr Broxtowe for redundancy was based on nothing more than their belief that he was not a 'high flyer'. The company accepted that he was not 'culpably inefficient' and he had never had any intimation from senior management that his performance was in any way unsatisfactory. He was not consulted about his future before the decision was made, nor did the company look to see if any alternative employment was available. An employee with 26 years' service is entitled to better treatment than he received in this case.

CASE 27: Spencer v Amalgamated Breweries Ltd

An industrial tribunal would be likely to uphold the employee's claim. In the similar case of *Shaw* v *Garden King Frozen Foods Ltd* (*1975*), an industrial tribunal held that, in the absence of an agreed redundancy procedure or customary arrangement, fairness under normal circumstances would demand that the principle of 'last in, first out' should be followed. In the present case, the company's departure from this principle was not justified by Mr Spencer's allegedly lower standard of performance. Before the redundancy arose he had never been warned that his level of performance was unsatisfactory, nor was there any evidence that his health was such as to make him unfit for work. Any faults he had might have been eradicated by further training and development. A tribunal might also take the view, however, that even with assistance of this kind he was unlikely to achieve the standard required to enable him to run the plant on his own. If the company was fundamentally dissatisfied with his performance it should have given him a formal warning and, if he subsequently failed to improve, dismissed him. Had the company done so, it is very doubtful that the action would have been considered unfair.

CASE 28: Green v Moonweave Ltd

An industrial tribunal would be likely to find in favour of the employer, Moonweave Ltd. In the similar case of *Guy* v *Delanair (Car Heater) Ltd* (*1975*) an industrial tribunal held that the way in which an employer decided to respond to a fall in the demand for its products was entirely a matter for that employer. It was not open to a tribunal to put itself in the position of the employer and say what it would have done had it been in the employer's position. This line of reasoning has since been confirmed by the EAT in several leading cases. In the present case, the alternative to dismissing the night shift would have entailed disorganizing all three shifts and rearranging employees' contractual hours of work. In the circumstances it was not unreasonable for the company to make the night shift employees redundant, even though there were other employees on different shifts with less service than those on nights. Nor did the failure to consult the trade unions make the dismissals unfair. This was a case in which the decision had to be made in a hurry and consultation would simply have delayed an outcome which was inevitable.

CASE 29: Haddon and Others v Grimtex Yarn Spinners Ltd

An industrial tribunal would be likely to find in favour of the employer, Grimtex Yarn Spinners Ltd. In order for there to be a dismissal on the grounds of redundancy, there must still be in existence at the time of the dismissal a situation in which the needs of the business for employees to carry out work of that particular kind have diminished or are expected to diminish. In the present case, the change in the shift system and the freeze on recruitment had together avoided the need for redundancy. From September 1979 to February 1980 the employer's need for employees to carry out that particular type of work had not diminished, nor was it expected to diminish. As a result, no redundancy situation existed at the time when Mr Haddon and his colleagues resigned.

The claim for constructive dismissal is also unlikely to succeed. There was no fundamental breach of the employees' contracts, only a variation of the terms of work which was agreed with the trade union and accepted by the employees themselves (see the EAT decision in *Dal and Others v A S Orr* [1981]).

CASE 30: Hardy and Bishop v Bleak Moor Engineering Ltd

An industrial tribunal would be likely to find in favour of the employers, Bleak Moor Engineering Ltd. In this case the two employees must have known that as non-union members they were more vulnerable in a redundancy situation than their colleagues. The company may not have consulted them directly, but it certainly made efforts to protect their position and there is no evidence in this case that consultation would have made any difference to the final outcome. (See the EAT decision in *Evans and Morgan v A B Electronic Components Ltd* [1981].) Once a redundancy situation arose, it is unlikely that the trade union would have accepted a last-minute application from the two employees to join.

CASE 31: Fox v Laze Around Holidays Ltd

An industrial tribunal would be likely to find in favour of the employee, Mr Fox. Since 1976 both the EAT and the Court of Appeal have stressed that it is no part of a tribunal's job to inquire into the justification for either a redundancy or a business reorganization. Nor, by the same token, is the employer invariably obliged to consult or negotiate with his workforce. In *Hollister* v *National Farmers' Union* (*1979*), for example, the Court of Appeal held that when an employer is obliged to reorganize his business he is not required by statute to consult those employees who are going to be affected. An industrial tribunal is, however, entitled to consider whether consultation, had it taken place, would have made any difference to the final outcome — *British United Shoe Machinery Co Ltd* v *Clarke* (*1977*). This has opened up a significant loophole in the legal protection against unfair dismissal, though this loophole has recently been narrowed (*Ladbroke Courage Holidays Ltd* v *Asten* [*1981*]). In this case, which is similar to the one used in the text, the EAT made it clear that, if an employer seeks to rely on business reorganization or commercial necessity as a reason for dismissal, 'he should produce some evidence to show that there was a reorganization or that there was some need for economy' and that the tribunal was entitled to know whether the company was making a profit or a loss. In the present case such evidence was not submitted. The failure to discuss the matter with the employee was also a factor which a tribunal would take into account.

CASE 32: Parkinson and Others v Oxenford Services Ltd

An industrial tribunal would be likely to uphold the employees' complaint. In the similar case of *Williams and Others* v *Compair Maxam Ltd* (*1982*), the EAT has reminded tribunals that it is not enough for an employer to show that it was reasonable to dismiss *an* employee; he must show that he acted reasonably in treating redundancy as a sufficient reason for dismissing *the* employee. 'Therefore', said the EAT, 'if the circumstances of the employer make it inevitable that some employee must be dismissed, it is still necessary to consider the means whereby the applicant was selected to be the employee to be dismissed and the reasonableness of the steps taken by the employer to choose the applicant, rather than some other employee, for dismissal.' The EAT then proceeded to enunciate five principles which reasonable employers would seek to follow in redundancy situations where employees are represented by a recognized, independent trade union:

1. 'The employer will seek to give as much warning as possible of impending redundancies so as to enable the union and employees

who may be affected to take early steps to inform themselves of the relevant facts, consider possible alternative solutions and, if necessary, find alternative employment in the undertaking or elsewhere.'

2. 'The employer will consult the union as to the best means by which the desired management result can be achieved fairly and with as little hardship to employees as possible. In particular, the employer will seek to agree with the union the criteria to be applied in selecting the employees to be made redundant. When a selection has been made, the employer will consider with the union whether the selection has been made in accordance with those criteria.'

3. 'Whether or not an agreement as to the criteria to be adopted has been agreed with the union, the employer will seek to establish criteria for selection which so far as possible do not depend solely upon the opinion of the person making the selection but can be objectively checked against such things as attendance record, efficiency at the job, experience, or length of service.'

4. 'The employer will seek to ensure that the selection is made fairly in accordance with these criteria and will consider any representations the union may make as to such selection.'

5. 'The employer will seek to see whether instead of dismissing an employee he could offer him alternative employment.'

These principles, the EAT emphasized, 'should be departed from only where some good reason is shown to justify such departure.'

In the present case, none of these principles was followed. There was no consultation of any kind with either the employees or their union and no attempt to agree either on selection criteria or on the method by which the criteria were to be applied. If there had been proper consultation, this would almost certainly have resulted in the adoption of fairer selection criteria. As the EAT pointed out in *Compair Maxam*, 'The purpose of having, so far as possible, objective criteria is to ensure that redundancy is not used as a pretext for getting rid of employees who some manager wishes to get rid of for other reasons. Except in cases where the criteria can be applied automatically (eg last in, first out) in any selection for redundancy, elements of personal judgment are bound to be required, thereby involving the risk of judgment being clouded by personal animosity. Unless some objective criteria are included, it is extremely difficult to demonstrate that the choice was not determined by personal likes and dislikes alone.'

CASE 33: Godfrey v Horton Transport Ltd

An industrial tribunal would be likely to find in favour of the employer, Horton Transport Ltd. In *Martin and Others* v *Automobile Proprietary*

(*1979*), the EAT laid down clear guidelines for employers who are faced with the need to change the contractual terms and conditions of their employees, if necessary unilaterally: 'In determining whether it is fair to dismiss individual employees who refuse to go along with a reorganization, the vital question is whether the employer acted fairly and reasonably with reference to the individual . . . the first thing that has to be examined is the contract of employment to ascertain whether or not there was a change in the original contract which was being enforced unilaterally by the employer. The next thing . . . is whether or not the enforcement of that unilateral variation was properly handled. Proper handling involves a patient understanding by the employer of the strongly held views of the employee. It imposes an obligation on the employer to demonstrate to the individual that this is a reorganization which is sensible and in the interests of the employees generally; to listen to and weigh up the representations of the employee; to exercise managerial judgment whether it may be possible to make an exception in the case of an individual and not force him into a collective arrangement. In some cases the individual may be demonstrated to have acted unreasonably and to have been unnecessarily obstinate. He may be caught by a collective agreement. In those circumstances the employer may be able to show with comparative ease that he acted reasonably.'

In the present case, the employee's objections to the proposed changes are likely to be regarded as unreasonable. The additional duties which management asked him to take on were well within his capabilities and his objections were frivolous. His intervention to discourage Mr Sloan from taking over the duties which he should have performed was even less defensible. He was given a clear choice between acceptance and dismissal and must therefore have known what was likely to happen if he continued to refuse to accept the changes. (See also the EAT decision in *Bowater Containers Ltd* v *McCormack* [*1981*].)

CASE 34: Burke v North End Builders Ltd

An industrial tribunal would be likely to reject the claim for constructive dismissal. Since 1978 the tribunals' approach to constructive dismissal has been shaped by the Court of Appeal decision in *Western Excavation (ECC) Ltd* v *Sharp* (*1977*) in which it was made clear that such claims would succeed only if the employee could show that the employer had broken a fundamental term in the contract and had thereby repudiated it: 'An employee is entitled to treat himself as constructively dismissed if the employer is guilty of conduct which is a significant breach going to the root of the contract of employment, or which shows that the employer no longer intends to be bound by one or more of the essential terms of the contract. The employee in those circumstances is entitled to leave without notice or to give notice, but the conduct in either case must be sufficiently serious to entitle him to leave at once. Moreover, the employee must make up his mind soon after the conduct of which he complains. If he continues for any length of time without leaving, he will be regarded as having elected to affirm the contract and will lose his right to treat himself as discharged.'

In the present case, the employers were obviously not in breach of contract in refusing to give Mr Burke an advance on his accrued holiday pay to cover a period of suspension without pay for which he himself, by his own misconduct, was responsible.

CASE 35: Wilson v Broadacres County Council

An industrial tribunal would be likely to reject the claim for constructive dismissal. Although the employer's behaviour towards Mr Wilson can be criticized on several grounds, it did not amount to a repudiation of either an express or an implied term in his contract of employment. In any case, the employee failed to indicate that he was resigning from his job because of his superior's conduct towards him. Indeed, he said that he was resigning because he had a better job. As the EAT said in *Walker* v *Josiah Wedgwood & Sons Ltd* (*1978*): 'Whilst a formal assertion by the employee to the effect that he is treating the employer's conduct as a repudiation of contract which is bringing the contract to an end is not necessary in order to claim constructive dismissal, the employee must leave because of the breach of the employer's relevant duty to him and this should demonstrably be the case. Nor is it sufficient if he leaves in circumstances which indicate some grounds for his leaving other than the breach of the employer's obligation to him.'

CASE 36: Lowe v Bullman's Brewery Co Ltd

1. An industrial tribunal would be likely to uphold the employee's claim that he was constructively dismissed. In *Pedersen* v *London Borough of Camden* (*1980*), the Court of Appeal held that a tribunal is entitled to consider all the circumstances when construing the meaning of a contract of employment. In the present case, the wording of the advertisement to which Mr Lowe responded was significant in so far as it strongly suggested that the postholder would primarily be a bars manager and would undertake other duties only when he was not required for barwork. The letter of appointment also stated that his working week would be 'primarily related to the preparation and operation of the bars'. These were facts which an industrial tribunal would certainly take into account. Moreover, the fact that Mr Lowe's superiors tolerated his occasional refusals to do catering work could be construed as an implicit admission that they had no contractual right to insist that he performed these duties.

2. The company also erred in failing to consult Mr Lowe in advance of the changes. This would have enabled an explanation of the changes to be given and would have afforded the employee an opportunity to express his objections. Some form of compromise might have been achieved and the contract altered by mutual consent. The company's unilateral action constituted a breach which went to the root of the contract and entitled the employee to resign.

CASE 37: Robson v Grimditch Mutual Insurance Ltd

1. An industrial tribunal would be likely to uphold the employee's claim for constructive dismissal. In *Woods* v *W M Car Services (Peterborough) Ltd (1981)*, the EAT held: 'It is clearly established that there is implied in a contract of employment a term that the employers will not, without reasonable and proper cause, conduct themselves in a manner calculated or likely to destroy or seriously damage the relationship of trust and confidence between employer and employee. To constitute a breach of this implied term, it is not necessary to show that the employer intended any repudiation of the contract. The industrial tribunal's function is to look at the employer's conduct as a whole and determine whether it is such that its cumulative effect, judged reasonably and sensibly, is such that the employee cannot be expected to put up with it . . . an employer who persistently attempts to vary an employee's conditions of service, whether contractual or not, with a view to getting rid of the employee or varying the employee's terms of service acts in a manner calculated or likely to destroy the relationship of trust and confidence between employer and employee. Such an employer has, therefore, breached the implied term and any breach of that implied term is a fundamental breach amounting to a repudiation since it necessarily goes to the root of the contract.'

2. In the present case, the employer had agreed to continue Mrs Robson's employment on terms 'no less favourable in any respect' than those she had previously enjoyed. The company's subsequent actions amounted to a repudiation of this undertaking and led to a breakdown in the normal relationship between employer and employee.

3. As the EAT pointed out in the *Woods* case quoted above, the emphasis which the Court of Appeal placed on fundamental breach of contract by the employer in *Western Excavating (EEC) Ltd* v *Sharp (1977)* has enhanced the significance of *implied* contractual terms. A strict construction of the Court of Appeal's reasoning might otherwise leave the employee vulnerable to behaviour by their employer which, however unreasonable, stopped short of a fundamental breach of contract.

CASE 38: Hameed v Calderdale Foods Ltd

An industrial tribunal would be likely to reject the claim for constructive dismissal. Despite the fact that the employers have broken Mr Hameed's contract, it cannot be said, taking into account all the circumstances of the case, that they acted unreasonably. The offer of promotion was rejected by Mr Hameed for reasons which he was not prepared to substantiate. The employers had sound reasons for introducing the reorganization and sought to persuade Mr Hameed to accept it. In *Savoia* v *Chiltern Herb Farms Ltd* (*1981*), the EAT said: 'It does not follow that once it is found that an employer was in fundamental breach of contract, a claim of unfair dismissal must succeed.' A tribunal is entitled to go on and ask whether, notwithstanding the breach, the employer still behaved reasonably. In the present case, the employer's behaviour was reasonable.

CASE 39: Patel v Brudderfax Clothing Co Ltd

An industrial tribunal would be likely to dismiss the complaint. In *Seide* v *Gillette Industries Ltd* (*1980*), the EAT held that: 'In determining whether there has been unlawful discrimination, the question is whether the activating cause of what happened is that the employer has treated a person less favourably than others on racial grounds. Where there is more than one ground for an employer's action, it might be enough if a substantial and effective cause for the action is a breach of the statute. However, it is not sufficient merely to consider whether the fact that a person is of a particular racial group is *any* part of the background or is a *causa sine qua non* of what happens.' It follows that Mr Patel's argument, that if an employee's racial origin is a factor in the chain of causation, it must also be taken to be one of the grounds on which the employer acted, must be rejected.

In the present case, although the whole sequence of events began with Mr Thwaites' racist remarks, there was evidence that a third employee, Mr Richards, who was not found in any way to be motivated by racial prejudice, was unwilling to work with Mr Patel because of the antagonism which the latter appeared to cause. It is also clear that the company acted fairly and in accordance with the grievance procedure. If this had not been so, there might have been material from which a tribunal could begin to draw an inference that there had been unlawful discrimination. But, in reality, the decision to transfer Mr Patel was not motivated by racial prejudice but by the difficult interpersonal situation which had arisen within the press-packing section.

CASE 40: Shaheed v Metropolitan Borough of Cleckleydale

An industrial tribunal would be likely to uphold the employee's claim. In the case of *Khanna* v *the Ministry of Defence* (*1981*) the EAT held that industrial tribunals should 'take into account the fact that direct evidence of discrimination is seldom going to be available and that, accordingly, in these cases the affirmative evidence of discrimination will normally consist of inferences to be drawn from the primary facts.' In the present case, the primary facts indicate that there has been discrimination of some kind. The employer must, therefore, offer an explanation of why the employee was not appointed to the job for which he applied. It is then up to the industrial tribunal to consider this explanation against the inferences drawn from the primary facts and reach a decision on the balance of probabilities.

In the present case the balance of probabilities indicates that there was racial discrimination against Mr Shaheed. There was no obvious reason why Mr Shaheed should not have been appointed to the post in 1981 and, in the light both of Mr Gregson's expressed opinion of his suitability for promotion and Mr Crawford's complete lack of practical experience in dealing with ethnic minorities, it would be reasonable to infer that a majority of the interviewing board were influenced by racial prejudice.

CASE 41: Winston v Cohen's Turf Accountants Ltd

An industrial tribunal would be likely to uphold Mr Winston's claim that he had been unlawfully discriminated against. In the similar case of *Hussein* v *Saints Complete House Furnishers* (*1979*) a tribunal held that to embargo potential employees because they lived in one particular area was indirectly discriminatory if such an embargo was likely to affect black or coloured applicants more adversely than white applicants. S4(1) of the Race Relations Act 1976 stipulates that: 'It is unlawful for a person, in relation to employment by him at an establishment in Great Britain, to discriminate against another in the arrangements he makes for the purpose of determining who should be offered that employment.' In this case the employer clearly broke this provision, although a tribunal would almost certainly find that he did not *intend* to discriminate either directly or indirectly against the applicant on racial grounds. A tribunal would recommend that the embargo on local residents be dropped and that suitable applicants should at least be interviewed.

CASE 42: O'Neal v Delgardia

An industrial tribunal would be likely to uphold Mrs O'Neal's complaint. First, there was no evidence to show that the employer's policy applied to men and women alike. According to the evidence his policy was not to employ women with young children, which directly discriminated against women under S1 of the Act. In order to establish whether a discriminatory condition is 'justifiable' within the Act, the

215

employer must show that the condition is necessary and not merely convenient. In the present case, even if it is conceded that some women with small children are less reliable than those without, it does not follow that the employer would be justified in excluding *all* women with children. In *Hurley* v *Mustoe* (*1981*) the EAT said: 'In general, a condition excluding all members of a class from employment cannot be justified on the grounds that some members of the class are undesirable employees. Parliament has enacted that women with children are not to be treated as a class but as individuals. No employer is bound to employ unreliable employees, whether male or female. But he must investigate each case and not simply apply a rule of convenience, or a prejudice, to exclude a whole class of women or married persons because some members of that class are not suitable employees.'

In the present case there was evidence to show that Mrs O'Neal was a thoroughly reliable employee. By failing to take this into account and omitting to make further inquiries about the arrangement she had made for the care of her children while she was at work, the employer discriminated against her.

Index

Index